THE GREEKS
THEIR PHILOSOPHY HISTORY AND CULTURE

By

Krishna P. Bahadur

Ess Ess Publications

4837/24, Ansari Road, Darya Ganj,
New Delhi-110002
✆ : 3260807
Fax: 3274173
E–mail: essess@del3.vsnl.net.in
url:http://essess.8m.com

First Published 1999

ISBN : 81-7000-260-5

Price : Rs. 500/-

Published by :

Ess Ess Publications

4837/24, Ansari Road, Darya Ganj,
New Delhi - 110 002
✆ : 3260807
Fax: 3274173
E–mail: essess@del3.vsnl.net.in
url:http://essess.8m.com

Printed at :

S.S.S. Printers, New Delhi

Contents

Dedication

for Shveta

Be good sweet maid, and let who can be clever;
Do lovely things, not dream them all day long,
And so make Life and Death, and that For Ever,
One grand sweet song.

Charles Kingsley

PREFACE

Aπανγasή παί παί δευσιs

ή μέρους γελεî

Culture makes all men gentle

Menander. Monosticha, 41.

Horace says 'Friends, when you write make Greece your model, and keep pondering over her volumes' Doubtless till the Greece civilization lasted, in Europe it overshadowed all others. The people of the Greece mainland soon found that it could not contain the growing population and hence moved out forming colonies, the Greek city-states. Sooner or later, these colonies began to fight. The colonists had their own cults, diatect, alphabet and so forth. The earliest colonies were founded in the first half of the eighth century B.C. by Miletus on the southern shore of the Black Sea. They numbered about a hundred. In the West and South the Colonies were in Italy and Sicily.

Unfortunately the greatest hindrance in the development of Greece was internecine warfare. The two great powers were Athens and Sparta. Sometimes they stood by each other, but often they could not resist rivalry, and this was suicidal to Greece, for as Sallust says (Juguratha) 'It is always easy enough to take up arms, but very difficult to lay them down'.

Another ill of the Greeks was the frequent rise of tyrants and tyranny. As we have quoted Aristotle 'Democracy is the acme of tyranny' (Politica, VIII, 10), and we find that this was a fundamental Greek evil. There was corruption too, and strangely a scruplously honest reformer, who did much for Greece, namely Solon, was taunted for not being corrupt! There was aristocracy too and often the aristocrats dominated.

Another disgraceful Greek institution was slavery, and the slaves were in large numbers. Curiously even Aristotle, a renowned thinker and philosopher, remarked that 'states are bound to have a population of slaves in large numbers'. All agricultural labour was to be conducted by them. Another philosopher, Xenophon, proposed that Athens should have three slaves for every citizen and employ them as mining labour. In working in silver mines, these slaves were treated more or less as beasts of burden. The impression of some scholars that they were well-off is quite mistaken. They had no rights as a Greek citizen had and led a miserable existence much like the Sudras and Chandalas of Hindu society.

However these shortcomings do not diminish the greatness of Greek civilization. The only thing worth pointing out is that its greatness is confined to Europe. India and the East had very little, in fact no real contact with each other, though some writers seem to insist otherwise. In the field of art the Greeks showed the utmost skill in fashioning vases, some of exqusite workmanship. As atheletes they had no competitors and gave the utmost attention to body building. Their homes were simple and so was their living, the food meagre, the meals consisting of break and plenty of green vegetable with very little meat. They ate to live, not lived to eat. They had a great fascination for the theatre.

The main object in writing this book is to place the philosophy, culture and history of the ancient Greek civilization in its proper perespective, even though it may diminish the ardour of those writers who extend the Greek culture beyond the confines of Europe.

I am obliged to my publisher in bringing this book in these difficult times, and in an excellent format.

Acknowledgements

The author acknowledges that this book is foam of the following books :

Greek Philosophers by M.E.J. Taylor

Oxford

The Greek Philophers from Thales to Aristotle London,

Methuen London 1950

Theology of the Early Greek Philosopher Werner

Jaige Oxford. 1947.

A History of Greece to 322 B.C. H.G.L.

Hammond, Oxford 1959

The Legacy of Greece Ed. R.W. Livingstone

Oxford 1921

The Greeks and their Heritage Arthur

Tonybee, Oxford, 1981

BIBLIOGRAPHY

Armstrong, A.H. Methuen. *Introduction to Ancient Philosophy* 1947.

Burnet, J. *Early Greek Philosophy*, Black, 1930

Cambridge Ancient History. vols. 4, 5, 6 & 7.

Field, G.C. Methuen. *Plato and his Contemporarlies*, 1948

Grube, G.M.A. Methuen Plato's Thought, 1935

Hicks, R.D. Cambridge. *Stoics and Epicureans*, 1910

Jaeger. W., Oxford. The *Theology of Early Greek Philosophers*, 1947

Sepheres, G. IIoinqara, Ikaros, 1964

Shodgrass, A.M. *The Dark Age of Greece*, Edinburgh University Press, 1971.

Starr C.G., Knopf. *The Origins of Greek Civilization* New York, 1961

Taylor, A.E., Constable. *Epicurus*, 1911.

PART I

INTRODUCTION

Egypt's might has tumbled down,
Down a-down the deeps of thought;
Greece is fallen and Troy town,
Glorious Rome hath lost her crown,
Venice' pride is nought.

But the dreams their children dreamed.
Fleeting, unsubstantial, vain,
Shadowy as the shadows seemed,
Airy nothing, as they deemed,
These remain,

Mary E. Coleridge

Among European civilizations that of the Greeks was certainly the most prominent and for the first time is Europe spirituality triumphed over materialism, and philosophy in its real sense was born. That implies that for the first time in Europe wisdom replaced mere ritual and superstition and the garb of civilization covered barbarism. As a historian says: 'The word "philo-sophos" in Greek means "lover of wisdom." The early lonian speculators ... were apparently not called philosophers but wise men, "Sophoi" or "Sophistai" ..... the terms "philosophos", "philosophia" seem to have started in Pythagorean circles, and from the fifth century B.C. onwards "philophos" was the ordinary word used in the Greek world to describe a man who devoted himself to speculation about the universe and about human good and evil'.[1]

This was so in Europe, which, however, is only one continent in our vast world. Many Western writers suffer from the myopic vision that all wisdom, science, literature, philosophy, astonomy architecture of the world had its origin in Europe. Some writers seem to think, in the words of V. Gordon Childe, 'Peninsular Europe was in fact marked out by nature herself as the womb of a favoured civilization. It enjoyed a temperate climate as contrasted with the extreme continental regime ruling in upper Asia.' The writer goes on to mention the what he thinks favorable 'land surface', seas, mountain chains, forests and grasslands, and concludes that because of all this 'a stable industry and civilization' could never have been possible in upper Asia.[2] Before commenting on this, another Western writer may be quoted:

> 'In particular, mystical speculation based on religious experience is not itself philosophy, though it has often influenced philosophy profoundly, and for this reason the pantheism of the Upanishads cannot be called philosophical. It is true there is an Indian philosophy, and indeed Hindus are the only ancient people besides the Greeks who ever had one, but Indian science was demonstrably borrowed from Greece after the consequent of Alexander, and there is every reason to believe that those Indian systems which can be *regarded as genuinely philosophical are a good deal more recent* still ...... Of course philosophy may culminate in theology, and the best Greek philosophy certainly does so, but it begins with science not religion.'[3]

As for Gordon Childe's observation, firstly the topography of a region hardly govern its culture or philosophy. Secondly if civilization were confined to the temperate zone, how could one explain its splendour and grandeur in the Indus valley c. 4000 - 2500 B.C. which reveals the existence of a thriving commercial life, well-planned towns, well ventilated streets built in geometrical proportions. The more recent excavations in the Vindhyas and the Ganga valley by professor Sharma show that civilization existed in India 8,000 years ago[4]. When Seleucus Nicator tried to subdue Chandragupta Maurya the great Indian emperor, he was defeated and a Greek princess married the Indian monarch as a result of alliance by marriage. Megasthenes the Greek ambassador of Seleucus came to India in the Mauryan period found that the Indians were highly cultured:

> 'The inhabitants in like manner, having abundant means of subsistence, exceed in consequence the ordinary stature and are distinguished by their proud bearing. They are also found to be well skilled in the arts as might be expected of men who inhale a pure air and drink the very finest water ... And while the soil bears on its surface all kinds of fruits which are known to cultivation, it has also underground numerous veins of all sorts of metals, for it contains much gold and silver and copper and iron in no small quantity and even tin and other metals, which are employed in making articles of use and ornaments, as well as implements and accoutrements of war .... it is accordingly affirmed that famine has never visited India, and there has never been a general scarcity in the supply of nourishing food ....
>
> 'It is further said that the Indians do not rear monuments to the dead, but consider the virtues which men have displayed in life, and the songs in which their praises are celebrated, sufficient to preserve memory after death. But of their cities it is said that the number is so great that it cannot be stated with precision .... The Indians all live frugally, especially when in camp. They dislike great and undisciplined multitudes, and consequently they observe good order. Theft is of very rare occurrence .... They live

> nevertheless happily enough being simple in their manners and frugal. They never drink wine except at sacrifices. Their beverage is a liquor composed of rice instead of barley and their food is principally curry and rice. The simplicity of their laws and their contracts is proved by the fact that they seldom go to law. They have no suits about pledges or deposits and confide in each other. The houses and property they generally leave unguarded. These things indicate that they possess good, sober sense ..... . The Indians neither put out money at usury nor know how to borrow. It is contrary to established usage for an Indian either to commit or suffer a wrong, and therefore they neither make contracts nor require securities'.[5]

Further a foreign visitor of India, Ktesias, wrote: 'The Indians are not afflicted with headache or toothache or ophthlamia, nor have they mouth sores or ulcers in any part of their bodies. The age to which they live is 120, 130 and 150 years, though the very old live to 200 ..... The justice of the Indians their devotion to their king and their contempt of death are themes on which he loves to expatiate'. Even the food and the wines are praised by him. 'He states that the cheese and the wines of the Indians are the sweetest in the world, adding that he knew this from his own experience since he had tasted both'.[6]

Thus we see that civilization in India was, contrary to Childe's mistaken view, in a far more advanced stage than in Europe. The highest mountain range, the Indo-Gangetic plain and the great perennial rivers, are not in Europe but in India. Coming to Burnet's view, it depicts a misunderstanding of both the Upanishads and Greek philosophy. The former - the Upanishads - are not pantheistic in the sense that God and the universe are the same (this is the definition of 'pantheism' in Longman Dictionary of Contemporary English). God, according to the Upanishads is both eminent and immanent and immanent. The world proceeds from Brahman (the Cosmic Absolute) and merges into it as the web from the spider. There are four principles of this Absolute - Brahman, Ishvara, i.e., the personified lord who can be worshipped, Hiranyagarbha and Viraj. The Upanishads say about it the same as Plotinus 'We say what he is not, we cannot say what he is'. 'At the root of all religion and philosophy', says Paul Deussen, 'is the thought that the universe is only appearance and not reality, i.e., our experience does not show us things as they are in themselves. This was the concept of the Upanishads as later of Plato and Kant ... According to Plato they (the objects that lie around us) are not the true realities but only shadows of them. And according to the doctrine of the Upanishads they are not the *ātman* (the "real self") of the things, but mere maya, i.e., sheer deceit or illusion'.[7] As regards Burnet's observation that the genuinely philosophical systems of India are a good deal more recent to those of Greece, the Upanishads (the ancient ones including the *Chāndogya, Brihadāranyaka, Īsha and Katha*) are considered to date back to the eight century B.C. (the Veda, *Rig Veda*) to about 3000 B.C.

Then there are the observation, 'Indian science was demonstrably borrowed form Greece after the conquest of Alexander' and 'the best Greek philosophy ... begins with science not religion'. As regards the first, the Arabs transmitted the sciences of arithmetic and geometry to the western world from India where it was already known. The Indian numeral system is not borrowed from the Arabic, it is the other very round. The people of the Vedic period knew about fractions because terms like *ardha* (one-half) *tripad* (Three-fourths) and so on occur in the Rig Veda (3000 B.C.). That knowledge of science was cosidered of paramount importance in ancient India is testified by a narrative which occurs in the *Chāndogya Upanishad* according to which the sage Narada approached the *rishi*, Sanat Kumara, to learn from his the supreme knowledge (*brahma-vidyā*). The rishi asked him what he had already learnt till then. Narada said 'Lord, I have studied the four Vedas, the history and chronicles (itihāsa-purāṇam), the sciences of grammar, rituals, numbers, chronology, logic, polity, etymology. Spirits, archery, astonomy and antidotes, the natural sciences, the sciences cognate to the Vedas and the fine arts - all these I know'. The Vedic Hindus knew geometry, rectilineal figures, measurements of areas and volumes, squaring the circle and vice versa and about similar figures.[8] They adopted the decimal system. An important theorem 'Theorem of the square of the Diagonal' which is associated with the Greek mathematician Pythagoras was in all probability enunciated by Baudhāyana (800 B.C.). Other notable achievements of Vedic geometry are about indeterminate analysis, surds and so forth. The Vedic Hindus comed names for the notional places corresponding to 1, 10^2 10^3, 10^4 etc. The *Rig Veda* speaks of the earth as spherical in shape and suspended freely in the air.[9] The sun was said to one, the maker of the day night, twilight, month and year, and the cause of the seasons.[10] This conclusion was reached in 3000 B.C. in India. While in Greece Anaximander was proclaiming much later (6th Century) that the earth was cylindrical like a drum! and the sun moon and stars rings of fire round the earth'. Another Greek concept was that of Anaximenes who 'thought the earth to be a disc floating on the air and the heavenly bodies as moving laterally round the earth, accounting for their apparent setting by their disappearance behind the higher parts of the earth in the north, the position of the earth itself being tilted.'[12]

As regards medicine the Ashvins were expert in surgery and medicine. A Vedic hymn speaks of a surgeon wanting to set right a fracture.[13] Another shows the use of herbs and plants in curing diseases.[14] Rebha, a sage, was revived after drawing, Paravrij was cured of his blindness and lameness, and Vishapala who lost of leg in battle was fitted with an artificial leg made of iron, which must have involved complicated surgery. Astrology was one of the six *angas* (*branches*) of the Veda. From India it spread to China, Babylonia** and chaldea, and then to Egypt, Greece, Rome and throughout the world. Vara**ha Mihira who is said to have lived in India in A.D. 507 is recognized as the greatest of Indian astrologers.[15] Ancient Hindus showed a great deal of knowledge of medicine and surgery round the 5th Century B.C. Uncommon operations like that for anal fistula were successfully performed. Carak and Susrut were the two great names. The instruments used by Susrut were essentially the same as used in modern surgery- the lion forceps were known then as *simhamukha yantra* and the speculum as *ashtanga-hvidaya sutra*. The ancient Hindus knew about complicated operations like removal of tonsils, and the Caesarean section. They could also perform plastic surgery and stitch back cut off noses which occurred quite often, being the punishment for adulterers! Some form of anaesthesia was also known. The patient was administered a substance called *sammohini* which made him unconscious. After surgery another herb, the *sanji**vani*** was given which brought him round. In A.D. 4th Century king Buddadisa of Ceylon performed an operation on a herdsman who had accidentally drunk water containing frogs' eggs. One of these entered his nostrils and went into his head. The egg was hatched and a small frog began to croak inside the skull of the poor man! The expert surgeon-monarch cut open the skull and removed the frog, and the man was all right again. Thus the idea that Indian science borrowed from Greece is completely wrong and baseless. Then there is Burnet's concept that Greek philosophy begins with science not religion. The Greek religion is certainly not mixed up with philosophy, and that is true of the Hindu religion also, for the *Gita* and Upanishads are undiluted philosophy. But the same great Greeks were scientists as they were philosophers and Leucippus, founder of the atomic doctrine of matter, and Democritus who expanded it, Pythagorus, Hippocrates, Plato, Aristotle, Theophrastus and others are the prominent fathers of science, medicine and of numbers. The dividing line between philosophy and science is indeed very thin: 'Science and philosophy, however was not originally distinct; the man described as a "philosopher" was also the man who attempted to give a scientific explanation of the phenomena of the world .... '[16]

This brief digression is by no means aimed at disparaging the contribution of Greece to the world of knowledge, wisdom, philosophy and science, which indeed has been immense and indisputable. It is only meant to correct the view that philosophy science and civilization starts with the Greeks. That may be true as far as Europe is concerned, but not when we are taking a world perspective. Foreign writers on philosophy often tend to err in thinking that philosophy starts with Aristotle and Plato. Such statements as 'the conception of the soul as the spiritual substance of human personality was a Greek discovery'[17] are mere encomiums and panegyrics betraying ignorance of philosophies and civilizations other than those of the Greeks. Before this concept developed, indeed much before this idea was conceived by Greek philosophers like Plato and Plotinus, we find in the *Brihadāranyaka Upanishad*, dating back to the eight century B.C. the following teaching about the soul given by the sage Yājanvalkya to his wife Maitreyi: 'It is the soul, dear Maitreyi which needs to be realized and heard of, reflected and meditated upon. One can know it only by hearing, reflection and meditation... This great reality is endless, infinite and pure knowledge'.[18] There are several other such passages in the Upanishads which testify to the soul's immortality. In the *Bhagavadgita*, which Western scholars give a date much late-3rd Century or so-but which is really thousands of years old,[19] we also find the same vies: 'The soul is never born, nor does ever die, and having come to be is never non-existent. It is unborn, permanent and primordial, and does not die with the body's death.... The soul which dwells within all bodies is eternal, and can never be slain'.[20] In the same way Dandamis, the ancient Indian mystic snubbed Alexander even as Diogenes had done. When the emperor's messenger offered him many gifts if he went to meet him or death if he refused he said, 'If I wish to keep gold, I destroy my sleep... And if he wish to cut off my head, he cannot take my soul; he will only take the fallen head, but the departing soul will leave the head like the portion of some garment,[21] and will restore it to whence it received it, namely to the earth.[22] But when I shall have become a spirit I shall ascend to God, who has enclosed it within this flesh. When he did this he wished to try us, how, after leaving him, we would live in this world. And afterwards when we shall have returned to him, he will demand from us an account of this life. Standing by him I shall see my injury, and shall contemplate his judgment on those who injured me: for the sighs and groans of the inured become the punishments of the oppressors. Let Alexander threaten with this them that desire riches or fear death, both of which I despise. For brahmins neither love gold nor fear death. Therefore go and tell Alexander this: Dandamis seeks nothing of yours, but if you think you need something of his, disdain not to go to him'.[23] It must be said to the credit of Alexander that despite his vainglory he never lost his sense of balance. Had a Moslem monarch approached Dandamis in this manner, beheading would have been the natural consequence, soul or no soul; for with them except with rare exceptions like Akbar, the dazzle of vanity blinded them to all else and 'the quality of mercy was seldom enthroned in their hearts'. Alexander was a lover of books and read the Homeric poems and the plays of Aeschylus, Sophocles and Euripides. He seems to have faith in astrology and often consulted his seer and sooth sayer, much as the ancient Hindu kings did their family priest (*purohit*). It is recorded that power never really turned his mind and as W. Romaine Paterson wrote: 'Once he stood silent beside the tomb of Cyrus, and read the inscription: "O man, whosoever thou art and whencesoever thou comest, for come thou wilt, I am Cyrus who won the Empire for the Persians. Grudge me not, therefore this handful of earth which covers me". And we are told that Alexander betrayed great emotion, being reminded of the undertainty and the transience of human life'.[24]

The concepts which foreign writers often have about Indian philosophy are usually motivated by a tendency to disparage it, and that would be excusable, for to the Western mind all that hasn't taken birth in Europe or the Western world is inferior, but what is in excusable is condemnation without knowledge of what is being deprecated; for one not knowing what he is belittling is really like a blind man groping in the dark. For example the surprising concept that *Brahman* (the Cosmic Absolute), 'is a word denoting the prayer or spell which commanded the gods'![25] The same writer goes on say that the doctrine of transmigration prevailed among 'aborginal tribes and is pessimistic and that of karma is 'destructive of human activity and responsibility'.[26] The statement is all the more surprising as it comes from a professor of Sanskrit and a scholar of note of Indian philosophy. *Brahman* is neither a prayer nor a spell and it does not command the gods. *Brahman* is described as being-consciousness-bliss, true knowledge and infinite bliss (*satyam jnānam anantam ānandam brahma*).

When every passion vanishes
That finds a home in the human heart
Then he who is mortal becomes immortal
Here already he has attained Brahman.

Then as regards transmigration of the soul, Deussen says: 'There can be three answers to the question "What becomes after death?" 1. Annihilation, 2. Eternal retribution in heaven or hell, and 3. Transmigration. The first supposition is in conflict with man's self-love and is impractical. The second supposition, which opens up the prospect of eternal reward or punishment for an existence so brief and liable to error, so exposed to all the accidents of upbringing and environment, is condemned at once by the unparalled disproportion in which cause and effect here stand to one another. Hence only the third supposition remains'.[28] Nor is transmigration or belief in karma 'pessimistic' or 'destructive of human activity and responsibility'. Arnold Tonybee says: 'Heritage is karma. This is a Sanskrit word whose literal meaning is simply "action" ...karma is a current account which is constantly receiving credits and debits. Karma is being changed, either for better or worse, by continual further action; and action will continue for so long as the human race survives... Even if we believe that death spells spiritual as well as physical annihilation for each individual, we must concede that karma will be transmitted either physically through genes or culturally through the transmission of a social heritage by education in the broadest meaning of this word.

'Karma is at work even if we have no conscious memory of our own past acts or of the acts of previous incarnations of ourselves or of our ancestors or of other deceased members of the human society to which we are parties. This is one of the senses in which "all history is contemporary history" [Benedetto Croce: "Ognivera storia é storia contemporan ca"]... The whole of the past is always alive and at work in the present, even if we are now oblivious of it'.[29]

As the *Bhagavadgita* says: 'One cannot escape the consequence of works by shrinking from them, nor can he achieve fulfilment by giving them up. Because not even for a moment can anyone abstain from work. He will be driven to it helplessly impelled by the qualities of Nature, [i.e., in accordance with his inclinations]. Do your prescribed duty for action is better than inaction; you cannot even exist if you do not work'.[30]

Thus contrary to Berriedale Keith's belief karma is inevitable. There is no escape from it and far from being destructive of activity it is the source and the raison d'être of all activity. Indian (read 'Hindu') philosophy has often been stigmatized as being pessimistic by Western writers like Dr. Albert Schweitzer, Oswald Spengler and keith (quoted aforesaid). It has been said it is life-negating, emphasizes suffering and has an atmosphere of gloom. As regards Schweitzer's comment of 'life-negatic ascetics imposing their gloom on their followers', perhaps the learned doctor has forgotten his Bible in which Christ says 'He that findeth his life shall lose it : and he that loseth his life for my sake shall find it'[31], and 'The care of this world, and the deceitfulness of riches'.[32] And then there is the account of what God said when he banished Adam and Eve from the garden of Eden 'cursed is the ground for thy [Adam's] sake; in sorrow shalt thou eat of it all the days of thy life; thorns and thistles shall it bring forth to thee; and thou shalt eat the herb of the field; in the sweat of thy face shalt thou eat bread, till thou return unto the ground; for of it wast thou taken : for dust thou art, and unto dust shalt thou return... Unto the woman [Eve] he said, I will greatly multiply thy sorrow asd thy conception; in sorrow thou shalt bring forth children, and thy desire shall be to thy husband, and he shall rule over thee'.[33] The author's object in quoting from the Holy Bible is not to disparage Christianity [as Dr Schweitzer does Hinduism], for he reveres it as much as Hinduism. The Hindu mind, often derided for its orientalism, shows reverence for all faith. An edict of king Ashoka, of whose reign H.G. Wells says it 'was one of the brightest in the troubled history of mankind'[34], reads: 'He who does reverence to his own sect, while disparaging the sects of others wholly from attachment to his own, with intent to enhance the glory of his own sect, in reality by such conduct inflicts the severest injury on his own sect. Concord therefore is meritorious, to wit, hearkening and hearkening willingly to the Law of Piety, as accepted by other people'.[35]

Besides, it would be relevant to point out that one of the greatest of Greek philosophers, Plato, believed in the immortality of the soul which he said 'was truly divine, a being immortal in its own right and not the gift of any higher divinity. It has existed, therefore, always, before its indwelling in any body, and will continue to exist of incarnations. It is altogether a higher creature and has nothing in common with the world of the senses in which it finds itself, and any "this-worldliness" or accommodation to earthly existence on its part is a sin to be punished in the periods of purification in the other world which intervenes between its successive incarnations. This doctrine of reward and punishments in the next world is taken very seriously and great stress is laid on the punishment of the wicked' [Hellenic Philosophy].

Plotinus, who with Plato and Aristotle, is one of the supremely great masters of pagan Hellenic thought, has a kinship to Hindu thought - the realization of our pre-exising identity with the supreme Absolute. His philosophy is contained in the 'Enneads' comprising fifty-four treatise. According to him the One is Unity-Absolute and admits of no duality. It is indescribable and beyond thought and language. There is a World Soul and the lower soul or Nature. The Soul contains the body and not the body the Soul. The soul's spiritual state depends on its attitude. If it devotes itself selfishly to the body it becomes entrapped in it, is isolated from the whole and finally sinks intobrutishness. The mere fact of being in the body does not imply imprisonment in it. That comes when the soul surrenders to the body. It is the inward attitude that makes the difference. Man can pass from the narrowness of earthly life to the university of the transcendent Soul and then pass beyond the Soul to take his rightful place in the world of the Divine Mind. Thence the can even pass higher, though rarely, to that ecstatic union with the one in which Mind attains to the highest by leaving itself behind.

We can see how close Plotinus' ideas come to those of the Hindus. The Upanishads postulate a higher Self and a lower.[36] The *Gita* says, 'Let not a man degrade his Soul, but himself uplift it; for the elevated Soul will be his helper, and if debased, it will turn against him. The Soul is a faithful friend when it is attuned to the spiritual, but the same Soul is an adversary when the lower instincts prevail. The Supreme Self abides in the man who has vanquished his lower self'.[37]

Then we come to transmigration of the soul which as aforesaid Berriedal Keith dismissed as a doctrine of aboriginal tribes and termed it pessimistic. About this, the view of Pythagoras and the Pythagoreans may be stated:

> '...the core of Pythagoreanism was a belief in the immortality of the human soul, and its progress through a series of incarnations not only as man but also in the bodies of other creatures. With this connected the most important of Pythagorean taboos, their abstention from animal flesh. For the beast or bird which you eat may haply be inhabited by the soul of your grandmother. If that is so, if the transmigration of souls in possible and usual, then all life is akin, and the kinship of nature is another Pythagorean tenet. It went further than we might think, for the animate world extended further for them than it does for us. They believed indeed that the Universe as a whole was a living creature.... The Universe was one, eternal and divine. Men were many and divided, and were mortal. But the essential part of man, his soul, was not mortal, and owed its immortality to this fact, that it was a fragment or spart of the divine soul, cut off and imprisoned in a mortal body.

> 'Man had thus and aim in life, to shake off the taint of the body and, becoming pure spirit, rejoin the universal spirit to which he essentially belonged. Until the soul could purify itself completely, it must continue a series of transmigrations, exchanging one body for another. This meant the retention of individuality so long as the allotted cycle of births was incomplete, but there can be little doubt that the ultimate aim was annihilation of self in reunion with the divine'.[38]

The Greek word for rebirth is 'metempsychjosis'. The cult that grew around Orpheus, the bard of Thrace (about 6th contury B.C.) contained the germ of this doctrine. Empedocles carried the Pythagorean doctrine further when he declared human souls migrating to subhuman organisms could even go into plants. He said 'Thus in former lives, I have been a boy and a girl, a bush and a bird and a fish without speech in the depth of the sea'.

In the Renaissance period with the revival of Greek philosophy 'metempsychosis' was introduced in European thought - Marsilo, Finico, Giordano Bruno and Emannuel Swedenborg. Reincarnation came to full fruition in the classical period of German literature. Goethe says to Frau von Stein:

> **'An in the depth of time gone by**
> **Thou wast my sister or my wife'.**[39]

A world famous biologist, Pierre Leconte du No*uy, writes: 'Any effort to visualize God reveals a surprising childishness. We can no more conceive Him than we can conceive an electron. Yet many people do not believe in God simply because they cannot visualie Him. They forget that this incapacity is not, in itself, a proof of non-existence, considering that they firmly believe in the electron...[40] According to the telefinalist hypothesis man must continue to evolve toward spirituality. He must free himself from the domination of his animal reactions and from the crude ideas inherited from his direct ancestors, vestiges of the first conflicts between primitive conscience and adverse nature... Let every man remember... that his own dignity, his nobility as a human being, must emerge from his efforts to liberate himself from his bondage and to obey his deepest aspirations. And let his above all never forget that the divine spart is in him, in him alone, and that he is free to disregard it, to kill it, or to come closer to God by showing his eagerness to work with Him and for Him'.[41]

The rebirth doctrine is accepted by all schools of Indian philosophy and as we have pointed out aforesaid some of the prominent Greek philosophers also conform to it. This being so, by what reasoning can the Indian (Hindu) philosophers be deprecated, as Keith's analysis does, for formulating exactly what the Greek philosophers did? It may be stressed that ideas, particularly in the spiritual plane are nobody's copyright, and they can be thought of, on their own indeed usually are by the deep thinkers of all religions and cults. The charge of pessimism is also unwarranted. The *Isha Upanishad* says 'Make renunciation your support. Do not covet the wealth of others nor thirst for it yourself. If you are unable to renounce, live a hundred years in this world performing good actions; there is no other way to escape the taint of evil deeds'.[42] And in the *Rig Veda* we have many passages radiating joy and happiness. The newlyweds are greeted by friends and relations thus:

> **'Here now remain, nor ever part**
> **Enjoy the whole expanse of life,**
> **With sons and grandsons joyous sport**
> **Be glad in heart within your house**
>
> **'In sons, O Indra, make her rich**
> **Give her a life of happiness**
> **Ten children grant and spare to her**
> **As a eleventh her dear spouse'.**[43]

The doctrine of rebirth, as has been said prevailed in both Greek and Indian philosophy. It is finding recognition gradually in Christianity too, as the following account in a booklet of the Christian Missionary Society of St Paul given by Father O'Brien records, about a paralyzed woman having cancer too tears she said to us "Father, these last four years have not been easy. At times the pain has been almost unbearable. I'have worked so hard for my children. I love them, and I hate to leave them now. But God knows best. And I bow to his will. But is I did not believe there is a God and a future life *I would go mad*".'[44]

There remains Keith's observation 'Longer experience perhaps of the fatal climate of his (Indian's) country reduced him to a more gloomy frame of mind, to which Death the ender, appears as the most insistence foe of Man'.[45] This coming from a distinguished scholar, is a startlingly preposterous observation, for firstly death is not related to climate and one wonders what a 'fatal climate' means. We have aforesaid quoted Ktesias as testifying to the fact that Indian lived in those times for 120-150 years and the very old to 200. Life and death are not climatic phenomena, but acts of providence. Secondly who does not fear death? Sophocles says:

> **'For even boldest natures shrink in fear,**
> **When they see Hades overshadowing life'.[46]**
> **And Shakespeare says much the same about death.[47]**

Thus the fear and gloom associated with death in not confined to any race, but universal. In fact, as we have related a foresaid, the sages and mystics of India, like Dandamis' reply to Alexander, had to a large measure overcome it. And to link death with climate is laughable.

Then we have another renowned writer. Hendrik van Loon (*The Story of Mankind* New York Pocket Books, 1926, pp, 234-5) saying 'the majority of the Indian people, therefore *lived in misery*... many people went into the desert and *lived upon the leaves of trees* and stravved their bodies that they night feed souls...'; all of which illustrates Pope's line 'A little learning is a dang'rous thing', for the Indians of that time never lived in misery (we have already quoted Megasthenes to show that they did not) and as for living on leaves, the historian shows a confused knowledge of the Hindu *ashramas* (life-stages) the third of the four of them being that of the forest-dwellers (*Vānapratha*) not desert-dwellers and he forgets that there are edible roots and fruits too in the forests, not just leaves. Those sages went to meditate on the soul to which Plato gave so much importance.

The objective in going into all these factors is not to belittle in any way Greek culture, philosophy and civilization. It is only to emphasize that there have been other civilizations, maybe not in Europe, which were equally developed and perhaps more, and earlier than those of Greece and Rome. There would be no need to point out that to which the Pyramids of Egypt and the Harappa excavations of and Mohejodaro (Indus valley) testify, but for the fact that most Western writers tenaciously adhere to the view that the cradle of civilization was Europe and Europe alone and philosophy began with the Greeks. The spiritual legacy of the world is much older. If we consider civilization to consist of the use of lifts (elevators), air conditioners, sound-proof chambers, electronically operated doors and other devices, automatic dish-cleaners, washing machines, discos, jazz, rock music, see-through dresses, toplesses, homosexuality, free and unrestrained sex in which virgins are prudes, and so much more that makes the developed countries stand a part from the developing; then mankind was never so civilized as today. But if we consider the search for the spirit, the musings and reflections on the divine, the quest for unravelling the mystery of the unknown, why one moment a man is a thinking, speaking, laughing being enjoying the world and its objects with all his senses, and the very next a corpse to be hastily buried or burnt-if we consider the delving into matters like these to be civlization, then it would be difficult to say whether the world is progressing forward or backward. The Vedas express so much wonder at elements like fire (*Agni*) air (*Vayu*) and so forth that the Vedic hymns especially in the *Sāma* and *Rig Vedas*. Wonder indeed is germ of philosophy. The Greeks too like the Hindus considered a sun to be a god (Apollo) and Artemis the moon goddess. Even though Western writers try to gloss over Nature worship in the religion of Greece, but it is certainly there. Plato said 'Wonder is the feeling of a philosopher, and philosophy begins in wonder'.[48] And Pythagords 'It was through philosophy, he said, that he had come to be surprised at nothing'. "('Ek φ c λ o σ o φ ć a s Ë φ η σ ε v a v́ r ῶ π ε ρ L γ ε γ o v έ v a c r ò) M η δ έ v θ a v μ ά ξ ε L v".[49] Civlization are born, exist and then are obliterated, but it is their material constituent that fades away. But what remains is the great thoughts of the great men, the poets artists, musicians and philosophers. These are the gifts of civilizations for posterity, not the pomp and majesty of kings or the wealth and grandeur of cities or the wars and conquests, the victories and celebrations. As Omar Khayyám says:

> **'Think in this batter'd Caravanserai**
> **Whose Doorways are alternate Night and Day,**
> **How Sultan after Sultan with his Pomp**
> **Abode his Hour or two, and went his way'.**[50]

The philosophers have left us wisdom and inspiration which has the capacity to elevate the mind and alleviate sorrows and to them we turn in our periods of tribulation. Philosophers have no race or nationality, even though one may brand them as Egyptian, Indian, Greeks, Romans and so forth. They have one creed - wisdom and truth. It is the misguided who divide them into narrow confines and then extol some and deprecate others according to their warped conception. And that is why irrespective of any contact the thoughts of philosophers of diverse civilizations are often alike. Among philosophers the Greek ones were doubtless very advanced in their understanding. But before we go on to state their doctrnes we proceed to give a brief account of the history and culture of Greece.

HISTORY AND CULTURE

> Thus the class-war plunged Greek Society into every kind of moral evil, and honesty, which is the chief constituent of idealism, was laughed out of existence in the prevailing atmosphere of hostility and suspicion. No argument was cogent enough and no pledge solemn enough to reconcile oppenents. The only argument that appealed to the party momentarily in power was the unlikelihood of their remaining there so long and the consequent advisability of taking no risk with their enemies. And the stupider the combatants the greater their chances of survival, just because they were terrified at their deficiences, expected to be outwitted and outmanoeuvred, and therefore plunged recklessly into action, while their superiors in intellect, who trusted to their wits to protect them and disdained practical precautions, were often caught defenceless and brought to destruction.
>
> *Thucydides (iii.83)*

What is narrated by Thucydides to be the condition of the Greek city-states near about the fifth century B.C. might well be applied to the India of today in the fiftieth year of its independence; politicians at each others', throats those in power adopting all means, more foul than fair, to keep on to it, law and order reduced to anarchy, a police force indulging itself in crime instead of tracking down criminals, a force feared and hated not loved, administrators slogging away at their files in their cosy air-conditioned rooms while prices skyrocket, population swells uncontrolled bursting at its seams, criminals sitting in assemblies and parliaments and the entire republic enveloped by the fog of corruption; a country where now nothing matters except money and that too mostly pelf, entirely cut off and oblivious of its ancient culture, practising cheap initations of Westernusm, a country whose conscience has died long back, rudderless, its spiritualism a thing of the past: and as the intellectuals of the old Greek states did so those of the India of 1998 watch this dismal spectacle helpless, powerless to turn the tide, though attempting to do so like Canute at the seashore trying to make the waves recede.

THE ACHAENS, AND THE DORIAN INVASION

Greek history starts from the time the name 'Hellene' appears in its records. Before that there were the Achaens who were known to the Hittites as the Abhiyavas and to the Egyptians as the Akaiwashas. The centralized power of the Achaens was in Peloponnese.

By 1600 B.C. Crete influence had monopolized Greece as far as the northern plains of Doris and the foothills of Pindus as well as the islands of central Aegean. As Crete's power waned its influence on Greece weakened. The Achaeans were warriors, and their only interest lay in producing weapons like small round shields and leather helmets, broad-bladed spears and long sharpened swords. Between 1200 and 1150 B.C. hostile armies invaded Greece. The new conquerors burnt down cities and reduced houses to rubble. For nearly three centuries after the collapse of the Minoan culture of Greece, there set in a void. Only a few discoveries were made. Wars predominated. About them Homer wrote O ï δ' ä pï σ a v, ẁ σ ε í r ε π v p í χ θ ὼ v π ā σ a v έ μ o c γ o – 'They pour along like a fire that sweeps the whole earth before it'. And:

> **'Gods! shall one raging hand thus level all?**
> **What numbers fell! what numbers yet to fall!**
> **What power divine shall Hector's wrath assuage?**
> **Still swells the slaughter, and still grows the rage".[51]**

For three generations the mercenary Achaeans and their successors were firmly established in Greece. But thereafter new hordes of Dorians swept the land. There exists no record of the centuries following the Dorian invasion. It was a dark age, a period of unrest, turmoil and migrations. However there was a great advance in art, particularly pottery known as the geometrical designed type with angular geometrical figures in arrow. These Dipylon vases were ornately decorated and symmetrical. Thus art and war seem to have intermingled, for the Dorians were making slashing swords, as well as pottery the linear design of which is unrivalled in vases of this kind.

The tongue spoken after the Dorian invasion was Aryan, which was more intelligible inasmuch as it simplified thought and put words in their natural sequence. The Semetic, Turanian and other non-Aryan languages were clumsy and could not convey ideas with the same facility as the Aryan tongue. No people in history developed so rapidly as the Aryans. They were most original in their methods and most inventive in their ideas.

A small tribe of shepherds living on the banks of the Danube were adventurous nomads who wandered southward from their homes. They called themselves Hellenes. According to mythology when the Greek god Zeus living on the Olympus mount found vice and immorality spreading in the world, he was filled with rage and caused a great flood to arise. All the inhabitants were drowned in it but somehow a man and a woman escaped it. These Hellenes who took their name from Hellen, son of Deucalion and Pyrrha, were very coarse and ill-bred with no sense of hygiene or cleanliness, in fact living a life as filthy as that of pigs. When they slew anenemy in war they flung the corpse to be devoured by wild dogs. They were haters of mankind and killed the Pelasgians as they termed the inhabitants of Greece, usurped their territory, took their cattle forcibly, made their wives and daughters serve them as slaves. In brief the were initially unprincipled murderous marauders.

THE MINOANS AND AEGEANS

Before these Hellenes or Pelasgians (inhabitants of Greece) there existed in Crete, the Minoan civilization, which was skin to that of the Aegeans. The Aegeans had built small sea-faring vessels worked by oars and having sails. They worshipped the double-edged are the symbol of the thunder god and offered sacrifices, pouring the blood of the sacrificed animal on the ground. While the men wore only a short loin-cloth, a tight-laced belt and high boots of supple white leather, the women were dressed in low-necked modern style bodices short-waisted and short-sleeved and wore very delicately fashioned jewellry. Fresco paintings, ivory carvings, stone and metal implements and cut gems given evidence of the Minoans being lovers of the ornamental styles in their household articles. In the Mycenean palaces simplicity was combined with luxury. Decorations once copied natural objects but soon began to be conceived on imaginary and fanciful patterns. Sports were of the atheletic kind, dangerous and even cruel like price-fighting, bull-baiting, combats with oppenes armed with broad and sharp rapiers and pointed lances. And as for the women as a historian says:

> 'Their women were worthy of these sportsmen; large-eyed, loose haired, hoydenish creatures in flounced and embroidered skirts and excessively low-necked jackets, who danced and played and hunted, it seems, like the men, and joined them in feast and worship, waved adieu to the fighting force as it marched out, and wept over an ownerless shield after the war was over'.[52]

Thus the Aegeans had weapons superior to those of the Hellenes who had only clumsy stone axes. For several centuries they (the Hellenes) wandered about their new habitation till all of it was occupied by them. Then they began to feel that they ought to find out about the Aegeans who were their neigbours and lived in the colonies behind the high stone wall of Mycenae and Tiryns. They were good learners and were quick to adopt the sharp swords, flexible leather shields, helmets made of the tusks of boars, rapiers and lances of the Aegeans. They also learnt how to build boats and havigate the seas. Having done so they proceeded to fight and plunder their colonies and soon they became the unchallenged rulers of Greece and the coastal regions of Asia Minor. The last stronghold of the old civilization, Troy, fell in the 11th century B.C.

THE GREEK CITY-STATES

The Hellenic civilization varies somewhat from the Minoan in many essential aspects. While the former observed nature and painted portraits of actual phenomena, the Hellenic artist drew men and beasts in the abstract as he imagined them to be. In Greece Sparta because the best and most representative of the Greek culture, and it was with city the outside world had its relations. By 700 B.C. it began to outrival the kingdoms of Lydia, the lonian cities and the Egyptian lives. Later, however, art and luxurious living gave way toe militarization and a spartan became a man of aggressive warrior-like instinct than one of culture. But what Sparta lost was gained by Athnes. The process of history is a kind of see saw and civilizations rise to the pinnacle of their glory and having done so decline and fall either slowly or suddenly. Another thing is that civilizations can never be wholly peaceful for man can never forget his law-of-the jungle instinct of survival of the fittest. Hobbes says:

> 'Hereby it is manifest that during the time men live without a common power to keep them all in awe, they are in that condition which is called war; and such a war as is of everyman, against every man. For WAR consist not in battle only, or the act of fighting; but in

> a tract of time wherein the will to contend by battle is sufficiently known : and therefore the notion of *time* is to be considered in the nature of war, as it is in the nature of weather. For as the nature of foul weather lieth not a shower or two of rain, but in an inclination thereto of many days together, so the nature of war consist not in actual fighting, but in the known disposition thereto during all the time there is no assurance to the centrary. All other time is PEACE'.[53]

The fate of the Greek city-states was much like that. It was not that culture and art did not exist in them. But beginning from cohesion they ended up in dissolution. Poetry, the visual arts, architecture thrived. Elegies were sung to the accompaniment of the flute. There were dringing-songs, camp-songs, love-songs and catches. Lyric poetry found expression. When Anactoria, a girl Sappho loved, deserted her to be married, she expressed her grief:

> 'Some say the fairest thing on the black Earth is a company of horsemen or of soldiers or of ships, but I say "that which one loves". To make this plain to everyone is so easy. For Helen who far surpassed mankind in beauty, left the best of men and forgot child and dear parents to destroy the whole glory of Troy; for the Goddness of Love led her astray at first sight. Easily swayed is the heart of a bride and lightly fluttered by Desire, which even now reminds me of the absent Anactoria-her lovely tread and the shining sparkle of her eyes fain would I see rather than the chariots of Lydia and the soldies in arms'.[54]

THE GREEK COLONIES

When population increased in the Grecian mainland the need was felt to inhabit other areas round about. This was the beginning of colonization on islands or coastal strips. For this the sailing vessels were improved, by providing them with low straight hulls and side-decks with platforms from which marines could fight. Corinth and her colonies could thereby become supreme in the waters between Greece and Sicily. The colonies thus established adopted the religions and political institution of their mother state. The settlers called *epoikoi* came in waves, but the colonies were small and never expanded much. The object was mostly trade particularly in metals. Piracy and the imposition of tolls were greatly prevalent. Fertile an d arabale land was sought and also the prospect of fisheries. Factors like poverty, drought, and dearth because of the expanding population on the mainland of Greece, were incentives for colonization. The colonies were accepted and often took native wives, but the Greeks themsleves adopted little from the native people. Once a colony was established it added to its territory by force of arms and became practically independent.

POTTERY AND COINAGE

Egypt had some commercial relations with the Greek city states. In the reign of Necho relations between Miletus and Neucratis were cordial Necho (609-593) B.C. was dedicated to the temple of Apollo in the Milesian region. Amasis (569-526 B.C.) allowed Greek settlements and gave land for building Greek shrines. He married a Greek lady and contributed to the rebuilding of the temple at Delphi. Greek pottery was prized by the Egyptians and the Greeks derived the sciences of chemistry and geometery and some aspects of the Orphic religion from them.

Another development was the evolving and use of coinage. In the bronze and early iron ages the barter system was in vogue, and the main articles thus exchanged were ingots or bean-shaped pieces of precious metals. In order to ensure the genuineness of these they were hammered in with a distinguishing mark. Thereafter furrows were made on the reverse of the pieces and in the third stage an emblem was inscribed on them. The the first crude and authorized coins appeared. The weight of the gold and/or silver was also fixed uniformly. There were rast amounts of electrum an alloy of silver and gold and this was used in various proportions by different colonies Gyges king of Lydia (c. 687-652) standardizes his coins bearing a lion's head on those of big denominations and the paws of a lion on the smaller ones. Other colonies like those of Miletus and Ephesus followed suit, but the coins of Lydia of pure gold and pure silver surpassed them all. The mainland of Greece, however had no deposits of gold or silver, so iron continued to be used in coinage. The first silver currency was established at Aegina from imported silver, with coins having the emblem of a sea-turtle. Aristotle mentions the orgins of coinage in Lydia and Aegina : 'For the purpose of exchange men made a compact to give and accept a substance serriceable in itself and easy to handle in daily life, such as iron, silver, and other metals; at first it was defined simply by size and weight, but finally it was stamped to dispense with the need for measurement, since the stamp was established as the token of the amount'.[55] However, the Greek city-states avoided uniformity in coinage just as was their general tendency in all matters, though despite this coins were valuable in furthering trade and commerce. It should not be imagined that they were the only people to evolve coinage-a misconcept of most Western writers-for in the latter Vedic Indian civilization there are reference to some kind of currency. The *Shatapatha Brāhmaṇa* mentions a gift (*dakshiṇā*) of three hundred gold coins. For example R.W. Livingston says 'Yet if the twentieth century searched through the past for its nearest spiritual kin it is in the fifth and following centuries before Christ that they would be found'.[56] Quite true. But that is only if we consider the twentieth century to comprise only twentieth century *Europe*. So too the remark 'The Bible, Homer, Shakespeare, Greek art, remain the stars by which we may direct our course over stormy seas'.[57] Again by 'we' the writer obviously means only the inhabitants of the West and by the 'seas' only those with which those inhabitants are concerned and find them to be rough. But the world and its culture is much vaster and includes other regions and civilizations too, some of them earlier than the Greek like the Harappan (Indus Valley) and Egyptian. To Continue, the Greek coins were very picturesque with attractive emblems of bees, turtles, foals, owls, elephants and horse and some of the Greek rulers and Greek gods.

THE WARS

Man can never get rid, it appears, of envy and distrust fulness which make his life, as Hobbes said, 'a continual fear and danger of violent death' and 'solitary, poor, nasty, brutish and short'.[58] And now when the Greek city-states had reached the apogee of their glory their minds were perverted by mutual distrust. Their songs of peace turned into those of war and as Walt Whitman wrote a phantom arose before them 'with distrustful aspect, terrible in beauty, age and power, the genius of poets of old lands, as to them directing like flame his eyes, with finger pointing to many immortal songs, and asked "What singest thou?" And they [the Greeks in our context] said:

> 'Know'st thou not there is but one theme for ever enduring bards? And that is the theme of War, the fortunes of battles, The making of perfect soldiers?'[59]

As the Greek city-states grew on the mainland and Greek colonies sprang up they got embroiled in mutual warfare. Sparta subdued the Messenians and after a weary twenty year's war brought them under its Subjugation. Corinth conquered south Megara. Megara, thus losing some of its land and under pressure of over-population subdued Salamis and settled 600 Megarians there. The Athenians smelt trouble and driving out the Megarians occupied salamis, but later 560 Peisistratus seized the island. Next was the turn of lonia and Aeolis, the two colonies squabbling among themselves. There were struggles for naval supremacy and also commercial exploitation. Sparta challenged Argos but Argos defeated it- Pisa broke away from Elis and gained Ohympia. The Phigalians repulsed Sparta. But Sparta soon made a come back and waged a nineteen years war, defeating Argos in 546 B.C. and adding Thyreatis to its territory. This made Sparta the most powerful state in the Peloponnese.

When the wars for supremacy died down the so-called 'sacred wars' began. The sanctuary of Appolo lay in Delphi and so it had become a kind of holy centre as we would for the Hindus consider called Benares, Prayaga or Hardwar. Twelve tribes of Greece called the Amphictyons controlled the sacred matters and formed the Council of Amphictyony, each tirbe having two votes each in it. Aparently Grecian religion and politics had a common bond, as indeed we have in the India of today even though politicians keep shouting themselves hoarse to deny it. Crisa was stronger than Delphi and both Delphi and the Council could not stomach this superiority and with the 'blessings' of the Pythaian oracle a crusade was declared against Crisa, which under this holy sentence was obliterated by war and bloodshed in the name of religion (a parallel would be the secularists vs Hindutva in present day India proof of the fact that the Indian civilization has gone back in time to about 2,500 yeras). The Sacred War gave Delphi izzat and Thessaly supremancy. Thus emboldened, Thessaly overran Phocis and Locris and entered Boeotia. Soon after, however, the Phocians rebelled and defeated the Thessalians in a night attack. Ere the Persian invasion which was imminent Thessaly's power was greatly reduced.

Wars between the colonies and the various states of Greece were fierecely and bitterly fought, and curiously enough the poets and statesmen like Solon and Tyrtaeus gave the warriors all encouragement in their compositions and speeches. To die in battle fighting with valour was extolled and honourable, even as long back in the *Gita* a Kshatriya warrior was eulogized:L 'And fortunate is the warrior for whom the opportunity for battle comes of itself; for such a Kshatriya, the gates of heaven stand wide open. Therefore if shunning your bounden duty you do not fight this righteous war, not only will you lose your reputation but will also incur sin. Besides people in time to come will ever speack of your infamy, and for the self-respecting man such dishonour is worse than death... Slain, you will go to heaven, victorious, you will enjoy earthly kingdom. Therefore arise, Arjuna, firmly resolved to fight'.[60] It was in the same spirit that the poets of Greece urged on their warriors, 'To die fallen in the front line, a brave man fighting for his fatherland is honourable; but to leave one's city and its rich/fields and live as a beggar is the depth of misery... We march to Salamis to fight for that loved island and cast off the burden of our shame'. Most wars were to survive or to be wiped out. Messenia, Crisa, Smyrna were wiped out of existence. Those vanquished were made slaves, often incorporated in the winning state or sold to other countries. Those wounded or rendered weaponless were put to death. Heralds and envoys were not attacked and the dead were allowed burial. Both the cavalry and infantry were effective, sometimes the one, sometimes the other. The type of fighting involved a great deal of prowess, strength and discipline. The wars were long destructive and costly. But they trained the Greeks in warfare and this training helped them to face the Persians later and defect them.

FROM KINGS AND TYRANTS TO SELF-GOVENMENT

In the beginning the city-states were small units with people who were more or less equal in wealth and property. But gradually differences came about. The changed situation was one in which kingship arose, for only monarchy could deal with people at war and migrating from state to state. And as the institution was the outcome of the needs of various states, it lasted in some, like Sparta Argos, Thera, Taras, Cyrene and Thessaly. But in the small groups of city-states of the Dorian, lonian and Aeolian *poleis* it could not take roof, and so too in the colonies where the *Olkistes* was is most cases not a king.

When kingship went, it paved the way for the aristocracy. At some place as at Argos, Athens and Corinth, the magistrate replaced the king, at others like Ephesus, the priest. And elsewhere, as in Elis, the heads of clans and phratries replaced the aristocracy. The central organ of these aristocracies was the Council (*boule* or *gerousia*). Generally these aristocracies existing by religions, social, economic and military sanctions, served the states well and were very stable for they had the support of the citizens and did not ride roughshod over them. The Assembly of citizens was not suppressed. Early lawgivers like Pheidon, Philolaus, Zaleucus, Charondas and others framed statues which prevented domineering, though sometimes 'the crooked judgements of corrupt kings', caused discontent.

In some states power passed into the hands of a single person who then became a tyrant. The tyrant's rule was called *monarchia* ('sole rule') or tyrannis. Tyrants flourished in states where wealth became concentrated in the hands of the few and the gulf between the rich and the poor widened. Thucydides wrote, 'Tyrannies were established in the city states as revenues were increasing when Greece was becoming more powerful and progressing in the acquisition of capital wealth'. Al caeus and Theognis cryptically observed, 'Money is the man and no pauper is highborn or respectable' and 'Wealth confuses birth'. As Goldsmith wrote in the eighteenth century.

> 'Ill fares the land, to hast'ning ills a prey Where wealth accumulates, and men decay'.61

The writers and poets of the period bemoaned the rise of tyrants. Heredotus wrote 'out of these factions [arising from groups of split up oligarchies] there arises bloodshed, and from bloodshed is one-man-rule'. Solon said, 'From the great men destruction comes to the state and the people in their ignorance fall into servitude to the single ruler', and Theognis observed 'From corrupt judges arise factions and civil bloodshed and single rulers'. The verse of Theognis and Megara sang 'Gone is Faith, goddess supreme, gone Moderation from mankind, and the Graces have deserted our land, my friend. Among men solemn oaths are no longer respected, and no one revers the immortan gods. the generation of religious men is destroyed; they recognize no standards of law or of piety'. Hatred, treachery and poverty prevail; man is at the mercy of gods whose will he cannot divine'. But in some tyrants there existed some good points too along with their wickednesses. Corinth was an example. There Cypselus ruled and after him his son Periander, and under him Corinth reached the highest point of prosperity Periander stopped the exodus of population, put curbs on extravagance, immoratily and local expenditure and ended the purchase of slaves. He got a passage (*diolkos*) made for taking ships across the Isthumus and proposed to construct a canal. He made conquests and expanded his territory by wars and marriage alliances, patronized poets such as Arion and Corinth's artistic goods became famous. So much so that Pindar later sang of the city's orderliness, justice and peace, the sweet-singing Muse and 'the war-god strong in the spears of her young men'. But he killed his wife and banished his son, Lycophron. Orthagoras of Sicyon, Epidaurus of Procles, Theagenes of Megara were other tyrants of the period.

The tyrants of Italy and Sicily were no better. Phalaris of Acragas killed leading citizens, seized the Acropolis and adopted terroristic way in getting rid of oppenets buring them alive in a huge bull made of bronze. Pythagoras who was initially not tyrnnical, became one. He voilated laws and plundered the rich, but used the money to aid the poor. He was therefore a kind of Robin Hood. Melas, Tynnondas, Pittacus, Thrasybulus were some of the other Ionian tyrants. Often they reviled one another, as Alcaeus said 'The low-born Pittacus was appointed tyranct of the spineless and ill-fated state by one and all with shouts of praise'. 'Now Myrsilus is dead, so make merry and drink deep'. The Ionain tyrants were worse than the

Dorian ones inasmuch as they destroyed but did nothing constructive. They also lacked self-restraint. Even though commerce flourished and to some extent the fine arts what the tyrants destroyed was liberty and free thinking which were much more valuable to the Greeks than wealth. The tyrants practised cruelties with an intensely base instinct and as Dionysius says, Τυραννίs θηίων ἁπάντων ἀγριώ γαγον - 'Atyranny is of all wild beasts the most savage'.[62]

The epoch of aristocracy and tyranny was, however shortlived and the first signal towards constitutional reform was given by the state of chios early in the sixth century B.C. There aristocracy gave way to a government with some democratic features. The people could vote and make the laws the wanted. There was a people' conucil which met every month and heard appeals and the executive functions were performed by magistrates (*demarchoi*). There were other officials too (basileis). Now when tyranny had exceeded all limits the people were sick of it and they turned to reforms, for as Aristotle said in Politica (VII, 10), 'Η δημοκρανία ἡ γελεναία γνραννίs εσγίν' ['Democracy is the acme of tyrany']. But it was not all smooth sailing. The task of publishing the laws was given to Draco and as the English word 'Draconian' suggests meaning laws 'rigorous harsh and cruel' [Oxford Dictionary] he produced laws severe, for he was a professional lawyer to whom a crime was a crime of whatever degree it may be. Stealing an apple was classed by him with murder and he considered the punishement for both was death! His laws of debt were another example of the Draconic. The clansman in the Greek state possessed land which could not be alienated, while the land of a guildsman was his personal property and alienable. Draco's debt laws laid down that though the clansman could not alienate his land he could pledge its produce while taking a loan, and if he became bankrupt he and his family had to pay one-sixth of the produce for ever. His land was then marked with a horos (a stone signifying that he and his family and his land would ever be 'enslaved' to the creditor). The guildsman could pledge his land *and* his wife and children and in case he could not pay the loan back the creditor could sell the guildsman, his wife and family either at home or abroad. The powerful class explited these laws and soon all the poor became indebted to the rich working for them as slaves and also deprived of a share of the produce of their lands. Solon, who was marked out to remedy the Draconian laws, himself observed: 'Swiftly has the state fallen into a base slavery, which awakens into life contention and a civil war that has destroyed the fair manhood of many... such are our ills at home... Many of the impoverished, sold and bound with shameful shackles, go to foreign lands'.

The task of setting right this sorry state of affairs created by Draco's misguided policies fell on the shoulders of Solon who was assigned the reformative work in 594-93 B.C. Some people were disappointed by his reforms, particularly those who had enriched themselves at the cost of the poor, but then it is always impossible to please all, and those who try to do so end up in pleasing none. Solon therefore remarked 'Should I stand before the bar of Time, Witness on my behalf would best be given by black Earth, Mother supreme of the Olympian gods, from whose breast I took up the record-stones which was planted far and wide; she, hitherto in bondage, now is free. I restored to Athens, their god-built fatherland, many persons sold abroad-some justly, some unjustly-and others fled through stress of debt, who spoke no more the Attic tongue, and others here in Attica I liberated from a shameful slavery, wherein they trembled at their masters' ways'. Solon consulted the cracle at Delphi.[63] The oracle replied 'Sit in the middle of the ship and steer a straight course; many Athenians are at thy side'. And that is what Solon did. He removed the disabilities of the clansmen and guildsmen, the institute of sixth-partners which Dranco had enforced as also the stone-pillars its emblems. All slaves whether at home or abroad were freed and the differences between clansmen and guildsmen removed. A temporary ban was put on export of natural products except olive-oil of which there was a surplus in Greece. Widows and orphans were cared for and to strengthen liberty trials were to be held by the Court of Areopagus. Commerce was boosted to mitigate poverty. Coinage was improved. Solon gave representation to all classes and while improving the peasants' lot did not eliminate the nobility for they could provide good soldiers. He devised a mode of taxation which would not be harsh on the poor. Apart from the Council of the Areopagus he established a Council of Four Hundred of which hundred members were to be nominated. The Council prepared the subject which would be discussed in the Assembly and either recommended the subject to be discussed or withheld it. The Assembly could only discuss as many subjects as the council sent up, none on its own. The Assembly could discuss, vote and decide but could not frame a resolution. Solon made the Assembly a judicial body under the name 'Heliaea'. Thus for the first time a body of citizens could act as the people's jurors and judges. He forbade selling women except those unchaste, slander of the dead. He gave responsibility to every class and expected them to exercise it. Social justice, liberty, reason and moderation were the pillars of his reforms, which he summed up thus: 'I gave to the people the privilege sufficient unto the people, not diminishing its rights nor demanding more, nor did I devise any unseemly position for those who held power and were respected for wealth. I stood holding my stout shield over both parties and I did not allow either party to prevail in despite of justice'. Any individual could sue for personal injury. Expenditure on dowries and funerals was regulated. A historian rightly praises Solon for his remarkable insight:

> 'But divine justice he [Solon] realized, differs from human justice-Like a storm in spring the wrath of Zeus descends upon a group, so that in a family the innocent

> children suffer and in a state the innocent citizens. Man is master only of his internal affairs... Neither state nor individual is master over outer circumstances such as health or plague, prosperity or disaster. Despite all one's hopes, merit and effort do not bring success; often a good worker fails and a bad worker successds. Merit is its own reward, and success in unpredictable. Solon himself was mocked for failing to explit his position and secure wealth for himself. He replied "Many bad men are rich, many good men are poor' but we shall not exchange wealth for honour, for money flits from man to man but hounour abides forever". He lived as he preached, in the light of his reason and his ideals. He saw both the glory and sadness of human life. Together with the Illiad and the Odyssey, the poems of Solon deserved to be, and were, an inspiration to lonian Athens'.[64]

Solon's principle was moderation, 'Μηδέν ἄγαν'. ['Nothing in excess'],[65] as in providing for the Council to moderate the Assembly he wished, as he said, that the 'Ship of state' should 'ride upon two anchors' to lesson its pitching in the surf and so reduce the turbulence of those who manned it. He was far ahead of his times and strangely his salutary reforms were not appreciated as much as they ought to have been. The oligarchs called them oligarchic, the democrats democratic and Aristotle called them 'mixed'. After framing the laws and declaring them inviolable for a hundred years Solon left Attica for ten years. But the Athenians had not learnt the advantages of peace and the value of the principles Solon had advocated. A scion of the aristocracy, Peisistratus, treachercously seized the Acropolis and with him tyranny revived. When Solon returned he was dismayed by these unsavory events:

> 'And much it grieved my heart to think What man has made of man'.[66]

Sadly he wrote, 'Clouds shed thick snow and hail, bright lighting produces thunder; so the leading men destroy the state and the people in their folly fall into slavery under one-man-rule. Hard it is for one who sails far out to come inshore again; one should think of all things in good time'. However, at this time the commerce of Athens expanded and craftsmen desirous of the citizen ship of that state came flocking to it.

GREEK THOUGHTS, IDEALS, ART AND WAY OF LIFE

Turning to the Greek way of thinking, we find that though their common aim was beauty and truth there was diversity in their methods of approach. Each Greek artist, philosopher or poet had his individual concept. Their art was not regimented according to a fixed pattern as Egypt's was. They considered this freedom of thought to be the main characteristic of civliztion and the suppression of this freedom, barbarism. From their point of view, therefore, the highly civilized empires of Carthage and Persia were as uncultured as the semi-savage ones of Thrace and Illyria. To them any restriction on the freedom of thinking was a sign of barbarism. By 800 B.C. this spirit of diversity made itself felt in Greece. Thus Athens, Sparta and other cities had their own characteristic patterns and designs. In fact each family had its own cults, shrines, politics, coinage and traditions. Due to various Eactros like wars, turmoil, overpopulation and so forth many Greeks round about 1000 B.C. left the mainland and settled in Asia Minor on the Anatolian coast. They called themselves lonians. During a short period they outshone the Athenians and Spartans in art, literature and the Sciences. In the seventh century B.C. Thales made advances in geometry and astonomy and Anaximander in geography. In literature there were Sappho, Alcaeus and Archilochus. Colonization was carried out spontaneouly and smoothly. Once a Colony was established they were content with it and had no desire for adding more territory to it, as Phocylides sang in his songs.

> 'A tiny city perched upon the cliff edge and living in wisdom is better far than all the folly of Babylon'.[67]

Such settlements were Cyrene, Istria, Byzantium and so forth. Temple architecture was greatly developed in the sixth century. Temples were colourful, made of limestone glazed with marble in red, blue green and such rich hues. But sculpture and paintings of the fifth and sixth century were so bad that it was hard to say what was what, and it had to be written below them 'this is a cow', 'this is a woman' and so forth. It was only much later that sculpture reached the highest point of its glory. But it was in literature that poets like Homer surpassed and 'moved the hearts of men to wonder'.

At the beginning of the fifth century the Greeks had been mainly agriculturists. But later under the administration of Pericles there was a social transformation and commerce and industry became predominant. The citizens began to take part in public meetings and discussions or diverted themselves by recreations like the theater, contests, games and so forth. Olive oil and honey were found in abundance and formed the chief items of export. Corn grown by the farmers could supply only one-fourth of the country's requirement but vegetables - cabbage, lentils, peas onions and garlic were plentiful and so too fruits, particularly figs. Roses were cultivated all over to provide wreaths for temple offerings and bouquets. Meat, except for that of pigs, was not popular, and oxen were meant mainly for sacrifices to the gods. Goats' milk was usually drunk (not cows) and cheese was made from it. Sheep were reared for their wool. The marketplace near the Acropolis presented the same state of confusion as an Indian village or small town hāt or bazzar of today. A popular form of entertainment was the theater. Soon every city had one. It was hewn from a rock cut out from a hereby hill. There was a chorus and behind it the actors who wore masks. The stage and stage effects were not there, at least as we find them later on in history. A writer says:

'The first arrivals secured their places soon after midnight, and since sunrise there has been a steady stream of spectators, climbing the steep gangways on the hillsides and distributing themselves upon the tiers of wooden benches which form the autitorium. Even so the theater is not yet quite full; for there is room in the spacious semicircle for nearly twenty-thousand people and the ushers are busy packing them closely together in the narrow seats. The more luxurious have brought cushions to sit on, and the more careful a supply of nuts and fruit, for this is an all day ceremony, and once in his place a man must stay there until the end of the afternoon. There is still some time to wait before the performance begins... The envoys [foreign ambassadors who are invitees] are followed by the ten judges, chosen by lot, who will decide the prize of victory to the best set of plays. Then the great theater falls silent; the aged priest of Dionysus is seen coming from sacrifice to the god. He walks slowly to his central throne with hands uplifted to heaven; a flute thrills out one silvery note; and the Agamemnon begins.[68]

A great occasion for the Athenians was the festival of Athena, patron goddess of the city. It celebrated once in four years. There was a weeks's celebration comprising competitions, processions, feasts music literary contests, sports and even beauty shown! A really torchrace was held in which two teams were framed, each one passing a lighted torch from hand to hand without its light going out, and the team which first reached the Cave of Pan just outside the city wall was declared winner. The men forming the winning team were presented an ornamented vase depicting athletic scenes and filled with olive oil. On the fourth day there was chariot racing and exhibitions of horsemanship, and on the fifth a beauty contest. But these were not the kind held now in our times for selecting a Miss World or a Miss Universe for to the Greeks considered male beauty superior to the female and the winner was Mr Greece. However the main event was not recreational but religions. And that was the reverent drapoing of the goddess Athena Promachos' ivory statue in the temple of the Acropolis. This was the only occasion when the Athenian girls also took part in the ceremony their job being to weave the robe meant for the statue of the goddess. Even the aliens joined in the city's rejoicing, though to remind them of their dependent status they merely bore stools and parasols for the Athenian girls. The drapoing was carried out after the white cows and the sheep with shining fleaces were offered in sacrifice to the goddess.

In daily living there was one very vital difference between Athens and Sparta inasmuch as while the Athenian women led a cloistered life confined to their homes, those of Sparta lived in the open and raced and wrestled with young men. So while the Spartan women were sturdy and blooming with health with deep firm bosoms and rounded limbs, those of Athens were of poor physique living within the four walls of their rooms and scarcely sharing companionship with their husband, merely bearing their children while the men were for the most of the time in the marketplace or the law courts or Assembly, engaged in some trade or vocation, or just strolling about on the streets; anywhere except under their own roof. Besides, the Athenian women were married early, at about fifteen years's age and this also took a toll on their health and liveliness. It would perhaps be too much to say as a historian does, that this cramped life of theirs 'was one of the main causes of the all too steady decay of the Athenian State', for Athens had her own glory too and produced great administrators like Pericles, Them istocles, Cimon, Demos thenes and Lycurgus. But the women were not by any means the equals of thier Spartan counter parts.

Every Athenian whatever his age, eighteen or seventy, considered daily exercise essential. He exercised naked, for even to wear a loin-cloth was thought to be a sign of barbarianism in the colonnade which was his gym. Everyone had an oil flask which Athenians always carried as one carries his umbrella. He rubbed his whole body with oil, this being an established practice as Lucian wrote:

> 'When their first pithless tenderness is past, we strip our youths and aim at hardening them to the temperature of the various seasons till heat does not incommode them nor frost paralyse them. Then we anoint them with oil by way of softening them into suppleness. It would be absurd that leather, dead stuff as it is, should be made tougher and more lasting by being softened with oil and the living body get no advantate'.

Thereafter the athlete went to the Konisterion and powdered himself with dust which was thought to close the pores of the skin, check excess of perspiration and keep the body cool. Then he was ready for exercise, punching keavy sacks or lighter balls before going out to run or jump or box or wrestle with his partner. This done he went to the bath-house a simple affiar without the luxury of Turkish hamman, scrubbing off the oil dust and dirt, and dressed again for the road. There were many diversions - a charming flute player, a military drill, a cock-fight and so forth. Or he played chess or a draught game, or discoursed with friends on various subjects. Thus the days passed in disciplining the body as well as the mind; days such as those which Aristophanes wrote of in his Clouds:

> **Then you will go to the Academe**
> **And under the olives contest with your partner,**
> **Small the fragrance of woodbines and lime blossoms**
> **When the plane tree whispers love to the elm in the grove**
> **In the beautiful season of spring.**

When at dinner the servants got scented water for the guests to wash their hands. Food was simple Cereals, plain bread and cheese, green vegetables and a little meat. They ate frugally and with their fingers. No knives and forks. Wine was drunk thereafter with first a libation to the gods. Drinking too was moderate and they hated someone being drunk. After the dessert there was the symposium. A ballad was sung with flute-girls playing on the flute. There was entertainment with boys playing on harps and girls dancing and somersaulting through hoops encircled with daggers, the mimicking of stories such as those of Area and Aphrodite. For the Greeks there were no long dinners with a variety of courses. It was not living to eat but eating to live. Rather the dinners were occasions for conversation and that too of an exalted kind, not bazaar rumours. As for example the account real or imaginary given by a historian as follows:

> 'Just as the actors are concluding their little play [part of the afterdinner entertainment] a noise of shouting is heard in the road and a violent knocking at the front door. A voice cries out "It is I, Alcibiades, and I am rather drunk [he couldn't have really been so otherwise he wouldno't has shown sobriety]. May I come in or shall I go away?" Callias leaps up from this couch and, after a little delay while the door is being unbolted, the rising young politician make's his appearance. His face is flushed, he is wearing a garland of roses and it is plain that his description is not altogether false. But the sight of his mentor, Socrates, somewhat cools his excitement, and when room is made for him on one of his couches he settles down quietly enough, and listens while his friend introduces a discussion, "Is wealth necessary to happiness?" Like most Socratic investigations, this lasts a long time... At the end Socrates convinces his auditors the philosopher alone is really wealthy and

really happy inasmuch as he alone is really self-sufficient, And so the symposium ends'[70]

As has been said, the Athenians had practically no family life. For taking their pleasure with women there were the free foreign women ('hetairai') who could lure with their come-hither looks but they were few and to have their company was an expensive affair. In the fifth century B.C. most Athenian women were wives or slaves, hardly claiming a man's affection. But in the Hellenic age there were vivacious courtezans like Thais, Cdycera, Phryne and others. The Athenian was very patriotic, always putting the country above self not like our own *netas* (politicians) in power today many of whom care a damn for the country and are busy amassing pelf. The Athenian's money was at his country's disposal and his life too, for up to his old age he would not hesitate to lay it down for it. But in his conjugal relations he was a complete misfit and he deliberately shut his eyes to the degenerate system of slavery.

Western writers have maligned the Hindu caste system, particularly its vilification of the Sudras or chandalas; and rightly so, one writer calling the Sudras pariahs and a class of 'despised and miserable slaves' who could never hope to be anything else. The same writer goes on, or rater goes back, to say about Greek slavery: 'The slaves were hereditary servants and waited upon the needs of their masters, and it was very pleasant to be a member of the organization'.[71] Baloney! How pleasant the Greek slaves found their slavery, is recorded by another hostorian, one of eminence, as follows:

> 'The mines could not have been worked without slave lbour, and of the adult slaves in Attica it has been calculated that more than half were thus employed. When a slave found himself at laurium he stayed there often for no very long period until he died. The conditions were bad, the hours long-ten hour's work followed by ten hour's rest-and the labour exhausting

The weaker men were kept above ground, where the ore was crushed in mortars and hand mills, washed and smelted; the stronger did the actual mining. In galleries three feet wide and three fect high, on their knees, their backs or their stomachs, they hewed with pick and mattock. There was no ventilation, no sanitation, the heat must have been cruel, the odours almost unbearable, and the iron rings can still be seen in the passage from which a worker whose output did not satisfy his overseer was trussed up for a whipping. A man of ordinary humanity... preferred not to visit his concession at Laurium; he regarded it as a necessity and thought about it as little as possible'.[72]

But was it? Was slavery, and particularly of this brutal kind, a necessity and justified. Even a philosopher and thinker such as Aristotle, while conceding that a Greek ought not to be a slave justifies this vicious institution by a reasoning so specious that one hearing it one may doubt his wisdom. According to him

> '...there are certain human beings who are natural slaves, without sufficient brains or intelligence to be worthy of self-realization. For such it may even be to their advantage to be governed by others rather than to misgovern themselves. He compares the use of slaves to the use of tame animals, the difference being that a slave can understand relatively elaborate orders'.[73]

In fact in the Greek city states the slaves were much more numerous than free citizens (E. Meyer estimates 55,000 citizens, 14,000 resident aliens and 100,000 slaves). All the dirty work and menial tasks were left to the slaves. To say that they were 'not on the whole badly treated' (W.R. Halliday) is a curious perversion of the truth. The Greek slave was much worse off than a domestic. It is said 'municipal services' were done by them. The term is vague, but it would include scavenging, cleaning drains, washing clothes, utensils, bearing heavy loats, and all because the free citizens needed leisure, discussions and so forth. And & slave had no legal status, he was 'a chattel which could be seized for debt; his family relations were not recognized, and his evidence in courts was given under torture' (W.R. Halliday). In view of this Hendrik Van Loon's aforesaid remarks about the Sudras in Aryan India would show that the Greek slave was only a super-sudra and much worse off that the Sudra of the Vedic era. In the *Gita* the classification of varna-caste was a later corruption-was based on occupation and nature *guṇa-karma-vibhāga* (Gita, 4.13). But the classification was not rigid as for the Greek slaves. In the *Chāndogya Upanishad* we come across one Satyakāma son of a low-caste woman named Jabāla. When the lad asked his mother about his family background she said 'I don't know, son. I earned by living the hard way serving as a maid in various households when I was young. You were born then. My job took up all my time and I had hardly any left to find out your ancestory. All I can say with certainity is that you are Satyakāma and I am Jabāla. Why not just call yourself Satyakāma Jabāla. The lad went to the sage Gautama, asking the sage to take him as a pupil. On being asked about his family he gave a directrephy exactly in his mother's words. The sage said, 'None but a Brahmin could speak so candidly (so by nature I take you to be a Brahmin whatever your origin may be)'. And the sage accepted him as his pupil.[74] Thus Hendrik Van Loon's observation in The Story of Mankind, 'The three highest castes were allowed to read these holy scriptures [the Veda] The Pariah, however, the despised member of the lowest caste, was not permitted to know its contents. Woe to the man of noble or priestly caste who should teach a Pariah to study the sacred volume!'[75] and this remark is not true of the period of development of Vedic knowledge in India and depicts the author's insufficient knowledge of Indian religion and culture. As another writer says with much truth 'it was a world empty of machines and full of slaves. This last fact cannot be over-emphasized. To see Hellenistic society as it existed, the slave background must never be lost sight of; and such aspirations as freedom and brother-hood-even the very revolutions-too often convey a sense of unreality when it is remembered that a large part of the population was, by most people, excepted from their scope'.[76] And even W.R. Halliday, quoted aforesaid, says 'But it is difficult for honesty to deny that ultimately Athenian democracy rested upon a basis of slavery...'[77] And the poet Byron who generally sang of the glory of Greece could not help condemning it for slavery:

> 'A land of slaves shall ne'er be mine-dash down you cup of Samian wine!'[78]

The Greek houses were simple and built on the otirnysl psyyrtn. They were single-storeyed, often without windows, and in the fort just one door in the sun-dried brick wall, which was mostly kept shut. Through this one passed into a courtyard with verandas no all sides. The rooms opened into this courtyard and their light and air from it.

Thus ventilation was poor and water supply pipes, plumbing drainage and sanitary arrangements, there were none. There was no chimney in the kitchen, just a hole in the roof, and so it was perpetually full of smoke. Three-legged braziers full of burning coal provided heat in the cold winter month. The flame of a lamp containing usually stayed indoors, a nurse looking after the children playing in the courtyard. The half-a-dozen slaves of such middle-class families did the chores like spinning and weaving, grinding corn, fetching water, preparing food and buying provisions.

LITERATURE, MUSIC AND ART

Literature

As we have remarked earlier, the Greek spirit of moderation on which was much like Buddhism's golden mean, permeated their life and living. And so it did their literature and thought. In politics they combined liberalism with conservatism revering tradition and old customs but also keeping their mind open to new ideas, reason straightforwardness and sincerity. In his famous *Republic* Plato brings out this quality in not praising the majesty of kings but their wisdom (recalling the renowned edict of Ashoka):

> 'Unless lovers of wisdom bear sovereign rule in states, or those who are now called sovereigns and governers become sincere and capable lovers of wisdom, and government and love of wisdom be brought together, and unless numerous natures who at present pursue either government or wisdom, the one the exclusion of the other, be forcibly debarred from this behaviour, there will be no respite from evil, my dear Glaucon, for states, nor, I fancy, for humanity; nor will this constitution, which we have just described in our argument, come to that realization which is possible for it and see the light of day. It is this which has for so long made me hesitate to speak. I saw how paradoxical it would sound. For it is given to few to perceive that no other constitution could even bring happiness either to states or individuals'.

There is no condemnation here of that which could be, but was never realized in Greece itself with the rivalries conflicts and intrigues of the city-staes, or earlier by Egypt and Babylon, or later by Rome or Britain with its bloody religious massacres, or Europe with the guillotine and Hitler's Jewish torture chambers, or the illiterate, poor miserable people of the undeveloped and developing world and the politicians in them at one another's throats, corrupt autocratic and anti-people, or the sword of Mohammet as Bacon said, to force consciences - there is no rebuke or admonishment in Plato's unsurpassed conclusion, only the ring of truth, long suppressed but glistening the more like genuine gold in the fire of falsehood.

As Livy says 'Justo et moderato regebantur imperio' nec abnuebant, quod num vinculum fideiest melioribus papere'.[79]

It should be made clear that though Greek literature had a great influence on English literature and that of Europe, such influence was confined to it. The literatures of the East developed on their own in Sanskrit or Arabic. And when Goethe is quoted as saying 'Where would one look for a greater orator than Demosthenes; or finer dramatic poetry, next to Shakespeare, than of Aeschylus or Sophocles not to speak of Euripedes' and that Herodotus was 'the most interesting and instructive book, next to the Bible, which had ever been written',[80] it is not only overstating but also ignoring the literatures of the other half of the world, like the Vedas, Upanishads, Brāhmaṇas the Sūtras, Mahabharata, Ramayana, the Ashtadhyāyī of Pānini of whom the Chinese traveller, Yuan Chwang observed 'Rishi Pānini was from his birth extensively informed about men and things' (*Siyuki*, 1.45), the plays of Ashvaghosha (*Shāriputraprakarana*) and Bhāsa, king Shūdraka's *Mrichchhakatika* Kalidāsa's *Vikramorvashī* and Shakuntalā to which Goethe himself paid a rich tribute:

> **'Wouldst thou the young year's blossoms, and the fruits of its decline**
> **And all by which the soul is charmed, enraptured, feasted, fed,**
> **Wouldst thou the Earth and Heaven itself in one sole name combine,**
> **Iname thee, O Shakuntalā and all at once is said'.[81]**

Dandin, Bhavabhuti, Bhartrihari, and so forth, to mention only a few names. This is not to belittle Greek literature, only to make it clear that since it forms only a small segment of the world's literature, any comparison of its excellence vis-ā-vis other literatures would be an exercise in facility.

Greek literature has simplicity and directness, with an economy of words. No circumlocutions and long-winded sentences or paragraphs. In this respect it resembles the Sanskrit sūtras for succinctness. In translations, therefore Greek expressions have to expressed in many more words than in the original. For example there is the enigmatic but bactual lines of Simonides on the dead Spartan warriors at Thermopylae:

ῶξεῖν', ἀγγ ἐλλειν Λ ακεδαμονίοις ογι γῆδε κεμεθα, γοίνων ρ́ή μασι πειθόμενοι,

'Stranger, go and tell the Spartans that we lie here, obeying their words'. As R.W. Livingstone says, where Byron, interpreted Sappho as:

O Hesperus, thou bringest all good things
Home to the weary, to the hungry cheer,
To the young bird the parent's brooding wings,
The welcome stall to the o'er-laboured steer';

Sappho herself put it as:

F'εσπερε πὰνγα φέρων ὅ σα φαινοις ἐσκδασ αὔως, φέρεις οἴν, φερες αἴγα φερεις ἄπν μαγερι παῖδα

'Star of evening, bringing all things that bright dawn has scattered, you bring the sheep, you bring the goat, you bring the child back to his mother'.[82]

Sappho's brevity is more eloquent than Byron's diffuseness, however effusive, Alexander Pope's version of the lliad of Homer is not really as effective as it could be:

'His beauteous princess cast a mournful look,
Hung on his hand, and then dejected spoke;
Her bosom labour'd with a boding singh,
And a big tear stood trembling in her eye
"Too daring price! ah, wither dost thou run?
Ah forgetful of thy wife and son!
And think'st thou not how wretched we shall be,
A widow I, a helpless orphan he?"'[83]

The version of Lang, Leaf and Myers quoted by R.W. Livingstone is much nearer to the original. The occasion is Hector's departure for fighting in the Trojan war, the possibility being that he is slain, and the reaction of his wife Andromache:

> 'So he spoke and laid his son in his dear wife's arms; and she took him to her fragrant bosom, smiling through tears. And her husband had pity to see her, and caressed her with his hand, and spoke and called her by her name. "Dear one, I pray thee be not of oversorrowful heart; no man against my fate shall send me to my death; but destiny I ween, no man has escaped". So spoke glorious Hector and took up his horsehair-crested helmet; and his dear wife departed to her home, often looking back and letting fall great tears. And she came to the well-built house of man-slaying Hector, and found therein her many handmaidens, and stirred lamentation in them all. So they wept for Hector, while he yet lived, in his house; for they thought that he would no more come back to them from battle'.[84]

Despite its simplicity Geek literature has great literary value. The Greek writers put their facts without needless comments. The death of his master doubtless overwhelmed Plato with grief was recorded by him with striking reticence more effective than any long and laboured epitaph: 'Such, Echecrates, was the death of our friend, the best man, I think, that I have ever known, the wisest too and the most just' [Phaedo, 118 BI]. Greek literature is truthful and unwanted impressions and verbosity. It portrays suffering without dwelling on its horror agony or disgust. As an example there is the occasion when Priam begs for his son's body from the man who killed him and Priam's other sons as well:

...'the king his entry made:
And, prostrate now before Achilles laid,...
Embraced his knees, and bathed his hands in tears;
....
"Think of thy father's age, and pity mine!
In me that father's reverend image trace,
Those silvery hairs, that venerable face;
His trembling limbs, his helpless person see!
In all my equal but in misery!...
Nineteen one mother bore-Dead all are dead!...
Still one was left... Him too thy rage has slain;
....
"Think of thy fater, and this face behold!
See him in me, as helpless and as old!...
Thus force to kneel, thus grovelling to embrace
The scourage and ruin of my realm and race;
Suppliant my children's murderer to implore,[85]
And kiss those hands yet reeking with their gore".'

Thus Priam, even while grovelling before Achilles, the killer of his many sons, for Hector's body, never loses his self-respect. And he would't even had seen Achilles' face had he known the barbarous manner in which Hector's dead body was treated, for the Greeks were no less than the Orient when it came to ruthless cruelty: 'He (Achilles) pierced the feet of the dead man and fastened them with thongs to the back of his chariot, letting the head trail. Then he lashed his horses and round and round the walls of Troy he dragged all that was left of glorious Hector'.[86]

As R.W. Livingstone observes in his very thoughtful and accurate analysis of Greek literature, the Greeks writer did not let his own feeling crowd out what his subject thought and felt, as an epitaph which a father put on his son's grave:

Δωδεκενη γὸν παῖδα παγηρ ἀπεθηκε Φίλππος
ενάδε γὴν πολλὴν ἐλπίδα Νικογέλήν.

Callimachus, Epigr.20: 'His father Philip laid here to rest his twelve year old son, his high hope, Nicoteles'.[87]

And Livingstone rightly holds the charming economy and brevity of Greek literature to be largely due to the fact that then hand-copying was the mode of transmission for printing had not till then been invented, and 'the habit of writing for money, which encourages abundant production, and the existence of the printing-press, which makes it easy, expose us to dangers from which the ancients were free'. The Greeks have many descriptions of the love of men and women, but none of the lurid sex and shameless details of lovemaking which gives popularity and best-sellership to our modern fiction which is considered 'great' in proportion to its capability to titatate lust and passion.

The Iliad and the Odyssey were composed in lonia (Western Asia Minor), composed, not written for it is unlikely that writing was then in vogue there. Both the epics centre round Troy, a city close to the Dardanelles Priam, the wealthy and powerful king of Troy had many sons, the foremost in valour and handsomeness being Hector and Paris. Paris came to Greece as the guest of Menelaus the Spartan king, whose wife Helen a very beautiful woman, he carried away by treachery, and took her to Tray. Menelaus and his brother captured Troy after a siege often years This was done by the stratagem of the wooden horse. A huge horse of wood was made in which some of the bravest Greek warriors hid and placed at the city's gate and the remaining Greeks went off to sea some distance. The Trojans dragged the horse in:

> **'Who of the young but hurried forth?**
> **Who of the old would stay at home?**
> **With song and rejoicing they brought death in,**
> **Treachery and destruction'.**

They thought they had driven the Greeks away. But at dead of night the Greek warriors quietly emerged from the wooden horse and fell on the unsuspecting Trojans rudely woken from their sleep. The Trojans thus caught unawares, had no chance to stave off the attack by night. The Greeks set fire to the city, and Troy burned. Helen was restored to Menelaus. Troy was in ruins. The Greeks killed Hecuba's young daugher Polyxena and cast Hector's son to death from the wall. The women were carried away as slaves

Troy has perished, the great city,
Only the leaping flames remain.

The long Trojan war was fought because of the abduction of Helen, who was considered to be superbly beautiful, as Marlowe later wrote:

Was this the face that laurched a thousand ships
And burnt the topless towers of Ilium?[88]

The Odyssey is the story of Odysseus or Ulysses, the craftiest of the Greeks, his ten year's wanderings along the Mediterranean and his return to Ithaca and his slaying of the native princes who meanwhile had been wooing without success his wife Penelope. As has been related after putting the wooden horse at the gate of Troy, the Greeks who had not got into it set sail. But on the way soon after they left the shore a great tempest arose. Many ships were lost, Menelaus' was wrecked on the shore of Egypt and Ajax was drowned. Odysseus' ship was cast adrift and he was forced to wander for ten long years before reaching home. At first he landed on the shore of the country of the Lotus-eaters who a few ate it and all memory of their land faded from their minds. They wished to live in the Lotus Land forever. But Odyseus dragged them on board and chained them there. Their next adventure was with the Cyclops Polyphemus a terrible giant and monster who devoured four of his men. Odyseus managed to make him drunk with wine and fall asleep. The with a huge timber log sharpened to a point by his men they heated it glowing hot and blinded the giant. The men trapped inside the giant's cave came out clinging to the back, underside of fleeced rams. The next adventure was their landing in the country of the Laestrygons, cannibals of gigantic size. The destroyed all of Odysseus' ships except his own which was yet at sea. the next adventure was at Aeaea the realm of Circe a lovely witch and enchantress who could change men into beasts. All except one of Odysseus' men were turned into swine. But Hermes pitied him and gave him a herb which saved him. Circe fell in love with him carried away by his handsomeness, and at his bidding restored his men to human form. After many other adventures including the dulcet songs of the Sirens heard only by him as he had asked his men to bind him securely to the mast, and got the ears of others waxed so that they could not hear. Finally after losing all his men when due to the Sun's vengeance, a thunderbolt sheltered his ship, Odysseus at last was home, and after killing all the suitors whom his wife, the lovely Penelope had resisted for these twenty long years and being united to her.

Other writers were Solon who wrote about his reforms, stated before in verse, Theognis of Megara a political poet, Archilochus the satirist, and Sappho a renowned poetess of love and beauty known as the 'Tenth Muse' and is fabled to have thrown herself into the sea from the Leucadian promontory as her advances were rejected by the beautiful youth Phaon, and of whom Byron wrote:

> **'The isles of Greece, the isles of Greece!**
> **Where burning Sappho loved and sung,**
> **Where grew the arts of war and peace,**
> **Where Delos rose and Phoebus sprung!**
> **Eternal summer gilds them yet,**
> **But all except their sun has set'.**[89]

The foremost writer of lyrical poetry of which there was a paucity, was Pindar who wrote feelingly of the pathos and sorrows of humanity and 'all that is inspiring and splendid in music and colour, the dazzling richness of wine, of gold, of the sea, of beautiful bodies and masterful action, all regulated and moulded by the Greek sense of measure, exemplified most admirably in his metres'.[90] There are four works of his of the Epinician Odes to celebrate the victories of the atheletic contests at Olympia, Pytho (Delphi) Nemea and the Isthmus of Corinth. Some popular songs were also composed which are extant as the harmodius sung at Athens as a national anthem and the Swallow Song of Rhodes chanted by the children as they went from house to house in spring:

The swallow is here again
Bringing with it fine seasons and good years;
White belly, back black as night!
Bring for us tarts wine and cheese
Or oatmeal and barley-cake
If you don't we'll thank you,
If you don't we'll carry away
Whate'er we can from your house, all we can,
Yes, even your wife, it'll be easy;
So give freely
Open up, hear the swallows' call
We are not grave old men, but merry children all!

Hesiod also wrote in verse though not of a high order. His *Theogony* gives an account of Greek deities. *Works and Days* is a handbook for farmers and a guide for sailors, interspersed with traditional subjects like the story of pandra's jar and the account of the Four Ages of the worldgold, silver, bronze and iron. Among the historians there was Heredotus, Thucydides who gave and account of the peloponnesian War in eight books-a masterpiece of history, Xenophon whose most well-known work is the Anabasis which narrates the romantic account of the ten thousand Greeks who baffled the entire Persian army.

The Greek theatre has already been described The earliest great tragic playwright was Phrynichus (about 510 B.C.) Aeschylus wrote about a hundred plays - the Suppliant Women, Seven Against Thebes (467 B.C.), Prometheus Bound and the trilogy relating the murder of Agamemnon, the vengeance of his son Orestes and the justification of Orestes for his matricide. The second great tragedian was Sophocles whose plays are balanced, having excellent diction and theatrical sense. He wrote eight plays. Euripides wrote nineteen plays having a great sense of beauty, cleverness and a questioning spirit and mind. For example in The Phcenician Damsels he wrote:

Jocasta. **Yet pause while;**
For haste is incompatible with justice;
But slow deliberation oft effects
Such schemes as wisdom dictates.
Polynices **Plain are the words of truth, and justice needs**
No Subtlety t' interpret, for it bears
Enough to recommended it: but injustice,
Devoid of all internal worth, requires
Each specious art.[91]

Another Greek playwright was Aristophanes of whom eleven plays exist. He has great Zeal, a riotous sense of fun an unsurpassed lyrical charm, gross at times, and magnificently inventive: There is the song supposed to be sung by the Hoopoe for the Nightingale, in his play *The Birds*, at the request of Peisthetairus a citizen of Athens disgusted with his own country and going to seek his fortune in the kingdom of the Birds:

A wake! awake!
Sleep no more my gentle mate!
Wake the tuneful echo Shrill,
On vale or hill;
Or in her airy rocky seat,
Let her listen and repeat

The tender ditty that you tell
The sad lament,
The dire event,
To luckless Itys that befell.
Thence the strain
Shall rise amain,
Up to the lofty palace gate,
Where might Apollo sits in state
In Jove's abode, with his ivory lyre,
Humning aloud to the heavenly choir.
While all the gods shall join with thee
In a celestial symphony.[92]

The Plutus (*Wealth*) the last of his surviving plays we have a different type of comedy, inclining towards the kind produced by Menander, more sophisticated and elegant appealing to the intellect quite unlike the riotous zest, jokes and buffoonery of Aristophanes. The plots of Menander's plays are clearcut and the characterization brilliant.

Among Aristotle's contempories was the great orator Demosthenes whose most famous works the Philippics, the Olynthiac and On the Crown deal with the rising power of Philip, king of Macedonia and the father of Alexander the Great. He tried by his speeches to warn the Athenians of it. But it was all in vain for plague and twenty-seven years of weary and disastrous wars had left them tired and indifferent. In desperation he fruitlessly tried to rouse them, even sarcastically berating their nonchalance:

You go about the marketplace asking one another for fresh gossip, 'Is Philip dead?' 'No, by Zeus, but he is ill'. what does it matter to you? Even if he dies, you will speedily make another Philip, if this is the attention you give to your affairs.

The end of Demosthenes was tragic. After the Macedonians triumphed over Athens they demanded the surrender of the orator: Demosthenes Macedon's inveterate foe took refuge in the temple of Poseidon where he swallowed poison to escape a fate worse than death. After Aeschylus the second great writer of tragedies was Sophocles, of whom we have already mentioned who pondered deeply over the mysteries of the universe. He wrote among other plays, *Ajax*, *Artigone*, and *Oedipus at Colonus* his last play written when he was ninety years old and produced after his death. He introduced a third actor, increasing the importance of dialogue and lessening the use of choral lyrics. He realized the significance of conscience guided by reason in decisions-such as the right of Ajax to commit swicide, of Agamemnon to deny him burial, of Creon to spurn the traitor Polyneices; the right of Antigone to bury her brother, the right of Oedipus as king, of Teiresias as priest, of Iocasta as mother-wife, or the problems faced by Theseus the Athenian king when evil Oedipus desired protectoin from the king of Thebes. Sophocles was a master of the Attic drama. The musical lyrics in it are in a reflective and philosophical vein as in the Oedipus at Colonus the chorus sings:

> Not be born is best,
> The second best to return speedily from where one came;
> For once youth is past with its passionate follies
> There remain troubles, envy, strife, war, sedition and carnage
> And finally old age
> In which one is unwanted, weak, friendless and disparaged
> And every ill becomes one's sole companion.

The chorus of Sophocoles' plays gave religious and social comments and discussed the philosophy of man's existence, its glorious achievements and limitations. The utterances of his characters-the pride of Ajax, the love of Antigone, the impetuosity of Oedipus and the tenderness of Deianeira - moved his audience as never before, with fear, pity and every imaginable emotion. In his *Poetics* Aristotle consided him unrivalled in handling Attic tragedy. After Demosthenes there were two other lesser orators, Aeschines the brilliant opponent of Demosthenes and Isocrates who greatly influenced Cicero and modern oratory.

Thereafter we come to the Hellenic period. An eminent group of writers flourished under the Ptolemias school of whom the most notable was Theocritus, the pastoral poet whose idylls are about the living of shepherds and other farmers, their sweethearts and their hopes and tiffs. He writes of the gossip of two women of Alexanda about servants, clothes, a letter to a lady to whom her lover sends the gift of an ivory staff, a girl singing to win back her faithless lover or of the most fascinating idyll of later Greece:

There we lay
Half-buried in a couch of fragrant reed
And fresh-cut vine leaves, who so glad as we?
A wealth of elm and poplar shook o'erhead;
Hard by, a sacred spring flowed gurgling on
From the nymphs' grotto and in sombre boughs
The sweet cicada chirped laboriously
Hid in the thick thorn-bushes far away
The tree-froq's note was heard; the crested lark
Sang with the gold-finch; turtles made their moan,
And o'er the fountain hung the gilded bee.
All of rich summer smacked, of autumn all:
Pears at our feet, and apples at our side
Rolled in luxuriance; branches on the ground
Sprawled, overweighed with damsons.[93]

Another idyllist wrote a Lament for Bion. Plutarch wrote his *Lives* and *Moralia*, a treatise on morals. The Graeco-Roman culture produced Lucian's satires. His best known work is the Dialogues of the Dead. A critical essay on the Sublime was composed n this period also. For the Greeks the novel and such fiction had no value, for whatever was written in it was absolutely 'untrue', except as allegory or politics. It was later in Roman times that the rudiments of fiction made their first appearance. Heliodorus wrote the *Aethiopica* ('A Story of Africa') about the perils the Anthology ('Garland') was made. These Greek epigrams were on love, death, art, and everything under the sun of human interest. They have directness and simplicity, following the style of Martial the Latin epigrammist.

The Greeks did not look upon death in any spiritual or reflective manner, but rather considered it to imply the skein of Ariadne, and quitting warm life with all its joys and pleasures, for even the slave's lot on earth was preferable to the kingship of Hades. For those left behind it meant the bitter pangs of grief and for those who depended financially on the one dead, poverty. In his funeral speech the only advice Pericles could give to the parents of those slain was to beget more children and if they could not do so because of age, life was over for them. Old age exhausted strength and took away health. Added dignity and respect were but poor compensation for lost youth, for age meant failing eyesight, pains in the limbs and toothless gums. One should make the best of the world and enjoy living while one could:

> 'Let us bathe, my Prodice, and crown our heads, and raising larger cups quaff wine unmixed with water. Brief is life for merrymakers, ere old age brings it to a close; and at the end waits death'.

The Greek philosopher Epicurus (b.341 B.C. d.270 B.C.) said that the worst pain was fear of death and the thought what may happen after death. For the Greeks beauty was something desirable and it was synonymous with goodness. In fact in the Greek language there was one word for both 'beautiful and 'good'. The Greek sense of beauty did not stop short of landscape, as some writers think, it went much beyond that as notices about it in their art and literature show Sappho said:

The stars about the lovely moon
Fade away forthwith
As soon as it shines
Spreading its light over the earth.

And describing the serenity of a waterfall the poetess says:

Roundabout,
A waterfall
Sends its coolness through the branches
Of the apple threes
And sleep flows downwards
Through the rustling leaves.

At Eleusis the cult of Demeter prevailed. She was worshipped as the bringer of the seasons. Her maiden daugher, Persephone, was abducted by Hades the god of death who emerged from a chasm of the earth and catching hold of her, as she had strayed away from her companions, bore the weeping girl to the underworld. In rage and grief, Demeter sent a famine on the earth. Zeus felt that he should intervene to end the misery of the suffering men on earth and sent Hermes down to Hades to bring the maiden back. But before she went she was made to eat and pomegranate seed by her abductor because of which she became bound to return to him. Persephone was united with her mother, but because of having eaten the pomegranate seed she had to spend a third of each year in the underworld. Zeus sent his old mother Rhea to comfort Demeter, and stand at the door of the temple she said to her:

Come, my daughter, for Zeus, far-seeing, loud-thundering,
bids you.
Come once again to the halls of the goods, where you shall have honour,
Where you shall have your daugher to allay your grief,

> **As in each year ended, bitter winter goes past**
> **Only for the third part the kingdom of darkness will be her's**
> **Yield now, and give men that which you alone can give.**

The origion of Orphism is somewhat obscure. It evolved perhaps from an ecstatic frenzy which Euripedes portrayed vividly in the Bacchae a frenzy in which a group of women tore up animals and devoured their flesh:

> **'I've seen the frenzied Bacchanals, who had fled**
> **On their white feet, forth goaded from the land.**
> **I come to tell thee and to this city**
> **The awful deeds they do, surpassing wonder...**
> **The young, the old, the maidens yet unwed.**
> **And first they loosed their locks over their shoulders,**
> **Their fawn-skins fastened, wheresoe'er the clasps**
> **Had lost their hold, and all the dappled furs**
> **With Serpents bound, that lolled out their lithe tongues**
> **Some in their arms held kid, or wild-wolf's cub,**
> **Suckling it with her white milk; all the young mothers**
> **Who had ldft their new-born babes and stood with breasts**
> **Full swelling...**
> **They with hands**
> **Unarmed with iron, rushed on the browsing steers.**
> **One ye might see a young and vigorous heifer**
> **Hold, lowiikng in her grasp, like prize of war.**
> **And some were tearing asunder the young calves;**
> **And ye might see the ribs or cloven hoofs**
> **Hurled wildly up and down, and mangled skins**
> **Were hanging from the ash boughs, dropping blood.**
> **The wanton bulls, proud of their tossing arms**
> **Of yore, fell stumbling, staggering to the ground,**
> **Dragged down by the strong hands of thousand maiokns**
> **And swifter were the entrails torn away**
> **Than drop the lids over your royal eyeballs'.[94]**

Dionysus was the god of wild animals and vegetation, the god of nature's fertility and the Satyrs and Sileni who worshipped him carried the emblem of the phallus (as in India Shiva's worshippers pay obeisance to the linga). In the Orphic myth the Titans devoured the limbs of Dionysus. The lightning of Zeus killed the Titans and from their ashes mankind arose. They were a mixture of the evil of the Titans and of the good from Dionysus. Therefore the divinity of the soul resides in man. Dionysus is also considered to be the god of the grape-bearing vine. So wine made from the grapevine can be good and health-giving if taken in moderation and if not one gets drunk on it and in a frenzy do atrocious acts.

Music

Music and dance among the Greeks was chiefly for the worship of the gods. The flute (*aulos*) and lyre (*citara*) were popular and were in all probability got from the Asia Minor. Each type of music was allied to a particular mood - the dorain with couorage, the Lydian with tenderness, and so forth. Music competitions were held at the Pythian games and on state celebrations. Dance often accompanied music and choric dances played a prominent role in ritual and worship. The actors danced and executed pantomimes to narrate the sacred legends (as we have the tableaus on Radha-Krishna or the Story of Rama). Corinth and Sparta were centres of music, dance and song. Processional songs (prosodia) were created by Emelus of Corinth. Arion of Lesbos who was patronized by Periander composed choral songs in praise of Dionysus (dithyramboi). At Sparta the choral lyric poetry of Alcman was created. An extant fragment is a maiden-song (partheneion) sung by ten maidens who took the sacred robe to the shrine of Artemis Orthia in the twilight between the setting of the moon and the rising of the sun. Alcman also composed the dance-song (*hyporchema*), the song of triumph (*paian*) and the drinking-song (*skolion*), apart from hymns. Stesichorus composed choral lyrics in Himera in the early sixth century B.C., based on the Epic Saga and in Sparta he produced an Oresteia for performance. In lonia and Lesbos elegies were sung to the accompaniment of the flute. These were songs of love, drinking-songs, political catches (*stasiotika*) and narratives, dedication-songs and epitaphs. Simonides and Archilochus were satirists, the latter devastatingly bitter:

> 'May the top-knotted Thracians take him, stripped of his kindly friends, where he willeat the bread of slavery and fill his cup with many ills. May they take him frozen stiff and strung with seaweed from the surge, his teeth chattering, his lips spewing the brine, his body sprawling doglike on his face by the edge of the surf. That is the sight I wish to see; for he wronged me and spurned his plighted oath, that he was my boon-companion'

Alcaeus wrote lyrics on politics, wine and love in the vivid Lesbian dialect. Sappho was inspired by Aphrodite and her attendant deities the Graces and the Muses to whose worship Sappho and the maindens were dedicated.

Art and Architecture

According to P.Gardner Greek art had eight characteristics-humanism, simplicity, balance and measure, naturalism, idealism, patience, joy and fellowship.[95] This writer, however, apparently is not content with analyzing Grecian art, but with the supercilious contempt of most Western writers must deprecate the art of India also, 'A Western mind can have little sympathy with the art which has moved on mystic lines, the art of India, in which such efforts (sic) has abandoned the search for beauty, and so given up the really artistic point of view. Mere prettiness no doubt is an unsatisfying ideal : but a loftier beauty in harmony with the world around us is another thing'.[96] The writer claims to be the representative of 'Western minds'. But all Western minds do not have the narrowmindedness of allergy to all that is Easter; not that such sweeping and gibberish ideas make any difference to the East:

> **'The East bowed down before the blast**
> **In patient deep disdain**
> **She let the legions thunder past**
> **And plunged in thought again'.97**

Of the sculptured figures of *yakshis* (hearvenly damsels) in the Gupta period contemporaneous with Alexander the Great Benjamin Rowland writes:

> 'In their provocative and frank display of the beauties and delights of the courtezan's art, these reliefs mark the culmination of a tendency already noted in the carvings of Sanchi and Bharhut. Not only is there a thoroughly convincing suggestion of solidity of form, but the articulation of body and limbs is achieved with complete mastery and no suggestion of the mechanistic joining of individual parts that characterized the archaic schools.... The sinuous and moving type of pose, as well as elquent and really flower-like gestures of the hands, suggest very strongly the active imitaion by the carvers of the poses and gestures of the Indian dance... Seldom in the history of peoples do we find a period in which the national genius is so fully and typically expressed in all the arts as in Gupta India. Here was florescence and fulfilment after a long period of gradual development, a like sophistication and complete assurance in expression in music, literature, the drama and the plastic arts. The Gupta period may well be described as "classic" in the sense of the word describing a norm or a degree of perfection never achieved before or since, and in the project balance and harmony of all

elements, stylistic and iconographic-elements in separable in importance'.[98] And about the famous temples of khajuraho in Bundelkhand (India) Kramrisch says, 'With every movement of the eye of the beholder a new perspective shows the images from a different angle; to avoid being bewildered he has to concentrate on each of them... and give his attention to the next'[99]

From the sixth century B.C. onwards originality had come to Greek art. The two marked features in it were atheletic sculpture in the Dorian style flourishing in Athens, Argos, Sicyon, Aegina and elsewhere, and the temple architecture which originated in Miletus and other cities of the Ionian coast and the Dorian temples of Greece and southern Italy. Paintings were produced largely in Ionia. But the zenith of temple and athletic architecture, fresco painting and the making of decorative vases was reached in the fifth century B.C. All of these were prominent in Athens, though Argos rivalled it in athletic art, Sicyon in painting and Saracuse in the art of coins and gem engraving. The temples of Samos, Miletus and Ephesus were very large being sometimes of 342 by 163 feet with a hundred columns each about fifty-five feet high and resplendent with artistic designs, those at Delphi, Athens and south Italy Smaller and Doric instead of Ionic. The great statue of the goddess Athena, a masterpiece by Phedias with a spear and shield in one hand a Victory in the other, in the Parthenoin was the embodiment of Athenian religion. The Greek temples were stately but at the same time depict simplicity in their style. The columns were massive resting on a firm foundation and having a human touch in their structure. The pillars were built in three patterns. The Doric pillar was solid and massive, the Ionic more slender, the Corinthian a variety of the Ionic more slender, the Corinthian a variety of the Ionic with acanthus leaves at the top in place of volutes. All columns were vertically grooved. The bases were plain but the gable spaces in front and behind and the lines of metopes under the roof carved or sculptured with figures. The figures which decorated the Parthenon were the highest achievement of sculptural art. Often these portrayed Greek legends, the victory of the gods over the titans of the Greeks over the Centaurs and the Amazons, and the conquest of Troy to avenge the abduction of Helen. The excavations at Delphi village brought to light many beautiful statues, sculptural decorations of the temple of Apollo and treasure houses with a number of small objects in bronze and terracotta. The bodies of atheletes were shown in detail with perfect proportion, rare specimens of human beauty. The muscles under the skin and the exact undulations they caused as Plato observed, beauty in the human form, not that of nature was predominant and the latter provided only a background to it:

> Since we have no accurate knowledge of such things, we do not closely examine or criticize the paintings of them; we are in such a case contented with a vague and delusive rendering. But when an artist tries to represent our bodies, we keenly perceive his defects, and in virtue of our constant close observation, become severe critics of one who does not render in all respects and accurate likeness.

It is true that the Greeks paid far more attention to the human form, the figures of athletes and youthful deities as Apollo and Hermes, than to material objects. Rhythm, balance and measure are marked features of Greek art. As has been said before male beauty found expression in Greek sculpture than that of the female. The Greeks had no inhibitions about nudity. Their statues both of men and gods were often in the nude depicting clearly the scrotum and sometimes even the penis as in the seven feet tall statue of Zeus casting a spear (National Museum, Athens), Athelete or Apoxyomenus of the fourth century B.C. by Lysippus of Sicyon (Vatican Museum) and the Doryphorus or Spear Bearer of Polycletus of the Argive school, fifth century B.C. (also at Vatican Museum). The beauty of the female form found expression later than that of the male and it originated chiefly in Ionia. The figures were mostly draped in a marvellous manner as the lovely Spartan woman, a competitor in the games in the Vatican Museum, but Praxititeles broke this convention in the 4th century B.C. and for the first time created the lovely nude statue of Aphrodite of Cnidus (Vatican Museum). Another statue of Aphrodite of Melos (2nd Century B.C.) was half nude (Louvre) and waist upwards, and that of the Medici

Venus (Louvre) fully nude. In painting, too, the Greeks produced many fascinating figure and designs on the picturesque vases of the 5th - 4th centuries B.C. The Greek vases were either black-figured or red-figured. In the former dating back to the seventh to sixth centuries B.C. the figures were drawn in black silhutte on the red or buff background. Touches of white and red were added. The markings on the vases were incised with a sharp instrument on the clay. In the red-figured vases outlines were drawn, and the whole background painted in black. The figures stood out in red against black and any further markings were made by a very fine brush with black or dark paint. The details stood out with a very lovely effect.

Religion

Sophocles observed 'Αεὶγάρ εὖ πίπτγνσιν οἱ Διὸς κνβοι ['The dice of Zeus have ever lucky throws']. Zeus was accepted as supreme among the Greek gods, particularly in the northern communities. However Athens and Attica were more devoted to Athena, while in Argos the pre-Hellenic goddess Hera, said to be the wife of Zeus, was more honored. A knowledge about the religion of the Greeks is mostly acquired by their literature and art, such as the Homeric epics, the odes of Pindar and the Attic tragedy. While Greek mythology has many lovely and inspiring legends, such as the story of Demeter and her daugher Persephone, Theseus and Ariadne, the virtuous wife of Odysseus, Penelope, who managed to keep away the suitors for twenty long years by a clever strategem and thus proved faithful to her husband; there are many instances in it which depict the gods and mythological heroes as licentious, cruel, immoral and unjust, such as the rape of Persephone by the lord of the underworld, Thyestes appropriating his brother's wife, who in revenge killed with horrible cruelty Thyestes' two little children, cutting apart their limbs, boiling the flesh and serving it in a dish thus making their father eat it by trickery, the awful murder of Agamemnon by his own wife Clytemnestra, the sacrifice made to please Artemis the goddess of Olympus, of the young maiden Iphigenia by her own father Agamemnon just for his ambition to conquer Troy and exalt Greece, a horrible human sacrifice for empty fame and honour

He dared the deed
Slaying his child to help a war...
All her prayers - cries of father! father!
Her maiden life,
These they held as nothing,
Thesavage warriors battle-mad.[100]

In Greek religion we find the gods and men often interacting on each other. In fact religion and mythology are closely connected. So too are art and religion, for we find many of the Greek gods like the omnipotent Zeus, Apollo, Asclepios (the god of healing, Dionysus (god of vegetation and ceremonies, and goddesses like Hera, Athena, Kore (the spring goddess), Aphrodite (goddess of love) and Demeter (goddess of the earth and fertility; all represented in various status and figures which have been found in excavations.

The Greek religion was distinctly polytheistic and below the personal deities we find a religious animism. The Hellene revered the sun, moon and the various winds. Some communities worshipped the stars, as the Sirius star. The worship of Nymphs, 'the Brides' was universal depicting the anthromorphic nature of Greek religion. It was not only in India that sacredness was attributed to rivers like the Ganga which due to the prayers of Bhagirath came down from the heavens, the Yamuna associated with Krishnaism and the Saryu with Rama. In Greece Hesiod advised the stranger when he is crossing a dangerous ford to bow and pray to 'the divine waters'. Offerings were made to rivers as of a bull or horse thrown alive in them. Gradually the concept of a river god emerges, anthromorphically conceived. Thus animism passes into theism and the river-god begins to be worshipped as a deity. The Romans too apparently worshipped rivers, for we read in the poem about Horatius:

> **'Oh, Tiber! fater Tiber!**
> **To whom the Romans pray'.**[101]

Hestia, the 'Hearth', was the divinity of the hearth who protects the household and the stranger and a small portion of the sacrifice was thrown into the hearth to appease her. The leading Greek divinities presided over the world of nature including vegetation, human society in its various aspects, the sphere of morality, of art and finally of the human soul. The lesser deities were concerned with individual departments only. The higher deities were also concerned with the growth of crops, care of herds the harvest, woods flocks and herds and even the protection of crops from mildew and mice

Zeus, the greatest of the gods had sway over the earth, the sky and the neither regions. In a vase found at Chiusi we have the figures of Zeus, Hades and Poseidon each one carrying symbolically lightning. This could be a pointer to the advance of poly theism towards monotheism, as with the Hindu religion - *ekam sad vipra bahudha vadanti* 'that which others know as many is known to sages as the one'

The monogamous union of the Greeks between the bridge and the bridgroom was based on the consecrated religious ceremony upheld by Zeus and his wife Hera. This 'Holy Marriage' was the counterpart of the human and was performed in a public ritual by the Greek states, and in private by the bridge and bridgroom. A relief from a metope of one of the temples at Selinus in Sicily and a fifth century B.C. vase in the British musewm show Zeus asn Hera as divinities of the monogamic marriage. The family gathered at Zeus' altar in their courtyard and the god was looked upon as the guardian of morality, maintaining the rights and duties of the parents, children and brothers to each other. Athena and Zeus also fostered good relations between kinsmen. Zeus was the 'father god' of the Dorians and the Aeacidae, Apollo of the Ionians, Poseidon of the Minyans, while Athena was looked upon as the patroness of the Athenians. The Delphic oracle, mention of which has been made earlier, was invariably consulted before undertaking any important event such as wars rituals, colonization and so forth. The temple service was solemn and elaborate and as has been said before the phallic emblem as the symbol o generation, was not considered obscene by the Greeks, particularly the Hellenic Greeks.

There was correlation between Greek religion and its legal system for the deities were considered to be guardians of the law also. The Hellenic religion fostered physical fitness, virtue, courage, patriotism, family unity, consideration to guests and strangers and even kindness to slaves. Thus it had a strong moral base.

The belief concerning the neither world and the fate of the soul after death were closely linked with the Greek mysteries and the Dionysiac cult which were revealed on to the initiated and those who were found suitable for such initiation. This implies rapport or divine communion with visions of holy things or sacred objects. The Orphics, who claimed Orpheus as their founder, had a large following in Greece in the sixth century B.C. They believed in the divine origin of the human soul, its transmigration through a series of rebirths in this world, the belief in eternal happiness and the power to attain through purification, complete union with God. Anacharsis says, Ψνχῆs γὰρ ὄργανον γὸ σῶ μα, μεοῦ δ'□ η ψνχή 'The body is the implement of the soul, and the soul of God'.[102] The Orphic doctrine stressed otherworldliness and was the first propagandist religion in Europe, for its appeal was Universal and free from the barriers of city, caste sex of family. It was similar to the teaching of the *Gita* which considered the soul to be immortal subject to *punarajanma* (rebirth) and the Cosmic Absolute (*Brahman*) to be *akhanda sukha* (eternal bliss).

Later private religious societies made their advent. In these called 'thiasoi' anyone could seek admission. Those who were its members believed in a divinity of their own. Sometimes this divinity was of the neither world and was the sources of happiness in the hereafter. The Greeks became thus more and more concerned with salvation as Hindu philosophy conceived emancipation or liberation (*moksha*).

WARS WITH THE PERSIANS

'Ω ξεῖν', ἀγγέλλειν Λακεδαιμονίοις, ὄγι νᾶδε
Κείμεθα, γῖs κείνων ῥημασι πεθόμενοι.

EPITAPH OF THE 300 SPARTANS AT THERMOPYLAE

'Go tell the Spartans, thou that passest by,
That here obedient to their laws we lie'.[103]

The Disunity of the Greek City-states

The almost continuous wars engulfed Greece about the end of the fifth century B.C when the Perians, taking advantage of the internal rivalries of the Greek city-states, launched waves of attacks on Greece. It was not that these city-states were weak, for ultimately they managed to repel the Persian invasin, the credit going mainly to Athens and Sparta; but their internal rivalries and infighting weakened them, and after their glorious victories over the Persians, made them vulnerable to conquest by the Romans:

> At a moment when the states of the World were laid out on the funeral pyre as the victims of their own fatricidial strife and turm oil, they were all at once presented with the [Roman] dominion and straightaway came to life again.[104]

It was indeed a heroic achievement on the part of Sparta combined with A thens this combination being not more than a fraction of the Greek city-states to have overcome the huge Persian armies and naval power that took part in this onslaught; and achievement which inspired Byron, the English poet, to write

> **'Earth! render back from out thy breast**
> **A remnant of our Spartan dead!**
> **Of the three hundred grant but three,**
> **To make a new Thermopylae!'105**

Patriotism was not lacking in the people of the Greek city-states, but it was misdirected inasmuch as it was limited to the state itself. Not only that it was patriotism in isolation. One reason for this was the nature and basis on which the states were founded. This was either due to overpopulation which led to migration to new areas, or to neglect of wider inter-state issues, or to the smallness of states like Phlius (70 square miles), Sicyon (140) and Corinth (350) or conflicting political ideoligies or wrong priorities even in periods of common danger. Athens and Sparta, two of the most powerful Greek city-states were often at loggerheads with each other In 458 B.C. there was intense fighting between Athens, Aegina, Corinth, Megara, Attica, the Peloponnese when Athens tried to weaken Sparta. Soon not only Athens and Sparta, but almost all the city-states were fighting with one another The Greeks were just as superstitious as the Indians or the Romans (Alexander had as his soothsayer, Aristander whom he often consulted), and the believed in omens. Before the Greek victory at Marathon, we are told, Callimachus made a sacrifice to the gods and the Greek attack was made as the omens were favourable. As has been said the oracle of Delphi which was just a stone wrapped in cloth, guided all their actions. But to have stuck to superstition even when faced with an emergency, was certainly not wisdom which quality the Greeks prized most. And the Spartans refused to proceed to Athens' aid when the Persian invasion came as they were celebrating the festival of Apollo Carneius and by convention no military operation could be undertaken till the full moon which was six days ahead. By that time the battle was over and all that the 2000 Spartan soldiers could do was to congratulate Athens on its signal victory! But as the fate of men is controlled by a higher power so is the destiny of nations, the outcome of battles and indeed the birth, growth, decay and extinction of civilizations. Otherwise there is nothing to explain why the battle of Marathon came when the moon was not yet full, or why the powerful Persian cavalry was delayed in joining the battle and were able to come in the last phase of it when the Persian infantry had already been worsted and the fighting was confused. So also was the case with the Greek city-state. The history of Athens in later years in one of vaulting ambition which, in the words of Shakespeare 'o'erleaps itself, and fall on the other'. Athens challenged Sparta, thus breaking an alliance which if preserved could have changed the course of history, attacking Sparta's Peloponnesian allies and at the same time intervening in the Egyptians' rebellion against Persia. Ultimately these tall aspirations, foiled by her naval and military disasters forced her to make peace with both the Peloponnesians and the Persians. To make up for its lost prestige Athens entered into an alliance with the Greeks who had been subjugated by the Persian empire. This alienated Athens' supporters who found that they had only changed one master for another. The result was another war between Athens and Peloponnesia in 431 to 404 B.C. Once again the fever of ambition which Athens seemed never to shake off, gripped it. By intervening in Sicily at the same time as it got involved in the second Peloponnesian war, it committed the same mistake again of fighting on two fronts, and eventually this led to the Roman conquest. The Romans did away the defets of Hellenic discord and adoped much the same policy as the Persians, banning inter-state wars and disciplining its subjects. Although the Hellenic achievement was great so too were its failures. Often when success was almost within their grasp, some sudden act of unwisdom turned it into failure. As Arnold Toynbee says, 'An untranscended achievement turns into a failure; and since the Hellene's achievements were outstandingly great, the severity of their nemesis was proportionate. The karma that the Hellenes bequeathed was far more potent than the karma they had inherited'.[106]

The Rise of the Persians

About 550 B.C. Cyrus, the Persian king of Anshan of the house of Achaemenes seized the crown of Media from his kinsman Astyages who according to legend had desired to kill him when he was a mere child, but was brought up hidden from him. However Cyrus, unlike some of the Greek tyrants as Periander who slew his wife, banished his son and sent 300 sons of noble families to Alyattes of Lydia to serve as eunuchs at his court, spared the king's (Astyages') life, thus proving Shakespeare's observation that

'mercy is above this sceptred sway
It is enthroned in the hearts of kings'.[107]

And what is more, returning good for evil, a quality found among saints, not usually among monarchs, and as we shall see, this was part of Cyrus' nature not a mere passing phase. A substantial body of Median nobles supported Cyrus. Croesus of Lydia who had made an alliance with Astyages crossed Halys early in 546 B.C. and seized Pteria. An indecisive battle was fought between the armies of Croesus and Cyrus. Croesus withdrew to Sardis and sending messages to his allies made ready for another attack. But Cyrus did not delay and capturing Sardis made the king prisoner, though, according to some, he treated him well. Lydia came under the Persian rule.

Cyrus next turned to Babylonia. There the rules of Nabonidus was not popular and when Cyrus invaded it, he was looked upon not as an enemy but as a liberator by at least half of the population there. Babylon was conquered. By 539 B.C. Cyrus added all the other Asiatic territories to his empire which extended from the shores of the Aegean to the Caspian and from the Euxine to the deserts of Arabia, a tremendous achievement.

Unlike many other conquerors Cryrus won over his subjects by his benignity. There were no massacres, deportations or flayings. Those deported by the Assyrians or Babylonians were left free to go to their old homes. The gods were restored to their shrines, people were free to observe their ancient rites. Clemency and tolerance replaced cruelty and terror. In brief it was an era of benevolence. Cyrus was busy protecting the eastern border of his kingdom from excursions of wild nomads and during one of these campaings he died in 529 B.C. leaving two sons Cambyses and Smerdis. Smerdis was secretly killed by his brother. Cambyses became ruler. In the spring of 525 B.C. he overran the Egyptian forces in the battle at the frontier fort of Pelusium. Eqypt became part of the Persian Empire. Although Cambyses was a Zoroastrian and worshipper of Amer, he got himself proclaimed as Pharaoh. His next target was Carthage, but the Phoenician sailors point-blank refused to sail against the Oasis of Ammon but his forces were lost in the desert sandstorms. So too was the fate of his expedition to the Nubian kingdom of Napata which he led in person. His convoys were cut off and he had to beat a retreat through the barren regions full of cataracts. Wild with the frustration of successive defeats, Cambyses went berseck, as the Greek historian says, cursing his religion, which he himself had betrayed, and the deities of it.

To make things worse the adherents of the old Magian religion, which was opposed to Zoroastrianism, revolted and put up a pretender, Smerdis as king. There was opposition brewing in Egypt also, and Cambyses went to suppress it with some prominent nobles, among them his cousin, A chaemenid Darius, and his army. However Cambyses died while he was on the march. The army went on taking his dead body with them. The Egyptian imposterfled and pursued by Darius and six of the Persian nobles, slain. There was none left except Darius to succeed to the Persian throne, and he established himself firmly on it. He had to face revolts in the first two years of his reigh-that of the Medians, Babylonins, Armenians and even of some Persians who believed that a grandson of Curus was alive. The satraps of Egypt and Lydia were minded to break away. But with the help of loyal Persian nobles, Darius suppressed them all. The satraps of Sardis and Egypt were supprressed and executed. By 217 B.C. Darius was the unchallenged ruler of Asia and Africa, as then known, with the exception of Carthage. The Aryan Hindus had long established themselves in India. Western records are silent about them, and so are the Indian records about the Persians. Darius never penetrated Indian territory.

Here we pause to consider the culture and religion of the Iranians and their relation to those of others, including of the Greeks. It is surmised by historians like C.B. Grundy (*The Persians and the Empire of the Great King*) that though no legend or myth going back to the period of separation [between various races of the Indo-European family] has survived' yer there is scientific proof of their original unity. In other word such a conclusion is merely a guess. But history is based on facts, not on guesses. While allowing the Aryans (Indian and Iranian) to be more spiritual than the 'crude Greek materialism', the writer expresses the view that by 'modern western standards, the Iranian developed a concept of religion higher than that which came to prevail in India'. Again pure quesswork for just before it is observed by the writer 'of the Indian it is not necessary to speak here'. The religion of the Greeks, the historian rightfully says was vastly different from that of the Persians and of the Iranians who believed in an afterlife, a divine judgment and the soul's immortality. Nonetheless these elements are also found in the Aryan Hindu religion and also the philosophy of the Greek philosophers Plato, Pythagoras, Empedocles and Plotinus, as well as in the Orphics. Also surprising is the observation of G.B. Grundy that in certain aspects the Persian civilization in the period of Darius 'was superior to the Greeks themselves'. What these aspects are is not mentioned, so it is difficult to comment on this. But it is hard to believe the Greek civilization with its rich literature - Euripedes, Aristophanes, Sappho Aeschylus, Sophocles and so forth and orators like Demosthenes etc., was inferior to that of the Persian.

To continue with the conquests of Darius. He led and army into Europen and marched through Thrace crossing the Danube and entered Scythia in an attempt to pentrate into Russian territory. But there he met with the same fate as other such enterprising invaders. His supplies were cut off and he struggled back to the Danube, his huge army a wreck.

Thereafter the confrontation was with Greece. All the Ionian cities-Dorian and Aeolian as well as Ionia-in Asia Minor and on the Propontis, with the exception of Miletus had submitted to Lydian rule and were therefore already part of the Persian empire. The Greek city-states had become weakened by their own internal rivalries. Besides tyrants like Peisistratus, who amassed great wealth, overran Athens and issued his own coinage, the tyrants of Naxos and Samos, made the situation worse and easier for the Persians to make invoad into Greecian territory. There was a conflict between the

Peisistratids' and the Spartans in which the sons of Peisistratids were captured Athens was free after thirty-six years of tyrannic domination. The Persians shut their eyes to these tyrannis. The city-states never could act concertedly and so the Persians kept them under subjugation with ease Both Bias, the sage of Priene and Thales of Miletus suggested measures for saving Ionia. Bias advised them to migrate collectively to Sardinia and Thales suggested union under one central government. But the Ionians dithered, and were ultimately overcome by the Persians and had to pay tribute and provide soldiers. The tyrants made friends with Persian satraps, as for example Histiaeus of Miletus. He preferred making his tyranny supreme than liberating Hellas. Thus to the misfortune of Greece, its tyrants, in a most un-Greek manner, worked against the interest of their own motherland! There will always be patriots and quislings in the world, but in the Greek administration, tyranny often kept suppressing democracy. Patriotism did not seem to be a Greek virtue. To the Persians the rule of despots and the tyrannies was a godsend.

In the Greek peninsula inter-state wars and rivalries continued unabated. Sparta emerged as the preeminent city-state. There was a devastating war between it and Tegea. Sparta won and Tegea became its vassal in c 560-550 B.C. bound to render it military service, although maintaining its individuality. With the subduing of Argos in the peloponnese Spartan hegemony was established Sparta was instrumental in establishing the Peloponnesian or, more correctly the Lacedaemonian League, an attempt to somehow unite the warring Greek city-states. The states formed an alliance with Sparta, and mutually agreed not to attack one another, and to render aid to a state when it called for it. In effect however, Sparta remained primus inter pares. It was under its command that the troops took the field whenever a state needed assistance. The non-Dorian state, Achae, on the southern shore of the Guld of Corinth was left out of the alliance as Sparta considered it of no practical use and Argos stayed away on its own. Though Athens became a member for some time, it considered itself a near rival to Sparta. Despite being a commercial and maritime state it was still weighed down by tyrannies and diversities of interests. Thus Sparta created a strong military confederation. Although it came into operation only in times of war, it had a salutary effect in reducing the oppression of tyrants if not wiping them altogether, for in Athens even after Solon's reforms constitutional government gave way to aristocracy and tyranny. In 555 B.C. Croesus, king of Lydia, finding Sparta mistress of most of the Peloponnese, concluded a treaty with her. Next year Argos was subdued by Sparta in a battle with heavy losses on each side. The Spartans we are told wore their hair long in triumph while the Argives cut theirs short in mourning'. Thus Sparta increased her power and prestige and Spartan valour became porverbial. However, despite the Spartan League, the Greek city-states could not end their squabbles and ambition, often self-destructive, on the part of those who were athirst for ascendancy was often their undoing.

Darius was emperor of a vast empire by the end of the sixth century B.C. and could not imaine any opposition or revolt. But for once the warring factions of the Greek city-states seemed to have combined to light the torch of freedom albeit only for a little while. It was a brief interlude and ironically this revolt, call it the struggle for freedom, was engineered by one of the tyrants, namely Histiaeus. His ambitions had aroused the suspicions of a Persian governor, and he was put under detention, though honourably, at the Persian court. He had time to ponder over the affront for captivity however luxuriously given is no match to freedom. He decide on an lonian revolt. His secret motive curiously enough was that first he should instigate rebellion and then be commissioned by Darius to suppress it! Bizarre too, was his way of conveying his message to his fellow conspirator, Aristogoras, his son-in-law and another tyrant of Miletus. He is said to have shaved the head of a trusted slave, tattoed it on his scalp and sent him to his son-in-law. Aristogoras was game but not from any altruistic motive. He saw in this an opportunity to establish his leadership and to get domain.

The conspirators seized the lonian captains of the ships coming back from Naxons and turning away the Persian-in fluenced by rants from the lonian states. Aristagoras promised equal rights to all in a proposed constitutional government. At first there were few takers. Sparta, the most powerful state refused aid for fear of dissipating its armed might in distant Persia. Athens, however, already engaged in acts against Darius, decided to assist with a squadron of twenty ships. Eretria, too, responded, though in a small way, with five warships. The Greek naval force made a surprise attack on Sardis burning down the buildings there including the renowned temple of Cybele, the Lydian goddess. However the Persian garrison under the command of Artaphernes, and the Lydians drove out the lonians and in 498 B.C. the Persian forces routed them completely. The burning of Sardis raised the morale of other Greek States of the Bosporus and Hellepont and the revolt gathered momentum. Darius drew up three army contingents under the generalship of Daurises, Hymeas and Artybius. The Greeks were unmindful of these preparations, and anyway failed to put up a united front. The Athenians withdrew their aid and Eretria did likewise. What was wrose, the troops of Curium and the war-chariots of Salamis deserted to the Persians. The Cyprians were routed, Cyprus fell, and in early 476 B.C. Soli capitulated after a long siege.

Daurises effected more conquests - the Greek states on the Asiatic shore of the Hellespont. Hymeas suppressed Troad. Finally the scene of battle shifted to the Asia Minor in a naval engagement near the Lade Island. The lonian fleet was drawn from nine states and comprised 353 oar-driven warships. The Persian commander offered to pardon the rebels if they capitulated, but the lonians refused to give in. The lonian fleet was raised mainly from Chios, Miletus, Lesbos and Samos. Again lack of concerted action lost for the lonians a winning battle. The ships of Samos hoisted sail and fled. So did those of Lesbos. Others followed their example of treachery. The remaining ones mainly of Chios fough valorously but in vain. The battle of Lade (495 B.C.) decided the end of the lonian rebels. Miletus, the cities of Caria and those on the coast south of Hellespont fell to the Persians. Histiaeus, who had masterminded the revolt, was impaled by Artaphernes and his head sent to Darius. The subjects of the rebellious states were cruelly punished. Their towns and temples were burnt down and the cities sacked. Boys and girls were sent to serve a eunuchs and handmaids at the court of Darius. Miletus was more severely punished. Men were massacred, women and children enslaved, and those left deported to the Persian Gulf. Those who fled like the Samians and others were spared. Thus treason was rewarded. The revolt failed due to the superior military support to the Persian navy. But not less because of treachery and the usual Greek failure to stand together when faced by a catastrophy. The Greek city-states seemed to be lack cohesion. Mere valour is not enough to assure victory. More important is to stay together, for as Publilius Syrus Says - 'Auxilia humilia firma consensus facit', Unity of aim gives strength to the feeblest aid.

When Miletus fell in 494 B.C. the Athenians bemoaned its fate. This was a good sign for Grecian unity. The mistocles fortified Peiraeu and wisely insisted on a naval policy for Athens. It was evident that the Athenians were not to be cowed down and were prepared to beat back any Persian attack. This common danger brought Athens and Sparta closer. When in 491 B.C. Aegina recognizing Persian suzerainty withdrew from the Spartan alliance, Sparta got those who were responsible arrested on Athens' appeal, and delivered them to her. This strengthened the resolve of the city-states to come together. Meanwhile the Persians were not idle. They managed to impose their suzerainty on the coastal colonies right up to Macedonia. This done, Darius got ready for an advance into Greece. As a preliminary he ordered the Thasians to dismantle their fortifications and send their fleet to Abdera on the Thracian coast. Darius's envoys demanded 'earth and water' as tokens of the submission of Greece. Many states submitted, the most significant being Aegina. A Persian assault was imminent.

The Persian Offensive - Marathon

The mountains look on Marathon -
And Marathon looks on the sea;
And musing there an hour alone
I dream'd that Greece might still be free.[109]

Under the command of Datis and Artaphernes the Persian fleet sailed from the Cilician coast in 490 B.C. Among the Persians were the subject peoples like lonians and Aeolians. Herodotus, the chronicler, gives the number of warships as 600. There were possibly somewhat less, but the force which embarked was doubtless formidable and could be almost 25,000 troops. The Persian force reached Euboea. Naxos which had gallantly opposed the Persians, was destroyed and those who could not escape, deserted. The Carystians, who refused to contribute troops, were forced into sub mission by the razing down of their town. While the Persian fleet was at the Euboic channel, Eretria asked Athens for assistance. The Eretrians veered between opposition and submission , finally deciding to resist. Again treachery proved their undoing and they were betrayed from within. Darius got their temples plundered and burnt and the people deported. Thereafter the Persian fleet sailed for Attica, and the troops embarked in the bay of Marathon. At Athens it was decided to march to Marathon, and a messenger was sent pasthaste to Sparta to secure help. Greek religious superstition, however came in the way. The Spartans were observing the festival of Apollo Carneius and a sacred law forbade military operations till the full moon, which was six days ahead. So they said they would send the help only then. As we shall see later, everything was over by the time the moon was full, and as the saying goes, time and tide wait for no man. Apparently the Greeks failed to understand that religion is quite apart from superstition and as Cicero says in *De Divinatione* (II., 72, 148) Nec vero superstitione tollenda religio tollitur, 'We do not destroy religion by destroying superstition'.

The Persian troops massed by the Oenoe stream which was dry then, when the Athenian army came to the foothills of Mount Pentelicus on the plain of Marathon. Plenty of water was available in the Great Marshes. The Persian cavalry and infantry were spread out on the plain and there were a large number of well-trained archers. The Athenians were in the west defending the town of Marathon and their right wing extended towards Heracles (See map sketched below).

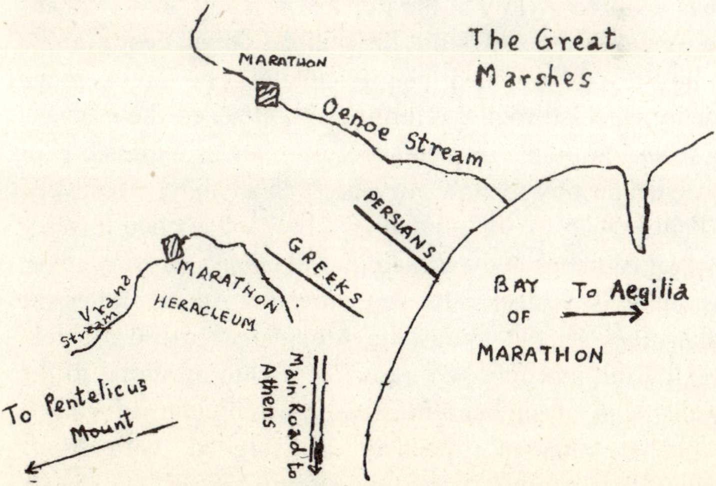

(Adapted from N.G.L. Hammond. *A History of Greece* Oxford, 1967)

The Greeks had brought supplies with them and had a supply-line by which more could be got if needed. There were 10,000 hoplites in the Greek force, but no archers or cavalry for in these they knew the Persians were far superior.

The Greeks were undecided as to when to launch the attack-forth with or after the Spartans had joined them. There was a council of ten generals on whom the decision rested. Five were for an immediate strike, five for after the Spartans' arrival. The former were he added by Miltiades who was familiar with the Persian fighting tactics during the Scythaian campaign. As the generals were equally divided, as was the convention, callimachus was called to decide. Miltiades, however, won him over and also got the operational command for five days. The Plataeans with about a thousand armed troops meanwhile arrived. The Greeks advanced to less than a mile away from the Persian line by felling trees and stockading them for cover. The lonian scooting force passed down news of the Persian cavalry being away. Miltiades immediately struck. Miltiades made his line of troops as long as than of the Persians and strengthened the left and right extremes. The Greeks charged swiftly at the Persian in fantry. The Persians were routed at the wings but the thinned Greek centre broke and the Persians pursued their advantage. The Greek wings suddenly wheeled round, reformed and attacked the Persians from their rear. In the resulting confusion it was impossible for the Persian cavalry by now arrived, to do anything effectively. The battle raged for long but at last the Persians fled towards the Great Marshes hotly chased by the Greeks. Losing seven ships, the Persian fleet sailed south towards Athens. When the Persian fleet set out to sea the Athenians noticed a shield reflecting the morning sun's rays as a kind of signal to the Persians. This meant that some treason was brewing in Athens. Obviously Athenian treachery outweighed with some Athenian patriotism. As tacitus says in *History* (I, 28). Is habitus animorum fuit up pessimum facinus auderent pauci, plures vellent ... 'Such was the temper of men's minds that while there were few to venture on so atrocious a treason, many wished it done ...'

Leaving some soldiers to guard the spoils, Miltiades rushed back with his force to Athens. When, acting upon the signal, the Persian fleet arrived off Phalerum, but the Athenian army was already lined up there and there was no possibility of their landing their troops. So they sailed away. The Spartans arrived then. They had marched immediately when the moon was full, covering the 140 miles distance in three days. The saw the dead lying on the battlefield - 192.

Athenians and 6,400 Persians. There was nothing to do for them except to admire the tactics of Miltiades and congratulate the Athenians. The victory of Marathon could not avert a future invasion of Greece, but it showed the efficiency of the Greek infantry. it also buoyed up the city-states with new hope and revived their flagging spirits.

In 487 B.C. Egypt revolted and Darius thought of raising a huge force against it and also to conquer Greece. But he died in the following year. It seemed the Greeks condemned just those persons among them who were the most praiseworthy-Socrates, Anaxagoras and now Miltiades. Whatever the motive, apparently the Greeks, instead of honouring their luminaries, hounded them to death or exile. Ironically enough in the case of Miltiades the charge was not the usual vague one of impiety but 'deception of the people', i.e., treason, and the one at whose instance it was brought by Xanthippus who had married A gariste of the clan of Alcmeonid, who had flashed the shield-signal to the Persians. Thus one who was guilty of treason to the Athenian Greeks was prosecuting the hero of Marathon whom he had sought to desist from making the Greeks victorious, and his countrymen upheld the trumped up charge! Probably no more disgraceful event could be found in the annals of any nation. Miltiades was so disabled because for a wound sustained at Paros, that he could not defend himself and it was only on the persuasion of his friends who pleaded for him as being the conqueror of Lemnos and the victor of Marathon that the judges, instead of the proposed death sentence let him off with a heavy fine which his son, Cimon, paid. Shortly after he died as a result of his wound and presumably the remorse caused to him by his countrymen. A well-intentioned good person was, against all wise counsel sacrificed to one evil – μηθ' ὁ πονηρὸς kαγεχέγω ξρησγοῦ γόπον,'Let not the bad man fill the good man's place' [Menander. *Fabulae Incertae, Fragment* 470]. With Miltiades out of the way, it was left to the Persians to renew their campaign against Greece, and the task fell in the hands of Xerxes, the successor of Darius.

The Invasion of Xerxes

Earth! render back from out they breast
A remnant of our Spartan dead!
Of the three hundred grant but three
To make a new Thermopy pæ.[110]

'Ὦξεῖν', ἀγγέλλειν Λakedaιμoνί ols, ôγι γαδε
kείμεθa, γoιs keίνων ῥήμασι πειθόμενoL'

'Go tell the Spartans, thou that pasest by,
That here obedient to their laws we lie'.

Epitaph of the 300 Spartans at thermopylÆ

Thermopylae

Marathon had taught the Greeks two lessons. First that for any warfare with the Persians a strong naval power was indispensable and second that unity among the Greeks city-states was imperative. Unless these two factors were there, victory against the formidable armies supported by Persian warships was difficult. Valour was not lacking. Athens had demonstrated that at Marathon and Sparta did not get the opportunity to do so. But it sincerity was never in doubt, for with the Greeks the gods were foremost both in peace and war.

A sacrifice was always made before taking any momentous act or decision and the omens as also the Delphi oracle were guides. Now the first task was taken up by Themistocles the acutest and most brilliant intellect in Greek politics. In 483 B.C. the Persians began to cut the canal through the neck of the Athos peninsula, making it obvious that in any future invasion of Greece the Persian fleet would be a formidable one. In 483-82 B.C a great source of silver was found in Laurium. Themistocles urged that this might be usefully spent in increasing the fleet to at least 200 warships. This was a wise proposal and luckily the Greeks acted forth with on it. Themistocles' wise policy did much to make Greece powerful both at land and sea.

Despite Marathon it was to Sparta, not to Athens that the Greek city-states looked for leadership. The had ultimately realized that if the Persians invaded again, only a strong military coalition could save them. The oracle of Delphi for once dampened their spirit for its verdict was a favour of the Persians - Your lot is unenviable, it said. The city will be put to fire. So the Delphi oracle presaged ill both for Athens and Sparta. However the Greeks wisely ignored this gloomy forewarning and the representatives of Greek states met at Hellenium in Sparta in 481 B.C. A Spartan Alliance was formed and its first meeting was held at the Isthumus. Each state was represented by its elected delegates, the *probouloi*, each one to cast one vote, and decisions arrived at by the majority. This, it may be said, was a curious Greek characteristic. Where democracy should be the norm it was tyranny, and where immediate and one-man decisions were required, as a Marathon, there was a council to deliberate! The League of Greeks or just 'The Greeks' as it was called, was a significant gesture towards Greek unity. Thirty-one states were included in the League.

When this joint body met at Corinth, Xerxes was advancing from Sardis towards the Hellespont. The

Thessalians were subdued and so were the Locrians and the Boeotians with the exception of Plataea and Thespiae, Phocis was the only state north of Attica that did not submit. Xerxes mustered a huge force said to be of 5000,000 by the chronicler-historian Heredotus, but perhaps only about 500,000 [as N.G.L. Hammond says], including the fighting men on both land and sea. The naval force was about 3,000 warships of Egypt, Cyprus, Phoenicia and also of the subdued Greek states. The Persian force reached Therma (Saloniki). Thereafter Xerxes delayed their advance for ten days as he was undecided from which direction to invade Greece, finally choosing an entry from the passes lying on the western side of Mount Olympus. The delay was not only on the Persian side, the Greeks to delayed, ultimately deciding on occupying the pass of Thermopylae and deploying their fleet at Artemisium. When Xerxes encamped in the Trachinian plain, Thermopylae was held by six or seven thousand heavy-armed Greek footsoldiers commanded by Leonidas a Spartan king. This was only an advance force, the main ones to come after celebratrating the religious festivals at Sparta and Olympia. History was to repeat itself and as at marathon ultimately it was destined that this advance force was the only one to immortalize thermopylae. But the gods did help as the Delphi oracle foretold 'pray to the winds for they will be staunch allies of Greece.' Off the coast of Magnesia of gale known locally as the Hellespontias destroyed 400 Persian woarships and many auxiliary vessels. Besides fifteen by some error sailed right into Greek hand and, along with the troops in them were captured. The Greeks, alarmed at the huge size of the Persian fleet and army were in favour of withdrawal but leonidas and Eurybiades supported by Themistocles stayed on determinedly. The Greek fleet decided to attack towards the evening.

Meanwhile the assault at Thermopylae began. Leonidas held the pass. A path by which the force could retire if needed was discovered nearby. A Phocian force which volunteered, was deputed to hold that path. Xerxes sent some scouts to reconnoitre. The saw some 300 Spartans quite unmindful, some combing their hair, others doing gymnastic exercises. Xerxes was amazed, hardly realizing the real stuff of which those valorous Spartans were made.

As the Median, Cassian and the Persian 'Immortals' passed through the narrow gap, the Spartan soldiers cut them down. The Persian cavalry were powerless to act. All day long the Persian soldiers tried in vain to overcome those handful of Spartans. Treachery again. It seemed that Greece would never be free of turncoats. A Greek of Malis informed Xerxis of the secret mountain path, who deputed Hydarnes to start from the Persian camp at nightfall.

The Persian fleet engaged with that of Greece. Despite being outnumbered they outnumbered they fought on. The gods again helped and lightning and a severe storm caused the Persian ships to be wrecked on the rocky Euboean coast. Fifty-three Athenian ships came to reinforce the Greek naval strength and in another attack many Cilician vessels were sunk. The remaining Persian ships, however, still outnumbered those of Greece. Xerxes ordered an assault next day at noon.

As the Greek quisling had leaked out information of the mountain pass, the Persians taking advantage of that got up the mountainside and began to rain arrows. Leonidas got news of this down below and asked other contingents barring the spartans and Thebans, to retire for Thermopylae was lost. The Thesbians and Megistias of Acarnania however refused the order and determined to fight on. Realizing that the Persians might attack from the rear, leonidas led his force throught the narrowest part of the passage, and faced the numerous Persian troops. The spears of the Greeks were broken but they fought on with their swords. Leonidas was killed. The Greeks with drew to a hillock for a last stand. The Thebans surrendered, the remaining soldiers fighting to the last man. The shower of missiles laid them all dead. Xerxes showed up the Oriental in himself which was to be the never ending horrible cruelties of the Turk and Mongol later in history, by cutting up the dead body of Leonidas and putting it on a stake.

The same day at noon the Persian fleet launched an attack. Many losses were suffered on both the Greek and Persian sides, clinias of Athens proving the most valorous captains among the former. Half of the Greek fleet was no more fit for battle and when news of the fall of Thermopylae cam it was decided to withdraw. About 20,000 of Xerxes' best troops and half of his fleet of battleships had been destroyed in these campaign. The losses on the Greek side were half of their naval power and 4,000 men at Thermopylae.

The Battle of Salamis

It was not only the Greeks who feared their gods and sought their help. The Persians wooed theirs, the chief of them being Ahura-mazda. The Persian army advanced through Doris into Phocis which they ravaged. Plataea and Thespiae were burnt down. Then they proceeded towards the sanctuary of Delphi. As they passed between the closely formed cliffs suddenly a storm arose and two huge rocks broke away and fell, killing some of them. The Persians took this to be an act of their gods, and those who were not crushed fled away.

The Greeks decided to anchor their fleet at the bay of Salamis and to build a wall across a narrow part of the Isthmus and hold it with all their strength. The commander at the Isthmus was cleombrotus, Leonidass brother, and at Salamis, the Spartan Eurybiades. The sketch below is roughly the battle array at Salamis:

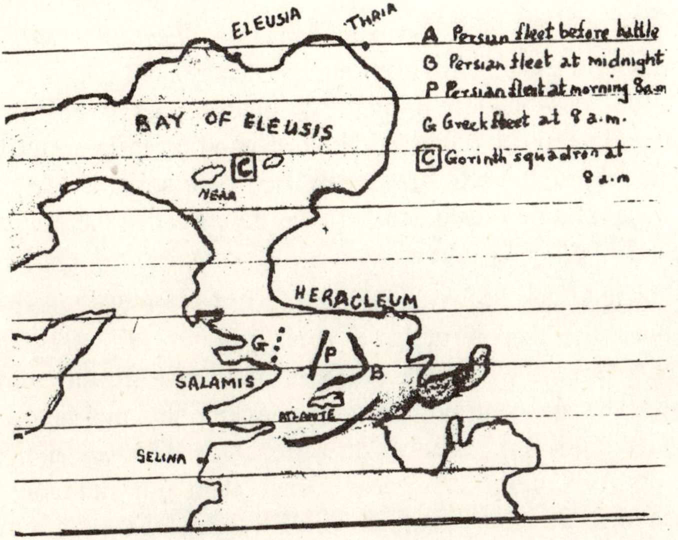

A Persian fleet before battle

B Persian fleet at midnight

P Persian fleet at morning 8 a.m.

G Greek fleet at 8 a.m.

C Gerinth squadrant at 8. a.m.

The Battle of Salamis

On the advice of Themistocles every citizen of Athens except those who were not fit, was pressed into the battle and Athens 'Entrusted to Athena'. Athens, Aegina, Salamis and Troezen were evacuated. Xerxes encamped on the Areopagus hiss and discharged fire arrows to flush out the Greeks who seeing the Persian force on the summit of the hill threw themselves down the wall leaping to their death. Others took refuge in the temple only to be pulled out and massacred. The smoke rising from the Acroplois was seen by the Greeks at Salamis. There was terror and dissension in the Greek navy. Most were for withdawal, but somehow Themistocles, despite many taunts, the captains were prevailed on to stay and fight. He also used stratagem, for as Herodotus (History III, 72) says-

"Ενθα γάρ γι δεί ψεῦδος λέγεσθαι, λεγέσθω 'Where something must be told, even though it may not be true, let it be told, even though it may not be true, let it be told'. Themistocles sent a trusted slave, Sicinnus, to beguile the Persian command that the Greeks being demoralized would sail away and be (Themistacles would go over to the Persian side!

The Greek fleet was 380 strong and these were pitched against more than three times their number. However, the Greek warships with three banks of oars were sturdily built, low-decked and with power to ram another ship and board it provided it got at the enemy ship's broadside. The Persian fleet saw no sign of the concealed Greek fleet but suddenly it emerged in Several columns. The Persian ships were more than 1,000 in number and ranged so close to each other that they could not move freely. Themistocles with his Athenian squadron of 180 ships waited till a current in the channel caused the high-decked Phoenician galleys to swing round their broadsides towards the Greek ships. The time to attack was now and the Athenian ships and those of the other Greek ones charged and rammed the Persian ships. After heavy reistance the Phoenician squadron broke up many being wrecked. Those captains who went to inform Xerxex faced his wrath and were slain. The shattered Persian navy sailed away pursued by the Greek ships, and many more were wrecked. It was the Greek tactics and superior fighting quality which won Salamis for them.

The Persian danger was, however, still there and the Persian fleet was still far more numerically than that of the Greeks. For the timebeing the war was over. But it was not the end and further battles were in the offing. From the spoils a huge statue of Apollo was made holding in his hand the prow of a trireme. The gods were praised, and the Delphi oracle which had filled them with hope and courage.

THE BATTLES OF PLATAEA AND MYCALE

> He acts most wisely who makes his plans with caution, recognizing that any untoward event may occur; but when the time for action arrives, acts with decision.
>
> *Herodotus Histories, VII., 49*

The Persian strength was still paramount despite their disasters at Marathon and Salamis. Mardonius their commander had the strong Thessalian cavalry and infantry. his forces had mobility, a firm supply-line, fodder for the horses and food for his men. The Greeks had no cavalry to boast of. Mardonius aimed at trying to turn Athens away from the Greeks, but he miserably failed to do so, and in a fit of rage razed all the buildings there and ravaged the countryside, thus giving vent to his frustation. Aristides and Xanthippes were chosen as leaders of Athens and Aristides declared that 'as long as the sun continued in its course' the Athenians would fight the Persians 'with the aid of the gods and the heroes whose shrines they had outraged'. Athens tried to wake up Sparta which was busy celebrating the Hyacinthian festival. The Spartans had indomitable valour but utterly lacked resolution and the capacity to perceive what was important when. They also seemed to attach more significance to their own hegemony, recluctant to fitter it away in opposing the vast Persian might. Sparta was for the Spartans, Athens for the Greeks. So Sparta's response was lukewarm and it dithered as usual, the price being the devastation of Attica and the seething resentment of Athenians at this lackadaisical attitude.

Mardonius put up camp by the river Asopus in the southern plain of Boeotia at the foothills of Mt. Cithaeron, clearing the ground and putting up a wooden stockade round his camp. He could get supplies there from Thebes (see map). His force consisted of about 300,000 men, 1,000 heavy-armed foot solders from Phocia, and 10,000 of his men in the cavalry. The Greeks had 38,700 foot soldiers and 70,000 light armed infantry. Of cavalry there was none worth mention Food supply was a problem for the Greeks as it had to come throught

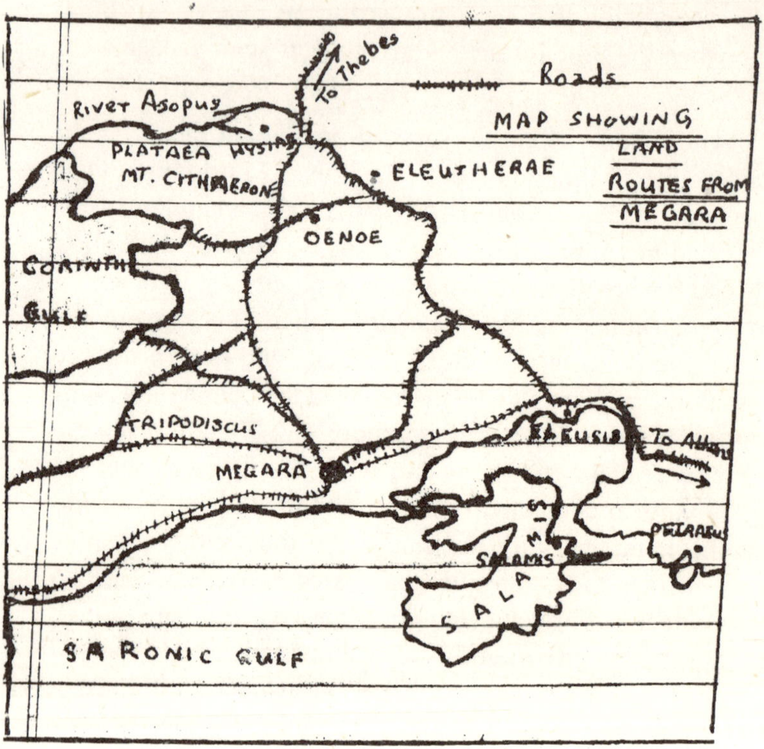

Adapted from N.G.L. Hammond. History of Greece Oxford 1959

the Cithaeron passes. Pausanias under whose command the army of the Greeks was, now waited taking up a defensive position for the Greek in fantry could not fight the Persian cavaly on a open plain. It was the Persian cavalry which first attacked driving back the Spartans from their source of water- the spring of Gargaphia. Pausanius then called a meeting and as decided moved to near Plataea. An obstinate Spartan officer however refused to move. The Athenians also stayed put. However Pausanias led his force along the foothills and the others reluctantly followed. Finding the Greeks divided (only the Tegeanes and lacedaemonians had steed firm), the Persian infantry attacked. The determined Greeks, now reduced by the uncooperative Athenians and Spartans, returned the attack with vigour, their deadly spears wrought havoc. Even a thousand chosen troops led by Mardonius were hewn down and Mardonius slain. The Theban troops however attacked some of the Greek soldiers killing 600. Whe the Athenians saw that the brave Lacedaemonians could not take the Persian post and failed to get throught the stockade, they joined them, which indeed they should have done much earlier. The opened a passage throught which the Greeks poured in and massacred the Persians for Pausanias had, in retaliation of their atrocities on the Greeks, asked them to take no prisoners. The Persian infantry were completely routed.

Simultaneously the Greeks secured a victory at Mycale on the coast of the Asia Minor. There were rumours of Samos breaking away from the Persian yoke and requests on behalf of the lonians to Sparta to liberate them. Though the Greeks did not move to assist either, Leotychidas exploited the situation by sailing his ships close to the shore and issuing a proclamation to the lonians in Persian service to join the Greeks in the name of Hera. The alarmed Persians disarmed the Samian troops. Another rumour spread that the Greeks had 'won a great victory', probably confusing between Plataea and Mycale. This filled the Greeks with new vigour. At Mycale the total Persian force was about 100,000. The Greek fleet had some 5,000 heavy-armed marines and 45,000 sailors for close combat. But the Persian army was a motley lot consisting of conscripts and mercenaries whose loyalty was questionable. The Greeks engaged the Persians, the Athenian foot soldiers driving back the Persian infantry. The Lacedaemonians, who had been delayed not joined the Athenians The Persian infantry, isolated into groups fought on till death and in the end 40,000 lay slain on the battlefield The victory of Mycale made the Greeks supreme in the Aegean Sea The Persian made some inconclusive sorties, but the end of Xerxes' invasion was clear. Xanthippus got Artayctes the Persian commander and his son put to death. The 'quality of mercy' was evidently neither in the Greeks nor in the Persians. It seemed that when the Bard of Avon considered it to be enthroned in the hearts of kings he perhaps never knew how few their number was. Xanthippus sailed away for home with rich spoils and with the cables of Xerxes' bridge which were probably dedicated to Apollo at Delphi and to Athena at Athens. The threat to Greece by a Persian invasion was by no means over and persisted.

AFTER MYCALE

> 'I shall fight to the death, I shall put freedom before life, I shall not desert colonel or captain alive or dead, I shall carry out the generals' commands and I shall bury my comrades-in arms where they fall and leave non unburied.'
>
> *-Greek Pledge Before the Battle of Plataea*

In times of necessity people take oaths to preserve unity, but when the time is past they are forgotten, for such oaths are superficial as Euripides says in Hippolytus, 612- 'Η γλῶσσ' όμωμοχ', ηδέ φρήν ἀνώμογος 'My tongue hath sworn but my soul is not bound by it'. And so it was with the Greeks, They would come together only to renew their animosities. Had they remained united the Greek civilization might have outlived that of Rome and lasted much longer. But it was not to be Dissensions persisted, and as Cicero says in *De Amicitia* VIII, 23. Quae enim domus tam stabilis, quae tam firma civitasest, quae non odiis atque dissidiis funditus possit everti?

'There is no house so strong, no state so firmly established, that it may not be levelled to the ground by internal hatreds and dissensions'. The leaders in the Greek city states were Athens and Sparta, and the Hellenic world found itself divided into two groups headed by the one or the other according as they were either maritime or continental, Dorian or Ionian or affected by petty jealousies. Athens favoured democracy, Sparta oligarchy. Moreover often other states kept changing from one group to another. The war with Persia had shown the necessity of an efficient and effective navy for Greece. Though the need for this was felt by Themistocles, the task of building up the navy was undertaken by Aristides and more particularly by Cimon, son of Miltiades. Athens gained prominence by theri achievement. It was necessary that the Hellenic navy should be supreme in the Aegean waters to meet the Persian danger. But there was lack of unity which was disastrous for the Greek states. There was no single high command no common fund for warfare no standard fixed for contribution in ships or money. The treasury was at Delos. Athens was the virtual protector of the Hellenic confedaration, though each state big or small, had one vote. Later in 454 B.C. the treasury was moved from Delos to Athens and this all the more made Athens the leader state.

However the prestige of Athens was weakened by Pausanias the victor of Plataea. Not satisfied with his position in Sparta he had joined the race for wealth at any cost, not disdaining pelf, as solon said in *Fragment*.

> 'Wealth I desire, but wealth unjustly gained
> I nowise covet'.

In his own selfish interest he intrigued with Persia, ending his life as a condemned traitor after hiding himself a fugitive from justice in a shrine, starved to death. More than what Greece owed to Pausanius, it owed to Themistocles who had guided it destiny in the days of the crisis. Still he was charged with conspiring with the Medes and ostracized. He fled to Argos and then to Magnesia where he was allowed to settle by the Persian monarch. It is a moot question whether Greece's great men were more thankless to Greece to them.

But worse was to come. It has been the tragic history of Greece that it punished those who benefitted her on the slightes excuse. With Socrates and Anaxagoras it was impiety, and the new excuse was ostracism, curiously enough both accomplished in a democratic manner by majority votes! No wonder Aristotle remarked in his *politica* that democracy was the acme of tyranny. Due to the influence of Simon of whom one historian says he was 'too honest to be an intriguer, too simple-minded to be a statesman, but with a genius for winning victories',[111] Athens and Sparta were on friendly terms. Cimon admired Sparta and was at the same time loyal to Athens and of course hostile to be common enemy, the Persians. In 463 B.C. there was a serious revolt of the helots of Messenia who had occupied the fortress of Ithome. Sparta appealed to her allies, including Athens. Cimon led a force to take the fortress, but failed. Athens lost face with Sparta and Cimon was ostracized. Hence forward Athens and Spartha were at loggerheads and Athens allied itself with Sparta's constant rival Argos of Peloponnesia, and very soon after with Sparta's allies corinth and Aegina.

THE PELOPONNESIAN WAR

Athens and Sparta were the two leading city-states and it was unfortunate that they started working at cross-purposes. Megara, at the north end of the Isthumus was threatened by the powerful neighbour, Corinth. When corinth attacked Megara, Athens came to her rescue. Aegina joined Carinth. The Athenians not only held Megara but overran Aegina as well and it became a tributary of Athens. In 457 B.C. Sparta entered the field and in unmistakable opposition to Athens. The Attic territory was invaded and the Peloponnesians suffered a defeat. At this time Themistocles had proposed an imperial conference of Hellas but Sparta was not agreeable. Thereafter he had raised a wall to fortify Athens, but the greater need was for a stong navy. There were a number of revolts and ultimately Boeotia, Euboea and Megara broke away. Thebes recovered her ascendancy. Megara joined the Peloponnesian League and Attica was again open to invasion. In 445 B.C. Athens perforce concluded a thirty years peace with the Allied Peloponnesians, surrendering most of her acquisitions on the mainland of Greece. We have related how disgracefully Athens treated the Well-meaning Themistocles.

Athens established new colonies from which contributions were raised, and these maintained her navy. Pericles was the new Athenian genius, and he developed a system of colonization in which the land occupied by Athenians was paid for by the reduction of tribute. Pericles was the uncrowned king of Athens. He favoured democracy at home but was an uncompromising imperialist in foreign affairs. He replaced the autocratic Areopagus by a body in which all citizens could participate. As an imperialist he planted colonies which increased the ascedancy of Athens and eased the economic burden of surplus population. The Greeks attached great importance to their sacred temples and so Pericles took on himself the task of restoring the ruined ones thus giving Athens prestige. However its hold on the new colonies always remained precarious. Such colonies were established in italy also - Thurii and 'New Sybaris'.

In one way envy or jealousy is in born in human nature and a failing of most human beings, as Socrates says - T òν φθόνον (εῖπεν) ε̎λkos εῖναι γη̄s ψυχη̄s 'Envy is an ulcer of the soul', and Greece having a disproportionately large number of tyrants and intriguers, had a large measure of jealousy too, for as Demosthenes (*Ad Leptineum*, 140) says - Φύσεωs kakías σημεìóν έσγιν ò φθόνοs, 'Envy is a sign of an evil nature'. Sparta was burning with this envy at the rising position of Athens in the Greek hegemony but her complacency and inertness, though keeping the fire of ill-will smouldering within, did not urge her on to let it break out. However circumstances provided her with the excuse. In 435 B.C. Corinth and her colony corcyra had a dispute about the

Corcyrean colony of Epidamnus and Corcyra won a naval victory against Corinth. Corinth decided to punish corcyra and it had the Peloponnesian League behind it. Thus cornered Corcyra sought the help of Athens. Athens agreed, but only if corinth attacked corcyra. However a small Athenian squadron saved the Corcyrean fleet from a possible disaster. Potidaea revolted and so did half of the Chalcidians. In 432 B.C. an Athenian force defeated the Corinthians and laid seige to the city. corinth appealed to Sparta. Pericles passed an order in retaliation forbidding Megarians to enter any port under Athenian Control, as Megara had aided Corinth at Sybota.

WAR AND PEACE

Sparta now entered the fray. Corinth was supported by the other Peloponnesian states. In the spring of 431 B.C. the first part of the Peloponnesian war started. In early summer 430 B.C. the Peloponnesian army invaded and ravaged Attica for forty days. At the same time a terrible plague broke out in the crowded cities of Peiraeus and Athens. Men died in thousands and the heaped corpses were burnt. Those who survived lived on a kind of life-in-death. Unaffected by all this horror and suffering, lawlessness and crime were rampant. But Sparta remained unmoved and refused any terms for peace. One third of Athens' first-line troops were dead and many disabled. In the citizen population it was impossible to count the dead. Yet the spirit of animosity was not wiped out About 100 Athenian soldiers, fifty Lesbian and China ones and a large cavalry ravaged the eastern countryside on the Peloponnese coast. The same force attacked Potidaea, but all they got in return was death by plague which they had carried with them from Athens. In 429 B.C. Pericles died. The Thebans tried to get possession of Plataea by stratagem. But it failed and Plataea appealed to Athens. However nothing substantian was done by Athens. The Peloponnesians laid siege to it and Plataea put up a valiant defence. But reduced to starvation half of the garrison escaped to Athens and the rest killed. Another episode was the revolt of Lesbos. The Peloponnesians promised them help but sent none and though the entire population of Lesbos was decreed to be massacred, timely second thoughts on the part of Athens prevented such a horrible happening, which according to Thucydides, the famous historian and chronicler of this period, was more due to political compulsions than to the 'quality of mercy'.

After Pericles the nature of Athenian democracy underwent a change. The democrats were so in name only. Lust for power, wealth and aristocratic birth became significant. War was to extend domain, the peace party's aim was only to thwart the warmongers and the Peloponnesians mainly wished to humiliate Athens. Demosthenes seized and fortified Pylos. The Peloponnesians tried to drive him out and a small Spartan force landed to assist, but had to surrender. Thus Demosthenes established Athens' waning prestige, and the Lacedaemonians stopped their annual forays into Attica.

Meanwhile the peacemakers were getting the upper hand though some, like cleon of Athens wanted the war to go on. With Cleon's death, however, the peace party gained ground and the Peace of Nicias was concluded which satisfied Athens and Sparta for a short time but had no durability and left Corinth, Megara and Boeotia dissatisfied. According to the terms of the peace some conquests on either side were to be restored. But Sparta's allies rejected this and so Athens too refused to carry out her part of the agreement. In this way it was a time for war and a time for peace, when the merry-go-round of conflict and cooperation kept rotating, till in 415 B.C. Athens embarked on the Sicilian expendition which was to result in its ruin.

Segesta its Sicilian ally appealed for assistance against Selinus and Leontini sought deliverance form Syracuse. This provide Athens with the excuse for interference. But the real objective was to absorb Sicily into the Athenian empire. The Athenians were very enthusiastic about the campaign but of the three persons put in charge of it only one, Lamachus, was a capable leader the other two were Nicias a half-hearted and diffident man and Alcibiades, reckless and rash.

In Sicily Syracuse was predominant, and Hermocrates the leading Syracusan wished to keep clear of the Peloponnesian tangle so long as there was no outside interference in its own affairs. But the Athenians were in no mood to leave it alone and prepare an attack by a huge force. Just then the sacred images of the Hermae were multilated and Alcibiades, and inveterate drunkard, was suspected of having done it. He was charged of the sacrilege but challenged trial. As this would have delayed the expedition the trial was postponed for later.

The dithering of the three commanders, each pulling his own way, however, was suicidal. The promised support, financial and military, from Athens never came. And to make things worse because of scheming by those against Alcibiades he was called back to stand his trial. Not at all the opportune moment for it. Anyway he doubted if he would get a fair trial and so escaped on the way home, and thoroughly annoyed by the Athenian decision, sided with Sparta, urging it to come out against Athens. Alcibiades was condemned to death in absentia. The Athenians blockaded Syracuse but Nicias omitted to close a gap and this enabled Gylippus who had been sent from Sparta, to effect an entry and with that the Spartans turned the tables on the Athenian force. Nicias asked for more men and Athens, unwilling to give in, sent a bigger force under the command of Demosthenes and Eurymedon.

The second expedition 413 B.C. found the AThenian force thoroughly demoralized and the Syracusans, Dominating both the Great Harbour (see map on next page) and the siege lines, in high spirit.

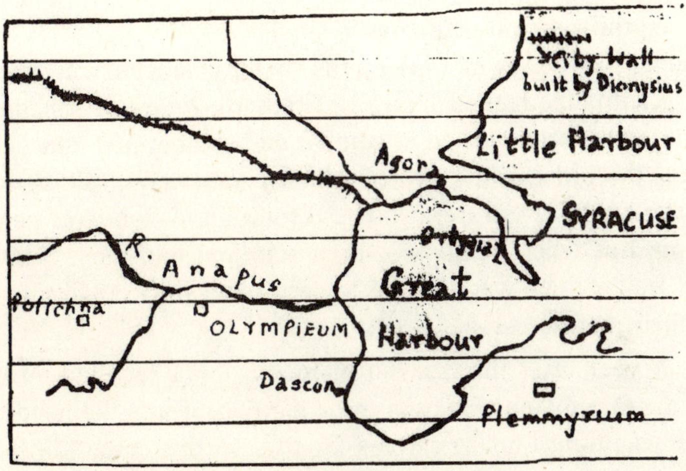

The disaster at syracuse

The Athenian fleet after a desperate struggle, was cooped up in the harbour, the mouth of which was blocked. And all internal routes were ambushed or blockaded so that escape by land was not possible. It was not merely a retreat. It was a great disaster. Those Athenian troops who survived the slaughter spent the rest of their days in abject sfavery. 'The Peloponnesians marched down and slaughtered them, especially those in the river [who tortured by thirst had gone to drink water] and the water was immediately spoilt, but all the same most of them were drinking it, bloody and muddy as it was, and even fighting for it. The Corinthians put Demosthenes and Nicias to death. Some 7,000 were herded into a cramped quarry shaft at Syracuse, where many died of exposure, malnutrition and disease.[112]

Although Athens carried on the struggle for another nine years. The disaster at Syracuse practically marked the end of the Athenian empire. Athens was left without a trusted leader, none who could inspire confidence. Her fighting reserve was completely depleted. Alcibiades had ability but no character, and though an admirer of Socrates as Plato's Symposium witnessed, it is not wisdom or wise speech which matters, but character, as Menander (*Hymis, Fragment* 1, 7) says: τρόπος ἔσθ' ό πείθων γοû– λέγονγος, οὐ λόγος 'The speaker's character persuades, not his words.' And character was just what Alcibiades lacked-Instead of rallying round in Athens innumerable factions tried to combat one another and treason became the order of the day, of which Tacitus says, 'all were ready to acquisce' in treason The resolution to fight was not lacking, but when persons of high standing and those who could lead armies were hostile to each other how could they lead their men to combat?

A year after the disaster at Sicily, lonia revolted, not realizing that thereby she was throwing herself into the hands of the scheming Persian satraps. Sparta, with its anti-Athens tilt was all set for intriguing with them bargaining Lonia for a price which would be high enough to maintain its fleet, Still, despite such odds Athens, though crippled, held on, and even won a 'notable victory at Arginusae in 406 B.C. in 405 B.C. however due to the unbelievable carelessness of her naval commander at Hellespont, Lysander a Spartan leader, captured practically the entire Athenian fleet while the crew were ashore at Aegospotamia. Shorn of its navy, completely blockaded both by land and sea and reduced to starvation Athens was a spent force. Her Peloponnesian rivals would have entirely obliterated her but Sparta came to her rescue. Hellas owed much to Athens and so long as Sparta's ascendancy was not in peril, she did not hesitate to help her. Fallen and humbled, Athens did survive and with her capacity to revive, resumed her place in Hellas in time to come.

On the fall of Athens Sparta fell into the hands of tyrants, Spartan officers called 'harmosts' whose rule was most oppressive. The lust for territory dominated her. At this time Cyrus was named by Darius as his successor of the Persian empire. Cyrus had established good relations with the Greeks and when his father died in 404 B.C. and his elder brother, Artaxerxes succeeded, he collected some Greek mercenaries and pressed them into an expedition to wrench the throne for himself. The unsuspecting Greeks had no choice as they came to know of the real purpose only after they had set out on the march, and Cyrus who was in pursuit of his brother would have succeeded in doing away with him were it not for the fact that he himself was slain.

An Athenian admiral, Canon, had taken refuge in Cyprus with Evagoras, the tyrant of Salamis who was under Persian influence. He was placed in command of the Persian fleet, which made him happy, for he saw in it an opportunity to humiliate Sparta. Corinth and Thebes, Sparta's erstwhile allies were now incensed with her.

In 395 B.C. war broke out between Thebes and Sparta. Athens, Corinth, Argos and other states joined in against Sparta. The Persian fleet under its Athenian commander won a decisive battle at Cnidus and Canon returned in triumph which was celebrated by restoring the Long Walls. Corinth succeeded in holding the barrier of the lsthumus largely due to the skill of Iphicrates an Athenian soldier. However Xenophon who recorded the exploits of the 'Ten Thousand' waxed eloquent over the Greek contempt for the 'barbarian armies' of Persia, an idea more fanciful than factual was greatly deceived. Persia's strong point was her cavalry, her wealth and her effective fleets. If the Persians were apprehensive of the Greek infantry, so were the Greeks of the Persian cavalry. If the Persians were really so inferior as Xenophon would have us believe, it is difficult to see why the Greek states were always eager to secure its assistance in their mutual conflicts. In fact Sparta now reversed her anti-Persian policy and brought in the Great king as arbiter in the Greek dispute and bided by his dictation. The Spartan, Antalcidas negotiated the peace of 386 B.C. which bears his name. It was the 'Peace sent down by the king'. Persia claimed all the cities and lands in Asia, and Cyprus. The Lemonos, Imbros and Scyros islands were to go to Athensa the remaining to beautonomous as were all other Greek states-which involved the overthrow of the Theban supremacy in Boeotia. The treaty also meant that Athens had deserted her ally, Evagoras of Cyprus, who was valiantly struggling for independence. The subject of Sparta before the war still remained hers.

Sparta was now the trusted agent of the Great king for the suppression of all leagues and democracies. She suppressed the Olynthian League which was a mistake for it could have become a barrier to the rising power of Macedon. Sparta also put her own friends in power in Cadmeia the Theban citadel, and this led to most of the patriots escaping to Athens which refused to surrender them. This again was a blunder, for event were to prove that it led to the overthrow of Spartan tyranny. Making mistakes is a human factor, for as Demosthenes (De corona, 289) says Μηδέν άμαργεὶν έσγι θεῶν – 'Only the gods make no mistakes', but making another mistake after one has been made could only be the dictate of destiny, as Aeschylus (*Agamemnon*, 68-*Chorus*) says τελεῖραι δ' ες γὸ περωμένον, 'The end shall be as is destined'. Pelopidas who was exiled, made a daring plot assassinathing the oligarchs. The great patriot of Thebes, Epaminondas, and a competent military organiser won a victory at Leuctra in 371 B.C. Though he was slain, Thebes had won a place of honour and Sparta's tyranny received deathblow.

The Greek states were vying with one another in seeking the support of Persia. Persia, however, was itself on the way of disintegration. Mean while Syracuse led by Hermocrates, secured the assistance of Gylippus, the Spartan, and reduced the power of Athens. But the struggle left her exhausted, and realizing this Carthage forthwith attacked Selinus and then Himera. Both the cities were ruined. Hermocrates occupied what was left of Selinus and attacked the Carthaginians. But he was killed in 408 B.C. Carthage launched another invasion. The presence of Italian mercenaries was significant. They were in the force of Aeragas which was not to be a base for a Carthaginian conquest of Sicily. In December 406 B.C. Daphnaeus a Syracusan, general, suddenly got Acragas evacuated by night At dawn the Carthaginians entered the city killing all who were still in town and spent the winter there. In this situation Dionysius saw his opportunity and got the people to depose the generals and set up himself as his successor, getting the people to proclaim him having absolute powers (*strategos autokrator*). He virtually ruled Syracuse for thirty-eight years and built a strong fortress as Euryelus and fortifications made by a labour-force of 60,000. Thus he made Syracuse more than double the size of Athens and even more impregnable. As a novel weapon he got large bows (catapults-*katapeltes*) made from which arrows could be discharged with a force that could penetrate the conventional shields, and realizing the importance of inefficient navy, he got timber by felling trees on Mt Metna or imported from Italy, to make ships. His forces on land and sea became more formidable than those of Sparta deployed against Persia, but they lacked discipline, cohesion and experience. He could challenge Carthage and cagole Sparta for assistance when needed. However he could not build a unified state and his armies were a mixed lot with hired mercenaries bound more by political servitude than by patriotic fervour. His success was a personal one and was always afraid of treachery. He was vain and even had statues of himself made in the guise of Dionysus, the god of tragedy! However finally he was honoured by Athens made an Athenian citizen and given the first prize at the Dionysiac festival of 367 B.C. He remained a heartless tyrant all through his life. Yet strangely enough he was admired too. Plato and Aristippus, who hated tyranny came to Saracuse, and withstood his harsh conduct with them, just to find out how this on man could achieve so much, forgetting their own dictum that kings should be philosophers and philosophers kings! Isocrates praised him as the saviour of Hellenism! It was remarkable that he could, with his callousnes yet impress intellectuals. He had no scruples in destroying Greek states. He cared only for himself, and as an eminent historian of Greece sums up his nature:

> 'He set poor against rich, slave against master, mercenary against citizen, even to the extent of forcing the wives of his victims to marry his minions... By fostering revolution and by uprooting populations he destroyed the moral no less than the material foundations of numerous city-states. By enfranchizing slaves and by planting settlements of mercenaries he brought about a mixture of races which tended to lower the standards of Hellenism. His personal example was malignant, he was perfidious, vindictive and cruel, and he recognized no secular or religious restraint. If his military power saved Greek Sicily from conquest, his political methods did it more damage than those of any other siceliote'.[113]

Depending for its existence on his own personality, Dionysius I's empire broke up in a few years. His successor, Dionysius lacked the ability to hold the empire together.

MACEDON, PHILIP AND ALEXANDER

The Peloponnesian was from 431 to 404 B.C. had left Greece weak and strife-ridden. Meanwhile Macedonia lying at the north of Greece was growing in power. Lower Macedonia consists of a coastal plain through which two prominent rivers the Axius and the Haliacmon flow into the Thermaic Gulf. Except eastward this plain is ringed by hills. Beyond the hills lies the plateau of Upper Macedonia which too is encircled by high mountains except toward the east, the mountains having just a few passes. In this way Upper Macedonia is well protected by a string of mountains and in the east the river the Stromy on river forms a continuous barrier. The people are a mixed race, sturdier than the Greeks and used to a strenuous living as peasants and highlanders.

In 359 B.C. the Macedonians elected as their ruler Amyntas, the infant son of Perdiccas, and as regent Perdiccas's brother Philip, then twenty-one years old. Philip had been at Thebes as a hostage where he had as his acquaintances Epaminondas and Pelopidas and so was adept in both war and diplomacy. He had no scruples also in establishing himself in power and much like the Moguls of Indian history, did not hesitate to wade through blood for it. He prevailed upon Berisades to slay Pausanias a pretender for the throne, contrived to have his half-brother assassinated, paid the Paeonians to desist from invasion. Athens was his most inveterate enemy, but her interests were concentrated in subduing the Chersonese and Amphipolis and she made peace with Philip hoping thereby to get his aid in the war against the chalcidian League and Amphipolis. Having made his position secure he proceeded to remodel his army. The war-chariots had been the conventional chargers in battles, much like the horse-driven *raths* of the Kurukshetra war of the mahabharata and along with the chariots the close-fighting infantry. There would be horsemen too but they followed no battle order and had no cohesion or discipline. Philip trained his infantry to fight in one mass, the Macedonian phalanx and his cavalry to move in formations. In this way the cavalry charge could dissipate the enemy's wings and attack from their rear. The bowmen would shoot at the chariots' horses making the chariots useless. Secure from any attack by sea, Philip invaded Paeonia in 358 B.C. and won a victory over them. Next he turned to Illyria and vang shed their entire army. The Illyrian king, Bardylis sued for peace. Philip made him hand over all his territory up to Lake Lychnidus and married Audata, an Illyrian princess. Illyria's defeat was a great relief to Epirus and in gratitude Philip obtained in marriage Olympias, daughter of Neoptolemus and she became queen in Philip's household. Thereafter he earned the gratitude of Larisa by subduing Pherae and he married Philinna a Thessalian lady, another entrant to his harem!

With his recorganized army thus Philip moved from Thessaly to Greece. Philip made overtures to Athens and Boeotia for peace initially, but largely with the dissent of Demosthenes, the offer was refused. That left Philip with no choice. The Macedonian army, modernized by his was the most efficient in Europe. At Chaeronea in August 388 B.C. the Greek and Macedonian armies faced each other. Philip had more than 2,000 cavalry and the entire field army of Macedon comprising 30,000 infantry. The Greek army of about 35,000 infantry extended from the bank of the Cephissus river to the foothills east of the walled acropolis of Chaeronea (See figure below):

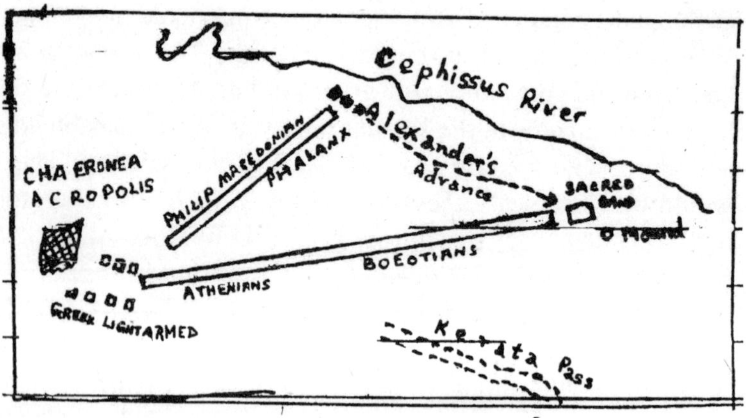

The Battle of Chaeronea

THE BATTLE OF CHAERONEA

The Athenians did not have much fighting experience while the Boeotians had. So Philip planned while the Boeotians had. So Philip planned to break the Athenian troops away from them. By his superior tactics he managed to create the required gap between the Greek foot-soldiers and the extreme right wing and Alexander charged through while Philip's general engaged the Athenians' extended line. A thousand Greeks were slain and 2,000 captured. Alexanders' cavalry annihilated the Sacred Band. The Greeks fled away. Peace was made. The Athenian alliance was dissolved. The Athenians retained Lemnos, Imbras, Scyros, Delos and Samos and get Oropus instead of Thebes. The Athenian prisoners of war were returned. Philip promised not to send troops to Attica or warships to Peiraeus Demosthenes had expressed the view that Philip intended to destroy Greece, but his liberal terms for the truce showed that wanted not its annihilation by its cooperation. In gratitude the Athenians give him their citizenship and put up statue of Philip in the Agora. In his funeral ovation for the dead Demosthenes urged Philip to bring coordination between the warring Greek city-states.

Polygamy was a common practice in Macedon and Philip had six wives but only two sons, Alexander born of Olympias being queen and of Greek blood, and Arrhidaes born of his wife Philinna, who was an epileptic. In 337 B.C. Philip married Cleopatra, niece of a Macedonian nobleman perhaps in the hope of begetting another son. Either because of Olympias's plotting to get rid of Philip because of this, her son. Alexander, already having been proclaimed heir, or due to some political intrigue, Philip was assassinated by Pausanias a young noble. Alexander was proclaimed king of Macedon.

Alexander's Campaings

Εί μή 'Αλέξανδρος ἤμην Διογένης ἄβημην

'If I were not Alexander I would be Diogenes'

Alexander (Plutarch, Alexander, XIV).

It is indeed remarkable that the pupil of Aristotle, the renowned philosopher should have turned out a military genius who at the age of thirty-three when he died, had an empire extending from the Aegean sea to the Indus, though he could not penetrate any further into India. True he crossed the Indus river but his so-called conquests came to naught after his death, leaving behind nothing except a chain of savage massacres. His successor, Selucus, had be humilited by defeat at the hands of Chandragupt Maurya ceding to him three rich provinces of his own-Paropanisai, Arachosia and Aria-and giving his daughter in marriage to Chandragupta, thus belying Vincent A. Smith's observation in his Early History of India (Oxford 1919, p., 112) about 'the inherent weakness of the greatest Asiatic armies when confronted with European skill and discipline'.

It seems that greatness carries with it an unexplained inconsistency of conduct. There are two main conquerors whom history gives the epithet 'the Great' Alexander in ancient times and Akbar the Mogul. Akbar, we are told, broke up a hunt even before he started it, setting all animals free and declaring that 'not the feather of a finch was to be touched'. Yet he was often heartlessly cruel to men. At chitor he ordered the massacre of 30,000 innocent peasants, getting a lamp-lighter killed just because he had fallen asleep near his bed, and getting Adham Khan thrown from the terrace, and finding that he was not dead though seriously injured, had him thrown down again spilling out his brains on the pavement. So too after a banquet at Saimarkand at which a great deal of wine had been drunk, Alexander slew with his own hands his friend and companion Clitus who had saved the king's life at the battle of Granicus. After he had done it he took out the spear with which had killed him and was about to plunge it in himself in remorse, when his bodygaurd snatched it away from him. He was ambitious and at times vain, egotistic and flaunted his self-importance. He had tremendous courage and endurance and retained the affection of his army. Once assailed by heat and thirst his men and horses were feeling fagged out A small amount of water was found and his soldiers brought it in a helmet to him. He took it but seeing the soldiers eyeing it eagerly, refused to drink saying if he did so his soldiers would lose heart. Thus he had both kindness and cruelty in equal measure. He got men convicted and killed men whom he suspected to be conspiring against him, like Philotus the commander of the cavalry, the son of Parmenio and Parmenio too even though he wasn't sure of their guilt. To the disgust of his friends he adopted Persian manners and dress and required prostration in the king's presence as they did.

Alexander's main achievement was the defeat of Persia with the help of the Greeks. He recruited Greek mercenary cavatry and infantry and managed to have a strength of 7,000 cavalry and 40,000 infantry. His first victory was at Gaugamela. He made an oblique march while Darius moved his huge army in a straight line. When the Persians repulsed the Greeks the Paeonian cavalry and the Greek mercenaries caused the Scythians and Bactrians to recede. His phalanx advanced steadily, Darius' chariots which were causing destriction were attacked by men wielding javelins. Alexander's troops charged in a wedge-like formation. Despite the loss of sixty Macedonians, they were on the winning side and the Persians fled, closely pursued by the Greeks and Macedonians. Darius took refuge in Media with part of his cavalry and a few of the Royal Guard of the infantry. The losses on both sides were heavy, but the Persian defeat was complete. Alexander was proclaimed king of Babylon. The royal treasury of Susa was captured king Meanwhile a rising by an Odrysian helped by a disloyal Macedonian with Athens' support too place. Sparta saw in this an opportunity for repudiating Macedon's control and establishing its authority in the Peloponnese Athens was asked to assist. Agis helped by Elis, Arcadia and Achaea overcame a Macedonian force and laid siege to Megalopis. However Antipater entered the Peloponnese with a force of Macedonians and Greek Allies. The rebellion was crushed. A gis was killed Alexander, who was asked to act as an arbitrator, pardoned everyone except the ringleaders levying heavy fines on them, and made Sparta join the Greek League.

From Sura Alexander advanced to Persia and reduced Uxii, Persepolis, Pasagardae and Ecbatana, and set fire to the palace of Xerxes at Persepolis. He sent home the The ssalians and the other Greek txoops rewarding them generously. The Greek League in return made Alexander their Mediator (hegemon) for life. In Athens, however, there was dissension regarding the attitude towards him, and hope of cooperation between him and the Athenians was getting less and less.

We have now concluded Brecian history in so fas as Greece is concerned. The splendour of its civilization continued for another 150 years or so. Unfortunately so did the conflicts between the Greek city-states, particularly Athens and Sparta. Greek history is not any different from that of any other civilization. Man's nature is more inclined to war than to peace. Peace appears to be just the beginning of fresh conflicts. As Thomas Hobbes says in Leviathan 'Hereby it is manifest, that during the time men live without a common power to keep them all in awe, they are in that condition which is called war; and such a war is of every man against every man'. Thus the sagas of civilizations unfold themselves with war and peace alternating more of war than of peace. Only the methods of war change from spears, swords and arrows, weapons, but the objective remains the same-lust for power, gold, domain and sometimes, as in the case of Helen of Troy, lasciviousness. There was no dearth of tyrants in Greece, though the Greeks professed democracy. Indeed a distressing feature of Greece democracy was the institution of slavery and the unforgivable feature about it was that even a renowned philosopher like Aristotle should consider it necessary were just chattels even as the Aryan slaves were. Another parallel between Greek and Aryan society was in the attitude to women who were delegated a subordinate role as we have narrated before. They were confined to home and often neglated by their husbands. As regards the Greek religion it was just as anthropomrphic as Hinduism with its plethora of gods in opposition to one another and Interfering in the affairs of men. The oracle of Delphi was invariably consulted on important occasions, and before venturing on a battle a sacrifice was always made to the gods. The Greeks were as superstitious as any other race and an infamous example was when at the battle of Marathon the Spartans who were celebrating the festival of Apollo declined to move to the assistance of Athens till the full moon and when they did it was too late.

SCIENCE AND CULTURE

> **As a rule, high culture and military power go hand and hand, as is evidenced in the cases of Greece and Rome.**
>
> *Baron Kolmar von Der Golt Z*

Something has already been said about the Greek way of life and their achievements in sculpture, painting temples, architecture and literature. These further observations are meant to supplement that. The nature of the Greeks, on the whole, remains inconsistent. The city-states, of which Athens and Sparta were the most prominent, were always at war with one another. Circumstances involved them in various wars with external powers like Persia, Rome and so forth, for the thirst for power and domain, like the greed for gold, is insatiable. Tacitus says in *History* (II.,38) 'The old passion for power which has always been innate in man icreased and broke out as the empire grew in greatness'. Marcus Aurelius wrote in his diary about the fight against 'barbarians' on the Danube and the sadness in his own soul (as Wolf exclaimed after the reading of Gray's Elegy that he would prefer to have written that instead of conquering Queberc). Marcus's observations are contained in his *Meditations* and have a already been quoted (Greek Philosophy, note 71).

The Greek way of life, the importance of athletics to them, their literature, religion, painting sculpture and their predilection for the theater have already been dilated upon. Scientific knowledge did not start with the Greeks. They owed much to the civilizations of Mesopotamia, Egypt and Persia. Yet it was the Greeks who developed the true scientific temperament inasmuch as they seldom distinguished much between science and philosophy and never put them into watertight compartments. Their philosophers were in some measure scientists also, as for example Thales, Anaxogoras, Heracleitus and Democritus contributed both to philosophy as well as to scientific knowledge.

The origins of science were not in Greece, but in the colonies established by the Greek emigrants, the lonians and Dorians particularly. Thales' signal achievement was in geometry. Though it was not the Greeks who invented it, it was Thales who found out that a circle is bisected by its diameter and that the angles at the base of an isosceles triangle are equal, that when two straight lines intersect, the opposite angles are equal, that the angle on the circumference of a circle of a circle subtended by the diameter is always a right angle, that the sum of the angles of a triangle is equal to two right angles, and that the sides of triangles with equal angles are proportional. Moreover Thales applied this knowledge to practical matters too. He was able to determine the distance of a ship from the shore, and to find out the height of a pyramid. In one way he may be said to be the father of science. Anaximander made the first attempt among Greeks to determine the details of the surface of the earth by the use of maps. He introduced among Greeks the use of the *gnomon*, an upright rod by which the length and direction of the shadow could be measured day by day, and the movements of the sun as well as the solistics, or the shortest and longest day be in this way be determined.

Anaximenes was interested chiefly in astronomy. He made an improvement in the calandar, making a better measurement of the solar year. It is significant, however, that as pointed out before most of these ideas originated in Mesopotamia and other civilizations and were introduced by the Greeks in their own land. We have already spoken of the atomic the atomic theory of Democritus, Anaxagoras explained celestial phenomena rationally and gave scientific accounts of eclipses, meteors and rainbows. Herodotus was a great traveller and gave an excellent account of geographical knowledge. He is the father of anthropology and history.

We have already spoken of Pythagoras. The Pythagoreans formulated the doctrine of numbers and made important advances mathematic. They created an interest in music and this led them to the observation that the pitch and notes in music depend on a simple numerical ratio in the length of the chord struck. They devised a system of plane geometry formulating theorems which concerned parallels, triangles, quadrilateral, regular and polygonal figures and angles. The great achievement of the Pythagoreans was their concept of irrational numbers Apart from their mathematical achievements the Pythagoreans made an important contribution to astronomy. They were the first to maintain that the earth and the heavenly bodies were spheres.

The Greeks like Alcmaeon of Croton (500 B.C.), a pupil of Pythagoras, discovered the optic nerve. He began the practice of dissection. He discovered the principle of the Eustachian.

Hippocrates, the physician, was born on the island of Cos in 460 B.C. Many medical works bearing his name have come down to us, though few, if any, are really his. He led a wandering life, dying at the ripe age of 100. We are all familiar with the Hippocratic oath, now a mere formality, and at least in India and the backward countries, not only disregarded, but also treated with contempt inasmuch as most physicians are only moneygrubbers and care a damn for their patients.

Hippocrates of Chios was a contemporary of Hippocrates of COS, though a little older, complied a work on the elements of geometry, a subject which was later to be allied with the familiar name of fuclid. We have already spoken of Plato and Aristotle who, apart from being eminent philosophers, were much interested in science. In Aristotle's view the egg or germ in its early stage. It does not have a soul even in a most elementary form. In a famous passage contained in his work On the Soul he says:

> 'The term life is used in various senses, and if life is present in but a single one of these senses we speak of a thing as alive. Thus there is intellect sensation, motion from place to place and rest, the motion... Hence even plants have life, for they have within themselves a faculty whereby they grow and decay'.

REFERENCES

1. Edwyn Bevan. *The Greek Philosophers: their Triumphs and Failures. The Universal History of the World* ed. J.A. Haminerton Vol. 3 London : The Educational Book Company. P., 1451.
2. V. Gordon Childe. *The Growth of Culture in Barbaric Europe. In Universal History of the World* ed. J.A. Hammerton. London: The Education Book Co. Ltd. vol.2., p., 961.
3. Philosophy J. Burnet in The Legacy of Greece. Ed. R.W. Livingstone. London: Oxford University Press, 1921, p., 58.
4. P.T.I. Dec. 22, 1978. Paper read in the post-plenary Symposium of the International Congress of Anthropological and Ethnological Sciences on Recent Advances in Indc-Pacific Prehistory 1978.
5. Megasthenes. *Ancient India* J.W. McCrindle
6. Ancient India as described by kte sias the Knidian, pp., 17-18, 30.
7. *The Philosophy of the Upanishads*
8. D. Mukopadhyaya. Notes on Hindu Astronomy. *Journal of the Department of Letters*. Calcutta University vol. 5.
9. Rig. Veda, 1:33: 8 and 4:53:3.
10. ibid. 7:58:21 and 1:95:3.
11. W.K.C. Guthrie, *The Greek PHilophers from Thales to Aristotle*. London: Methuen & Co. Ltd., 1950, p., 28.
12. Margarct E.J. Taylor. Greek Philosophy London: Oxford University Press, 1924. p., 17.

13. Rig Veda. 9:112:1.
14. ibid. 10:970
15. *Brihajjatakam of Var*aha Mihira*. Trans.; Swami Vijnanananda Allahabad : Indian Press, 1912 Foreword, p.,i.
16. *The Greek Philosophers : their Triumphs and Failures*, E dwyn Bevan *Universal History of the World* ed. J.A. Hammertor. London: The Educational Book Co. Ltd. 3, p., 1451.
17. ibid. (What the Modern Owes to Greece by H.A.L. Fisher) p., 563. Also Werner Jae ger. The Theology of the Early Greek Philosophers. Oxford, 1947. p., 73.
18. *Brihada*ranyaka Upanishad* 2 ; 6. Trans.; author's.
19. See Trans.; by author, New Delhi : Sumit Publications 1993, pagel Introduction.
20. *Bhagavadgita*, 2. 20 and 30. Trans., author's.
21. Cf. *Gita* 2.22. 'As a person discards old clothes and wears new ones, so too the embodied soul leaves useless body and acquires one that's new'.
22. Cf. Holy Bible, 'For dust thou art and unto dust shalf thou return'. *Genesis*, iii, 19.
23. Megasthenes. *Ancient India*, McCrindle, pp., 127-29. (As told in Megasthenes' *Memoirs*).
24. W. Romaine Paterson. *Alexander as World Hero* : A Study. In *Universal History of the World. London* : The Educational Book Co. Ltd. vol. 3. p., 1450 (Cyrus was the founder of the Persian empire).
25. A. Berriedale Keith. *Rising Religions in the Far East.* In the *Universal History of the World*, London, vol.2 pp., 1206-1208. The Educational Book Co. Ltd.
26. ibid.
27. *The Philosophy of the Upanishads*. Paul Deussen.
28. ibid.
29. Arnold Tonybee. *The Greeks and their Heritages*. Oxford University Press, 1981, pp., 1-2.
30. *Bhagavadgita* 3:4, 5, & 8.

31. *St Malthew*. x. 39.
32. *St. Malthew*, xiii. 22.
33. *Genesis*, 3.14.
34. H.G. Wells *A Short History of the World* England : Penguin Books.
35. 1922, p., 105. Edict of Ashoka, quoted Aldous Huxley. *The Perennial* Philosophy London : Collins, p., 206.
36. *Mundaka Upanishad* 1.1.3-5.
37. *Bhagavadgita*, 6:5-7.
38. *The Greek Philosophers*. W.K.C. Guthrie. London : Metheun & Co. Ltd., 1950, pp., 34-36.
39. From *Yoga* by Kavoor T. Behanan
40. Cf. Ramakrishna: 'Thou seest many stars at night in the sky but findest them not when the sun rises. Canst thou say that there are no stars? So o man, because thou beholdest not the Almightly in the days of thy ignorance, say not that there is no God. Max Miller : *Ramakrishna. His Life and Sayings*.
41. Lecomte du No*y. *Human Destiny*. London : Longman Greene. Signet Books, 1947, pp., 133, 138 & 189.
42. *Isha Upanishad* 1-2.
43. *Rig Veda*. 10.85.42 & 45. Indra is heaven's deity and the god of the firmament and the atmosphere.
44. John A. O'Brien. *Shall We live Again*? Paulist Press, 1964, 18-19.
45. A. Berriedale Keith. *Rising Religions of the Farther East. Universals History of the World*. ed., J.A. Hammerton. London : Educational Book Co. Ltd., p., 1027. vol.2.
46. Φενγουσι γáρ γol Χοἱ θρασεῖs, ὄγαν πέλas ἤδη γθόν "Αιδηv εἰσορῶσι γοῦ βίον. Sophocles. *Antigone*, 580,-(*Creon*). Tran; Plumptre.
47. *Measure for Measure*. 4:1
48. Plato *Theatetus*, XI (*Stephens*, p., 155,D.)-(Socrates).
49. Pythagords (*Plutarch de Reca Audiendi Ration*, XIII).
50. Trans; Edward FitzGerald.

51. The Ieiad. Book VIII. The Iliad of Homer. Trans.; Alexander Pope England. Oxford University Press, 1902, p., 158
52. J.L. Myres. The Minoans and Mycenae : Civilization Comes to Europe. Universal History of the World ed., J.A. Hammerton London : The Educational Book Co. Ltd vol. 2; pp. 784.
53. Thomas Hobbes. Loviathan.
54. Sappho. Quoted N.G.L. Hammond. A History of Greece Oxford, p., 173.
55. Aristotle *Politics*. C. Settman. *Greek Coins*, 1933 pp. 24 f.
56. Editor. *The Legacy of Greece*. London : Oxford University Press, 1921.
57. ibid. P. Gardner. *The Lamps of Greek Art*, p., 396.
58. Thomas Hobbes *Leviathan*.
59. Wait Whitman. *Leaves of Grass* ed. S. Bradley and H.W. Blodgen. New Delhi : Prentice-Hall, 1986, p., 2 As I Ponder'd in Silence.
60. *Bhagavadgita*. 2 : 32 - 34, 37.
61. Oliver Goldsmith *The Deserted Village*.
62. Dionysius Halicarnassensis. Cicero, de office, III., 23.
63. The Greeks often consulted the oracle at Delphi before undertaking any important task. It was believed that the oracle actually spoke and gave its command, much as the goddess Gauri is believed to have spoken to sita in the *Ra*ma*yana*. Delphi or Delphos was a town of phocis, at the foot of Mount Parnassus (the modern Kastri), famous for a temple of Appllo and for an oracle which was silenced only in the 4th century A.D. by Theodosius, and was celebrated in every age and country. Delphi was looked upon by the ancients as 'the navel of the earth' and in the temple was kept a white stone bound with a red ribbon, to represent the navel and umbilical cord. (Brewer's Dictionary of Phase & Fable. London : Cassell, 1959, p., 274).
64. N.G.L. Hammond. *A History of Greece*. London : Oxford University Press, 1959, pp., 163-64.

65. *Diogness Laertius*, I., 2, 16, 63.

66. William Wordsworth. *Lines Witten in Early Spring.*

67. Greece on the Eve of her Greatest Glory. Stanley Casson. *Universal History of the World*, ed. J.A. Hammerton. vol., 2 p., loss. op. cit.

68. ibid (Universal History of the World vol. 2), pp., 1267-68.

69. F.A. Wright. *The High Tide of Greek Life. Universal History of the World.* Ed., J.A. Hammerton. London. The Educational Book Co. Ltd. vol 2. p., 1279, op. cit.

70. ibid. F.A. Wright *The High Tide of Greek Life.* pp., 1984-85.

71. Hendrik Van Loon. *The Story of Mankind.* New York : Pocket Books, Inc., 1921, p., 61.

72. F.A. Wright. The High Tide of Greek Life. Universal History of the World, vol, 2, p., 1263 (Chapter 4). It is significant that the Athenians who were given mining contracts made huge fortunes from the deal. All the more reason why they should have cared for better conditions for the slave miners.

73. *The Greek City States at the Time of the Persian War.* W.R. Halliday. *The Universal History of the World* vol. 2. p., 1123.

74. *Chāndogya Upanishad.* 4. 4-9. (Trans; author's).

75. Hendrik Van Loon. *The story of Mankind* New York : Pocket Books Inc., 1921 p., 234.

76. Sir William Tarn and G.T. Griffith. Hellenstic Civilization London : Methuen & Co. Ltd, 1927, p., 4

77. *Universal History of the World* Ed. J.A. Hammerton, vol. 2., 1123.

78. George Gordon, Lord Byron. *Don Juan.* C III l xxxvi

79. Livy. *Histories*, XXII., 83. ['They lived under a just and moderate government, and they admitted that one bond of their fidelity, was that their rulers were the better men'].

80. Wordsworth. *Table-talk. The Legacy of Greece* ed. R.W. Livingstone. Oxford, 1921, p., 251 op. cit.

81. Krishna Chaitnya. *A New History of Sanskrit Literature.* Manohar, 1977, p., 315.

82. *The Legacy of Greece*. Ed., R.W. Livingstone. Oxford, 1921, p., 265 op. cit.
83. *The Ilied of Homer*. Trans.; Alexander Pope. Oxford 1902, Book VI.
84. *The Legacy of Greece*, ed., R.W. Livingstone. Oxford, 1921, pp., 256-57, op. cit.
85. *The Iliad of Homer*. Trans; Alexander Pope. Oxford, 1902, Book xxiv.
86. Edith Hamilton. *Mythology*. New York; Mentor Books, 1953, p., 191.
87. The Legacy of Greece. ed., R.W. Livingstone Oxford. 1991. p., 271.
88. Christopher Marlowe. *Fautus*.
89. Geoge Gordon, Lord Byron. *Don Juan*. Ib l xxxvi
90. Gilbert Norwood. Greek Literature and the Theatre. Universal History of the World. ed., J.A. Hammerton, vol. 2, p., 1342.
91. *The Plays of Euripedes*. London : J.M. Dent & Sons Ltd, 1908, vol., 2 *The Phoenician Damsels*. Trans.; Wod hull, p., 236.
92. Aristophanes, *Four Plays*. Trans.; John Hookham Frere. London : Oxford University Press. 1907. *The Birds*, pp., 181-82.
93. Trans.; C.S. Calverley. Gilbert Norwood. *Greek Literature and the Theatre*. Ch., 43. *Universal History of the World*, ed., J.A. Hammerton, vol., 2. The Educational Book Co., Ltd, p., 1361.
94. *The Plays of Euripides*. Trans.; Shelley, Dean Milman, Potter and Wodhull. London : J.M. Dent & Sons Ltd. vol. 2 pp., 19-20. (*The Bacchanals*). [A Messenger tells this Pentheus].
95. *The Lamps of Greece* Art. *The Legacy of Greece*. ed., R.W. Livingstone-London : Oxford University Press, 1921, p., 335.
96. ibid, p., 365.
97. Matthew Arnold. *Obermann Once More* h. 109.
98. Benjamin Rowland. *The Art and Architecture of India*. Penjuin, 1953. pp., 121-22.
99. Kramrisch. *The Hindu Temple*, p., 370.

100. Edith Hamilton. *Mythology*. New York : Mentor Books, 1953, p., 182. op. cit.

101. T.B. Macaulay. *Horatius*.

102. Anacharsis. *Plutarch, Septem Sapientum Symposium*, XXI.

103. Simondes of Ceos. Fragment 92 (151).

104. Publics Aelius Aristeides. *In Roman* * 69. Arnold Toynbee. *The Greeks and their Heritages*. London : Oxford University Press, 191, p., 65. op. cit.

105. George Gordon Byron, Lord Byron. *Don Juan* 1xxxvi Ib. 7.

106. Arnold Toynbee. *The Greeks and their Hentages*. Oxford University Press, 1981, p., 72.

107. *The Merchant of Venice*. Act IV. scene I.

108. *Universal History of the World* ed., J.A. Hammerton. London : The Educational Book Co., Ltd. CLIO, vol., 2, p., 1128.

109. Lord Byron. Don Juan.3

110. Lord Byron. *Don Juan*.

111. *Universal History of the World*. Ed., J.A. Hammerton London : The Educational Book Co., Ltd, vol., 2, p., 1234.

112. N.G.L. Hammond. *A History of Greece to 322 B.C.* Oxford University Press, 1967, p., 399.

113. ibid., p., 482.

GREEK PHILOSOPHY

Μάλα γὰπ φιλοσόφον γοῦγο γὸ
πάθος, γὸ θανμάξειν οὺ γάρ
ἄλλη ἀρχή φιλοσοφίας ἤ αὔγη.

***Plato**. Theaetetus, XI. Stephens, p., 155. D.) - Socrates*

['Wonder is the feeling of a philosopher, and philosophy begins in wonder'.]

The Development of Philosophy

As soon as man came on the earth and began to muse upon what he saw around him he tried to analyze those things and give them some sort of a meaning. And the first things that engaged his questioning spirit were the elements - water, air, fire, earth and the sky - and natural phenomena such as the sun and the moon, light and dark, the stars and planets and so forth. That, we might say was the beginning of philosophy in its most elementary stage - the spirit of wonder, as Plato calls it. But the philosopher could hardly stop his quest with thinking about these things for if he did he would only remain a materialist. There were other things more significant like death and sleep and the amazing process of conception and birth, and when Greek philosophy advanced, it traversed the path which other philosophies had taken before it the Egyptian, the Aryan and the Dravidian. Despite the fact the philosophy had a much more ancient beginning most Western writers keep on stubbornly affirming that even as they think civilization, all philosophy began in Europe. As we go along we will be pointing out similarities in the Greek and Vedantic concepts. From the thoughts about material things Greek philosophy went on to more vital matters like life and death and that unknown but indisputable entity, the soul, the exit of which from the body meant death.

Therefore in 481-406 B.C. find Euripides about two hunded years after the lonian philosophers Thales, Anaximander and Anaximenes had puzzled over water, air and the 'Boundless', Meditating on life and death:

> 'T ís δ' oἶδεν, εἰξῆν γοῦθ' ὅ κέκληγαι θανεῖν, γὸ ξῆν δέ θνήσκειν έσγὶ;'
>
> ['Who knows that 'tis not life which we call death, An death our life on earth'][1]

Plato (b. 427 B.C., d. 347-6 B.C.) later in his doctrine of the soul believed in its immortality divinity and also in afterlife, much like the teaching contained before in the *Gita* and Upanishads and the idea of karma. Thus while the origin of Greek philosophy lay in materialism its culmination was in spiritualism. Empedocles observed:

> 'For in no way can anything come into being
>
> From that which is not
>
> And that which is can never cease to be'.

The word 'philo-sophos' in Greek means 'lover of wisdom' and the early lonian philosophers, of whom we will speak presently, we called 'wise men', (Sophoi or Sophistai), and from the fifth century onwards philosophos was the word used in Greece to describe one who mused over the universe and about good and evil in human beings.

The Beginning of Greek Philosophy

We have narrated the continuous process of the springing up of the Greek city-states. They were colonies which gradually grew in the areas surrounding the Black Sea and the Libyan coast of Africa. When the colonies themselves expanded they planted further colonies. Such colonies in the North-east were Sinope, Trapezus, Amisus Miletus. Tomis Odessus, Istrus on the Danube, Tyras on the Dniester, Olba on the Bug and Borysthenes on the Dnieper. The colonies of Miletus with their sub-colonies numbere about a hundred. Other Ionian states found colonies along the Black Sea, such as Apollonia Pontica and Phanagoria. Dorian colonies were planted by Megara at Heraclea Pontica and Mesembria. On the European side of the Hellespont small colonies such as Sestus, Limnae and Colophon Cardia. In the West and South the earliest colonies in Haly and sicily came from chalcis and Eretria. Corinth founded colonies at Molycrium, Macynia, Chalcis and Oenidae, all at the entry to the Gulf of Corinth. In Illyraa Corcyra founded Epidamnus and Corinth, Apollonia *c.* 600 B.C. The earliest colonies in the West were planted on the Island of Pithecusae. The chaldeanms founded the earliest colony, Rhegium, at the very toe of Italy. In Sicily also a few colonies sprang up such as Naxus with colonists from Chalcis, mainly Ionians. There were a number of other such colonies varying in size and all sovereign in themselves and self-contained.

Thales

It was in the colonies in Asia Minor and then in Sicily and Italy that the first schools of Greek philosophy arose. The mainland of Greece was still busy with constitutional reforms first of Draco then of Solon, which have already been narrated, and so there was no intectual atmosphere there favourable to the growth of philosophy. In colonies, however, there were no such problems and there being greater stability and the opportunity for thought and meditation, the earliest Greek philosophers arose. Thales was among the earliest Greek thinkers. He was an inhabitant of Miletus in the Asia Minor and lived in the earlier part of the sixth century B.C. Miletus was populated by the Ionian conquerors. Thales furthered the spirit of inquiry and of the curiosity to know about things. There is not much in his doctrine that is truly philosophical in the Greek sense of a love of wisdom. He merely initiated the spirit of inquiry and that too a concept more crude than intellectual and quite off the mark as far as actuality was concerned, the concept that all things are water. But another saying also attributed to him was γγάνγα πλήρη θεῶν 'everything is full of gods'. Thales was fond of magnets and so Aristotle conceives him to be thinking, in this saying about magnetic attraction, and that everything is full of some force that is mysterious and that all reality is one, as the ancient Vedic Hindu thinkers thought - 'that which others call many, the sages know as One'. The Greeks had so far conceived gods as separate and individualized. It was Thales who in holding 'everything is full of gods' thought of that Oneness which transcends the many. The idea that all is God had found expression in the Vedantic philosophy long back round about 600 B.C. The *Isha Upanishad* says 'Whatever there is changeful in this ephemeral world must be enveloped by God'.[2] According to Thales the world is all-inclusive and divine in itself and so does not need any external divinity.

Anaximander

Anaximander of Miletus is considered to be Thales' disciple. He gave a different doctrine, not agreeing with thales that all things were water. If that was so, he reasoned, why should other things be found to exist in the world? The conclusion he arrived at was a positive advance to Thales' way of thinking. If all things were inter-connected, he reasoned, there must be a 'real' that comprised all. he considered this to be a 'boundless something' from which the opposites like hot and cold, dry and moist and so forth were separated. This Boundless (*apeiron*) is that thing from which all Becoming has its existence. Aristotle said that the 'Boundless' and the 'beginning' exclude each other. Thought everything has a beginning or is a beginning, the Boundless is beginningless. Here again we have the Vedantic concept of the eternal Brahman. Simplicius says that Anaximander was the first philosopher to hold that the Boundless or *apeiron* is the 'principle' or *arché* but others, like Burnet, think this was not so for *arché* in the sense of 'principle' was first conceived by Aristotle. Aristotle himself says about Anaximander's *apeiron*:

> 'As a beginning, it must be something that has not become and cannot pass away. For that which has become must necessarily come to an end and all passing-away likewise has an end. Thus as we have said, it is itself without beginning, but is rather - so it is thought - the beginning of everything else. And it encompasses all things and governs all things, as those persons declare who posit no other causes besides the apeiron such as mind [voûs] or love [φιλìa][3]

By saying that the Boundless governs and encompasses all things and is immortal, he also seems to point out that it is divine; as Aristotle observes; 'and this, (*apeiron* of Anaximander) they say, is immortal [áθávaγou] and indestructible [àνώλεθρον]'. Thus we come much nearer to the spiritual with Anaximander's concept of the Boundless. The scientific theories of Anaximander are somewhat unrealistic. He thought the earth was cylindrical and hung detached and motionless in the centre of the universe equidistant from all parts of the heavens. There are, he said, rings or wheels of fire enclosed in husks of dark air. Each of the husks is open in the middle and the fire is visible through these. As the wheels go round and round, the heavenly bodies become visible through them. The fire at the circumference of these wheels dried up parts of the earth which got separated from the water surrounding them. File arose on this warm mud. so life originated, and the first creatures were fishlike enclosed in scaly coverings. From these evolved animals and finally man. So man's ancestors were fishes. Why does the earth not fall? If it rested on water as Thales said, then what did the water rest on? Anaximander said that as the earth is at the centre of a spherical universe it is equidistant from all points, so it keeps on where it is. 'It is in the position of the donkey placed exactly half-way between two bundles of hay. which dies of starvation because it cannot decide which way to turn."[4] Curiously writers have praised this fantastic account of the earth, the heavenly bodies and the origin of life as 'a remarkable achievement'! despite its utter irrational thinking. What was remarkable was not this even thought it could be said to be 'interesting', but his doctrine of the Boundless (apeiron), which in one way was the precursor of Xenophanes' idea of the one God, was certainly a commendable advance towards philosophy, which is essentially something spiritual.

Anaximenes

Anaximenes, who came after Anaximander, considered that the transformation of the 'Boundless' into hot and cold was not separating out. It was definite transformation. The various forms of nature were only different degrees of intensity of one substance, and Anaximenes considered this primary substance to be air (aer). This (air) is 'Boundless' because it can be transformed and is amenable to rarefaction, condensation extension and incessant motion. Most likely like Anaximander understood divinity, he too ascribed divinity to air. As air was the life-breath of the should of a human being, so too the world, he said, was comparable to a human being and the air around it sustains it. The world is sustained by this envelop of air just as the soul is by breath. 'Air' meant both that literally as well as fog and mist. Anaximenes said that air could be condensed into mist and water and even further into solid substances like earth and stones. He was interested in the changes thus taking place and progressing towards the world's creation, which he called 'separating out'. When one breathed out with the lips close together the breath which emerges, he said is not so warm as when one breathed wide the mouth wide open. So, said he, air can increase in heat and becoming hotter, turn into fire. Homer used the word soul - ψνχή as 'breath' or exaltation', though some believe by 'soul' he meant just life. However Ernst Bickel in his work Homerischer Seelenglaube

(1925) was of the view that in Homer the word αποψνξω means to exhale or breathe out and that the phrase ψνξήν καπνσσαι, can be translated only as 'to breathe out his soul'. Anaximenes used the word ψνχή in the sense of 'soul' not 'life'. Xenophanes did not believe in Anaximenes' doctrine that the world is sustained by the air around it, but the Orphics speak of the soul entering the new-born child on 'the wings of the wind. Anaximenes said that 'the soul rules us' - σνγκραρεî ήμas - and this implies an intellectual element. In its rarest and purest form Anaximenes said, air, the ultimate world substance is also the stuff forming life. A small portion of this world-substance which surrounds the world enters the creatures on earth and is imprisoned in each body. The Hindu theory of *prāṇa* - the vital air that sustains life is much allied to Anaximenes' ψνχή (the soul). The physical concepts of Anaximenes do not have any originality and are even more fantastic than those of Anaximander. The earth was thought by him to be a disk floating on air. The heavenly bodies move laterally round the earth setting and disappearing behind its higher northern parts. The earth itself was tilted.

Pythagoras

The two main line of ancient Greek thinkers were the lonian and the Italian. The Italian tradition begins with Pythagoras who though born in Eastern Greek, left his native island of Samos early in life. He went to South Italy near about 530 B.C. Settling down in Croton. He is said to be the founder of religious brotherhood of which both women and men were members, bound together by strong personal ties and some doctrines which were secret, not to be revealed to all. The Orphics and Orphism had an affinity with the Pythagorian doctrine. Orphism is based on the Sacred Discourses and Rhapsodies a long poem consisting of twenty four cantos. The founder of Orphism was the mythical singer, Orpheus. It consisted of a kind of religious rites (γελεγαί).

The Orphics observed abstinence and were pure vegetarians. Theirs was, therefore, a strict way of life (Bios) of which some rites of sacrifice, exorcism and Plato later were greatly influenced by Orphism. They also believed in the immortality of the human soul and its progress through its incarnations in not only humans but also by entering the bodies of other creatures. Therefore their strict abstention from flesh. There is a kinship in nature according to their belief and the animate world extends further than we think.

The mystical rites of the Orphics and their closeness to Pythagoras cannot be dismissed as foreign to the Greek psyche, for as we have seen, the Greek mysteries had the element of secrecy and only the initiated and those prepared for initiation could be admitted them. Pythagoras' doctrine of the soul's divine origin, rebirth and transmigration were thus certainly not un-Greek for the Greek religion itself saw the gods as the participants and controllers of human destiny. Nor can the Oriental influence be denied for the Hindu-Aryans also believed in these very things and even though the Greeks may have developed these separately, the similarities cannot be negated. The dance of religious ecstasy of Dionysian origin could be very much likened to the kirtan (Community dance and religious chanting of Chaitanya and other, adopted by the Hare-Krishna movement in the West in our times). The doctrine of transmigration means also the unity of the life-soul (ψνξή) and consciousness, and so too divine judgment (allied to the Vedantic karma), as, going back to the philosophy of Anaximander, we find him saying, 'But from whatever things is the genesis of the things that are, into these they must pass away according to necessity; for they must pay the penalty and make atonement to one another for their injustice according to Time's decree'.[5] The Orphic belief is also in this respect similar to the view of Aristotle that human life is a kind of punishment for some great guilt. Anaximenes and Anaximander had held that the universe as a whole was a living creature. The Pythagoreans considered that further the breath of man and that of the infinite and divine universe were in essence the same. The body died but the soul was immortal for it was a fragment of the divine spark which was imprisoned in the body. The Pythagorean belief was analogous to that of the *Gita* (2:20), that the soul is immortal. Or we may liken the Pythagorean view about the soul being a spark of the divine to wordsworth's ode:

> **Our birth is but a sleep and a forgetting:**
> **The Soul that rises with us, our life's Star,**
> **Had had elsewhere its setting,**
> **And cometh from afar:**
> **Not in entire forgetfulness,**
> **And not in utter nakedness,**
> **But trailing clouds of glory do we come**
> **From God, who is our home.**[6]

Pythagoras, therefore believed that man's aim was to remove the taint of the soul, become pure and merged with the World-soul. Until it could do that it would have to undergo a series of rebirths in various bodies. Thus the end for man and the termination of these series of transmigrations was union with God, which in the Vedantic terminology was known as *moksha*. Pythagoras drew up two columns separating good things from the bad. In the good column he put light, unity and the male as the limit of goodness, while in the other column comprising the bad he put darkness, plurality and the female! as the unlimited. As we have noted before for the Greeks men were of greater significance, even as far as beauty was concerned. Male chauvinism has a very ancient origin indeed! The classification of female under the bad limit seems to be quite odd.

The religion conceived by Pythagoras was a sort of pantheism. The world is divine and good. It is unified and limited displaying cohesion and order. The organisms in it show order and methodical arrangement (Greek *organon*, meaning tool or instrument). The regularity of the phenomena of the world proves this order. Day follows night and then day again. The seasons come and go with regular succession. The stars, planets and the moon all keep their places. The moon waxes and wanes with regular precision Pythagoras called this by the name *kosmos*, and he was the first to use this word in the sense of order, fitness and beauty. To understand the essence of *kosmos* one has to make a keen observation of it. And by doing so one is led to be close to nature. Pythagoras believed that like the universe each human being is also a *kosmos* in miniature. He believed in the imposition of the limit (*peras*) on the unlimited (*aperion*), the limited being good and the unlimited evil. The imposition of limit and the kosmos through which one conceived the world as a whole made evident goodness and beauty. This *kosmos* or order was also the virtue of music, the importance of which was emphasized by Pythagoras. The Orphics to whom he was close were also charmed by music. The Bard of Avon wrote:

> **Orpheus with his lute made trees,**
> **And the mountain-tops that freeze,**
> **Bow themselves when he did sing:**
> **To his music plants and flowers**
> **Ever spring; as sun and showers**
> **There had made a lasting spring.**
> **Everything that heard him play,**
> **Even the billows of the sea,**
> **Hung their heads, and then lay by.**
> **In sweet music is such art,**
> **Killing care and grief of heart**
> **Fall asleep; or hearing die.**[7]

Pythagoras discovered the intervals of the musical scale expressed arithmetically in numbers adding up to ten. This was called the tetraktys, the octave represented by the ratio 2:1, the fifth by 3:2, and the fourth by 4:3. In this way he saw a in herent order in sound which was expressed in the Universe too perhaps a pointer to 'the music of the spheres'. Pythagoras also made advances in mathematics and his discoveries, although unconnected with philosophy, are remarkable and display a rational spirit in consonance with that of the Hellenic Greeks.

Pythagoras has apparently been given short shrift by his critics, perhaps because of his Orientalism, for Western writers are by and Large so taken up with everything Western that the refuse to believe that anything Eastern, even though existing before the beginning of civilization in Euope, has any substance or merit. Pythagoras' doctrine of the soul's divinity, transmigration, particularly the view that it can migrate to animals or lower life, was galling to them. As one writer comments, these ideas came 'rather from mystical religious than from rational sources'[8]. Another says, 'But the belief in immortality in the form of the doctrine of the transmigration of souls, which is specially associated with the name of pythagoras, was for him rather a religious than a philosophic doctrine'.[9] Empedocles believed that the should takes new bodies as a man changing his clothes, a concept exactly identical with that found in the *Gita* (2:22)[10].

So too empedocles repeat Pythagoras' concept of the soul entering bodies other than human.[11]

Plato, one of the greatest of Greek philosophers, considered the soul as divine in the Greek sense, a being immortal in its own right. It has existed always, before its indwelling in any body, and will continue to exist after it has won final release from its chain of incarnations. It is altogether a higher creature and has nothing in common with the world of the senses in which it finds itself, and any 'this-worldliness' or accommodation to earthly existence on its part is a sin to be punished in the periods of purification in the other world which intervenes between its successive incarnations. This doctrine of rewards and punishments in the next world is taken very seriously and great stress is laid on the punishment of the wicked.

We see that the views of Pythagoras about the removal of the soul's impurity, reincarnation and after several rebirths in various bodies, union with the Absolute was the belief of many other prominent Greek philosophers and to deprecate Pythagoras for holding the same view was not at all justified. The Orphics too were firmly entrenched in Greek culture in the sixth century B.C. The divinity of the soul and its transmigration and the belief in internal happiness and eternal damnation as also the complete union with God, were Orphic tenets and had been assimilated gradually in Greek religion culture and literature. And as the bard wrote:

> **Such harmony is in immortal souls;**
> **But while this muddy vesture of decay**
> **Doth grossly close it in, we cannot hearit.**[12]

It was this harmony, which Pythagoras termed as 'divine' which lay hid in the immortal soul of which the body was only the temporary receptacle.

Xenophanes

It has been said Religentem esse oportet - 'To be religious is a duty'. Religion consists of mythology, rites and observances, scriptures and philosophy. The Greeks did not have a scripture in the sense that the Christians had the Bible and the Moslems the Quaran, but the other elements of religion, namely mythology rites and philosophy were very much with them. Here, of these elements we are speaking of philosophy, which is a reflection on the seen and the unseen. The seen comprises the world around us which, when we are awake, we cognize through our five senses. When Thales said all things are water or Anaximander that they are air, they were thinking of the seen for they saw or felt these elements. But when Thales went on to say that all things are full of gods or

Anaximander spoke of the Boundless, they were taking a step toward the unsee, for the unseen is that which, even though not experienced by the senses, can't be denied - as dream, sleep and death. The domain of scientific investigation is the seen, that of philosophy the unseen - as Will Durant says in *The Story of Philosophy*, problems like good and evil, beauty and ugliness, order and freedom, life and death. One of the unseen elements is God or some power which holds the world in order. And the idea of God is consequent to death which some conceive the final end of life and others only an episode in the drama of 'life after life'. All this is said here because many who have written in our times about Xenophanes as having no claim to being a philosopher. One critic, W.K.C. Gutherie (*The Greek Philosophers from Thales to Aristotle*) completely ignores him, while another, Margaret E.J. Taylor (*Greek Philosophy, an Introduction*) 'Xenophanes then, like Pythagoras stands outside the main stream of philosophic thought'.[13] However even if we consider Xenophanes speaking of the nature of God more than anything else, he can't be excluded from the line of Greek philosophers because while the mere worship of God or the gods may be just religion, the concept of them and the Divine and the Soul certainly comes within the domain of philosophy.

Xenophanes came from Colophon on the coast of the Asia Minor, leaving his native city after its conquest by the Medes and thereafter settling in Italy. He had a strong personality and was full of the wander-lust going about the Greek cities for many years even till the advanced age of ninety-two, spending most of his time in Western Greece. He was very interested in philosophy even though much of what he wrote (generally in verse) was not philosophical. He put forward his views on the various aspects of philosophy in his poetry, and a large part of his verse was of historical events such as the founding of Colophon, and the colonization of Elea in South Italy. He also wrote of the nature of the gods, nature, truth doubt, the falseness of authority and the origin of things, in satirical verse known as the silloi. As was the practice then he recited his verses himself to his audience. What we have said earlier will show that if a proper and all-inclusive view of philosophy is taken, Aristotle's and Theophrastus' reluctance to acknowledge him as a philosopher is not justified. The Greek philosophers often contradicted one another. For example Aristotle, Plato's pupil, rejected Plato's Theory of Forms and along with that his idea of the soul's divinity, but while doing so he ignored the soul theory altogether without substituting a clear one in its place. Xenophanes was very much himself and he was eager to pursue the truth. He was an intellectual revolutionary and realized the great value of poetry in influencing thoughts. He infused new philosophical ideas in the Greek way of thinking. Anaximander had mooted the idea of the Boundless as divine, but it remained a nebulous idea, for one of the fundamental practices of the Greeks was the worship of many gods, till Xenophanes boldly declared that One God is the highest and neither in his form nor in his thought is he like the mortals. The human mind, he said, was incapables of grasping the infinite. He may not have said in so many words that God is without form but positively repudiated the concept that God's form is human. That, by implication, would conceive God as formless. God, he said, sees as a whole, thinks as a whole and hears as a whole. God's consciousness does not depend on any sense organ. He abides at one place, but a effortlessly controls all things by the power of his mind alone Aristolle's idea of 'the unmoved mover' seemed to have originated with Xenophanes. He (Xenophanes) was opposed to anthromorphism because to give human attributes to God would mean endowing them with human weaknesses and vices also like adultery, theft and deceit. he was critical of the idea of dressing up the gods as humans and making them wear garments, as we see in their statues which have come down to us. Rather out of context he also criticizes the animal-gods (they were revered in Egypt not Greece) and goes on to those of the Ethiopians and Thracians. The Ethiopian gods, he says, are 'black with snub noses, and those of the Thracians blond with blue eyes and red hair', and about animal gods he says, had the cattle and horses the ability to paint with their hands the horses would paint the gods in the form of horses and the cows in the form of cows. Those Greek philosophers who were inclined towards monism (ἑνίζονγες) were intrigued because he was the first to enunciate the highest principle. This concept was anagolous with Parmenides' theory of the One Being and the philosophy of the Eleatics.

Heraclitus

The next philosopher is Heraclitus nicknamed 'The dark one' and 'The Riddler' who came about the end of the sixth century B.C. with him we return to the lonian school. He was independent in his beliefs, fearless, a man of likes and dislikes, a lonely man who while having an admiration for a very few intellectual persons but, in general a Hobbes-like contempt for men. 'Fools even when they hear are as if deaf and even though they may be present, their presence is of no account. He was somewhat different in his thinking from other philosophers, for he castigated the multitude saying. 'They have neither the capacity for clear thinking nor for wisdom. They consider senseless crowds as their guides unaware that there are only a handful of good persons in them, for only a very few seek the immortal and the rest only think of filling their bellies as beasts do. he who is the best of the lot is for me like ten thousand of the others. There is non who considers widom to be apart from all else. I have sought the word myself while other persons neither seek it nor know what it is, despite the fact that all things happen in accordance with it. Men have no consciousness of what they do while waking just as they have no remembrance of their dreams. Do not listen to me, but to the word. Thought is no one's domain. It is everyone's preserve'. Strangely enough he said that 'war was the father of all, and strife is justice' thus contradicting Pythagoras' view of a harmonious and peaceful world. Thus he negated the idea of permanence and stability which most philosophers emphasized. All things, he said, live by the destruction of other things, Fire exists by destroying the wind, air by extinguishing fire. Water lives the death of earth, earth that of water. There can be no harmony between opposites. All things seem to be at rest but they are really under tension, as when one sees a bow leaning against the wall one thinks of it as a static thing at rest, but it is really under tension and if by chance the string breaks it will suddenly stretch out. In this way Heraclitus was the great denouncer, a prophet of doom, castigating those who had no originality of thought, led like blind men by the blind. His often spoke in maxims, aphorism and epigrams in which he resembled the Indian mystic Dādū.[14]

So too Heraclitus spoke in riddles and paradoxes, such as 'Good and evil are one' and 'Time is a chile playing draughts; the kingdom is a child's, 'Way up and way down - one and the same'.

Heraclitus often spoke of the *logos*. It is, he says, true for ever and identical with thought (*gnome*). Men fail to understand logos, he comments, even though it is eternal. It is truth and reality. Heraclitus speaks strongly of men who deliberately avoid knowing it:

> 'For while all things come to pass in accordance with this Word, men behave as if they had no experience thereof, putting to test such words and deeds as I set forth when I explain things each by its own nature and point out the real state of the case. But other men are just as unaware of the things they do when awake as those that do in their sleep'.[15]

The analogy of awareness to sleeping and waking has been often used by Heraclitus. What persons devoid of intellect call waking, he says in rcally for them not different from sleep. The *logos* lies at the basis of things and is common to all just as insight [φρονεῖν] is, but still the many live as though each had his own private wisdom. The organ of the *logos* is the mind [νοῦς]. Apart from being common to all the *logos* is knowledge of the divine. This concept is much like that of which the *Bhagavadgita* says (2: 69) 'What is night for ordinary beings is wakefulness for the disciplined soul, and that which other beings take as wakefulness is for the enlightened sage, night'.

Heraclitus holds that the *logos* is not only common to all [ξυνὸν] but also is the divine law, even though it remains hidden from mankind. it is the highest law of the cosmic process. Of war he says 'War is the father of all and king of all. Some he makes gods, others men, some he makes slaves others free'. He considers God to be everything - day, night, winter, summer, war and peace, hunger and surfeit. he becomes fire he says which when burning various kinds of incense becomes the fragrance of each. On the one hand he believed in incessant change - 'All things are flowing; nothing abides', 'You cannot step twice in the same river for the water is always flowing and fresh water taking its place', and idea that could be likened to the Buddhist one that nothing in the world persists save the fact of change; but while Buddhism denies that there is something unchanging and unending. Heraclitus does not. What keeps asserting itself in change is what he calls God. All change keeps working back to the unchanging. 'There is always one and the same even in the pairs of opposites, living and dead, the awake and the sleeping. Young and old. For these by their changes are those, changing back again to these'. This unity of opposites is a nexus or a contiguity [σύναψις], a harmony [ἁρμονία], or a coming together. From all is one, he say, and from one all. People fail to see that what draws apart also agrees with itself: a mutual fitting as well as opposite tension as that of the bow and the lyre. This notion of the union of opposites is expressed by Heraclitus in pithy observances like

'Good and evil are one', 'The way up is the way down', 'Mortals are immortals, immortals are mortals, living the others' death, dying the others' life'. Thus he sees unity in diversity. He applies this even to cosmology: 'All things are exchanges for fire and fire for all things, just as gold ornaments are exchanged for gold and gold for gold ornaments. Fire is transformed into sea and half the sea is earth, half whirling wind'. Of human nature he says, it has no insights, but the Divine has them. All human laws are kept alive by one law, the Divine. So man's character is his fate, for when he overcomes all selfish and petty interests for the common good, he becomes master of his self and circumstances. Compared with God, Heraclitus says, the wisest of man is childish and like an ape in wisdom and beauty and all else. Everyone has his opinion, but there is only one wisdom and that is to have that insight which governs all. The Greek idea of law is that which governs all, and since Greece was a democracy, this would have been framed according to the majority vote. Aerialists' belief, however, was in a universal norm which would not depend on this principle but transcend it. So he reconciled the two by declaring that law also means obeying God, the perfect Ruler who is perfection himself.

If was the Greek spirit of tolerance and independence in thought and ideas that considered the harangues of Heraclitus with broadminded forbearance and gave him due recognition as an outstanding philosopher, for in ancient Greece unlike the psyche in our country after fifty years independence, knowledge is put on the back-burner and we have evolved a democracy in which fear, hate and arrant corruption reign supreme.

Parmenides

With Parmenides of Elea we find an original departure from the philosophical thinking before him. This is particularly in his theory of the Existent (ὄν). The view of Karl Reinhardt in his book on Parmendes is a little too narrow in characterizing him as 'a thinker who knows no other desire than knowledge, feels no other manacle than logic, and is left indifferent by God and by feeling'; if this comment is meant to extol him as a philosopher, for this would exclude Plato and Aristotle who speak of the Divine in man and immortality, from the domain of philosophy. Parmenides set forth his doctrine in the form of an epic 'On truth' and 'On opinion'. He asserted that he learnt what truth (aletheia) was from the goddess herself, and so his 'truth' must be taken to be of divine origin. In fact he says the he is the only mortal to whom the goddess revealed it. He was led there, he says, on a chariot driven by maidens. He was conducted through the portals and welcomed by the goddess to the place far away from the reach of men. When the had reached there the goddess took his right hand in hers and said:

> **'And now you must study all things:**
> **Not only the unshaken heart of well-rounded Truth**
> **But also mortals' opinions, in which there is no true reliance'**

It is clear that the chariot is driven by higher powers and the road is 'far from the pathways of men'. The divine maidens must unveil themselves from the veil which covers them from this world of night and the person particularly chosen by the goddess is told to remove the delusion of the minds of me. The whole poem is thus and allegory and its purpose is to assert that the duty of removing such delusion is cast on Parmenides. The poem is therefore just a stage setting for his philosophical doctrine as the first chapter of the Gita is for Lord Krishna's teaching following it. Parmenides regrets that people roam about misled or blame their wandering minds as responsible for not visualizing the truth. The eyes and the ears are not capable of getting at the truth:

> **Seeing, they saw in vain;**
> **Listening, they fail to hear.**[16]

Parmenides uses religion as the basis of philosophy. What is this knowledge which he claims to have got from the goddess? This he conveys in his poem which, after the religious prelude of getting the Truth from the goddess which in contrary to people's opinions, is surprisingly very down-to-earth. It is contained in a poem of his, but before we quote it, it would be well to understand what he is getting at. The verb 'to be' in Greek meant 'to exist' no 'to be' for example *to be* black or white as we say now in English. To Parmenides 'is' meant 'to exist. The Ionian philosophers had held the view that the world was one thing but became many and this involved change as air to water to fire. But to change would mean to become what it is not. How can what is be what is not? That would be an untruth. So we can only say the One exists, the rest follows from it. The real world is changeless and so it remains. Only the mind can grasp the truth and the mind positively proves that reality is quite different. he expressed his mystic conundrum thus:

> **Come then, I shall tell you (and please listen well to my words)**
> **Which ways of inquiry alone can be thought.**
> **The first maintains that *it is* and *cannot be*;**
> **And this is the path of conviction which follows the truth.**
> **But the next asserts: *it is not* and *this not-being must be.***
> **This latter path, I must tell you, cannot be explored.**
> **For that which is not you cannot know**
> **(For it is beyond our achieving)**
> **Nor can you express it in words, for thinking and being are one and the same.**[17]

Parmenides proclaims the truth about Being, which he considers as eternal, beginningless, opposed to appearances and what mortals cannot conceive (much like the Vedantic *Brahman* or *atman*):

In the pure crystal of non-Being,
Being itself is the only flow.

Although Parmenides speaks specifically of Being and non-Being, he recognizes also a third way. it is clear that both Being and non-Being exist, still there are fools of wavering minds who go about trying to reconcile them although Being cannot be reconciled with non-Being, hoping to first go one way and then be back from it and go the other. These deluded men are the know-nothing (εἰδόγες οὐδέν). The Being never comes into existence nor ever passes away. True Being has nothing in common with non-Being. Neither can it be many, for anything which is manifold is subject to change and motion which can never be characteristics of Being. Thinking and Being are one and the same. The non-Existent cannot be known. The Being is one alone and the world of multiplicity arises from duality-the primal opposition of light and night as the two forces balancing each other. The world of becoming is mere appearance and that of Being is truth itself. Those men are in error who substitute duality in place of the one as something primal and put motion in place of the unchangeable. Parmenides associated knowledge of existence with the sphere of religion. The Existent (ὄν) he says cannot perish and is whole, single unshakable, limitless and complete. Thus he is conceiving and absolute Being beyond the realm of sense experiences. We can see thus that Karl Reinhardt's view about him being 'left indifferent by God and by feeling' is mistaken.

Empedocles

Empedocles was a native of Agrigentum in Sicily. He was politically very active there and championed democracy against tyranny and won the gratitude of the people. They wanted to make him their king, but he declined this honour. Later those very people who extolled him became inimical. he died in exile in the Peloponnesus.

He was said to be endowded with superhuman power, a healer of diseases and a miracle-worker, besides being a poet and an orator. Stories went round that he could divert the course of rivers, control the winds and weather and bring the dead back to life. It was said that he disappeared mysteriously at a banquet and was never again seen. Others, who were his detractors, said that he had cast himself into the crater of Etna to create a belief in his divinity. He publicly gloried in his superhuman power calling himself an immortal god, honoured, crowned with ribands and flower-garlands. Reverence was paid to him by everyone, he said, men in great numbers following him asking him to guide them, desiring oracles, seeking cures their diseases and removing their sorrows. He spoke about transmigration believing that the soul can descend into the bodies of creatures other than humans-birds, beasts and aquatic creatures. Therefore one should abstain from animal food. he said 'From what honour have I fallen, and what height of bliss have I left to go about thus on earth among mortal men'. And about not killing creatures for food, 'Will ye not cease from this accursed slaughter? do ye not see that ye are devouring one another in the thoughtlessness of your hearts?' He said that through serving their fellow men those who were fallen can rise to share the life of the gods 'free from the woes of men, safe from destiny, immune from hurt.'[18]

There were two strains in the philosophy of Empedocles, that of the scientist and that of a diluted religious. Orphic pietism. In his poem *On Nature* he follows Parmenides' idea of the impossibility of knowing 'that which is not'. His other poem, *Katharmoi*, or 'Purifications' depicts the influence of Orphism, though in a subdued form. Divergent views have been given to account for these two opposed trends-the rational and the mystic. According to Eduard Zeller the two namely belief in pre-existence. metempsychosis and abstaining from meat, and the 'mechanical physics' of *On*

Nature, had no connection with each other and were even contradictory.[19] Others like Diels and Bidez were of the view that the two poems depict the transition of Empedocles' thought from one period of his life to another.[20] The most likely explanation seems to be that initially he tried to expound the external world in mechanical terms, but later found it an impossible task and veered towards Orphism for his salvation. Ettore Bignone considers Empedocles in the dual capacities as a student of nature and as a religious mystic.[21] He was in fact a perfect representative of the intellectual culture of his time in west Greece, having distinctness and a colourful personality. Plato regarded him to be a close representative of Sicilian culture, and his poem and philosophy he classed as 'the Muses of Sicily.' Lucretius considered him to be 'the greatest product of the rich Sicilian soil'. The *Katharmoi* has a mystico-theological style and Empedocles calls upon his Muse to give him knowledge, even as Parmenides had been conveyed to the goddess on the chariot. But he does not go to beseech her but begs her to come and endow him with the gift of poetry. He admits that rationality has taken him nowhere and so turns to his Muse imploring her thus:

> **And may not the glory and honour**
> **By which men pay you obeisance**
> **make you ascend the pinnacle of wisdom**
> **Which puts its trust in what is more than holy.**

True Being cannot change, so we cannot say that the world *is*. On the other hand that which is must lie hid somewhere beneath coming-to-be and passing-away. There is no absolute coming-to-be or passing-away in this world, only things that are fundamental and beyond change keep coming together and separating. These things which mingle and separate are basically four-water, fire, air and earth. These principles are deified by Empedocles by naming them respectively as the gods Zeus, Hera, Aidoneus and Nestis.

Nothing, he says, can come into being from that which is not, nor can that which is be destroyed. These four roots or basic things denoted by their respective gods mingle and separate by the interaction of two powers which he declares are also gods, namely Philia representing Love and Neikos standing for Strife. He also personifies Love as Aphrodite corresponding to Hesiod's Eros.[22] Empedocles makes his Philia or Aphrodite the cause of pairing into male and female and also in the whole of nature which, he says, is organized similarly. Everything, sun, earth, heaven and sea, plants, beasts and men, trees, birds and fishes are all bound together in Love; even the entire cosmos. But as soon as this unity is achieved, the power of Hate or Strife seeks to break it up again. One may not see this happening but the mind's eye feels it going on and on. Still the Love element persists for long, and Empedocles calls it Sphairos because of its imagined spherical shape, equal on all sides. The *Sphairos* has the quality of remaining at rest at one place, as Xenophanes' god and also of the Permenidean Existent or 'that which is' (ὄν). In the repose of the *Sphairos* divine Love which sustains the world, is fully achieved. Gradually there is growth of strife and in the conflict between it and Love, the later maintain its sway only when the former lays low and is unable to have power. Strife is evil and villainous and brings hurt and sin into the world. The two, Love and Hate, alternately rule the world.

As we have said, empedocles was considered to be a healer of diseases and a kind of miracle-worker, and he makes no pretence to be modest about it. He says:

> **I go about among you as a deathless god**
> **No more a mere mortal, honoured by everyone;**
> **With head-band and decked with flowers and garlands,**
> **I am revered as a god by women and men.**
> **Some pursue me for gain, other desire oracles,**
> **And yet other to be cured of distressing deseases**
> **And bring back health to their afflicted limbs.**

quite understandably his critics frown upon this sort of vainglory. However it proceeds form his genuine belief that he has been chosen for divine salvation that comes when the soul is reunited with its divine source. But before that happens it has to suffer continual torment, urged on by Strife, separated from the divine taking all kinds of mortal forms, spurned by Air, Sea, Earth, Sun. He says:

> **Now I an, too one of these who are despised,**
> **An exile from God, a wanderer,**
> **Putting my trust in turbulent Strife.**

Thus the soul has been parted from the Divine, and after trials and tribulations, returns to the Divine. This doctrine asserts that firstly the soul in unmistakably linked with the Divine, and secondly that because of some iniquity it has to be far removed from its divine origin.

Empedocles, like Pythagoras, insists on abstention from meat-eating and the killing of living creatures whether for food or sacrifices to the gods, a common practice in Greece. In his *Katharmoi* he says:

> **Will you not desist**
> **From this heartless murder?**
> **Do you not see that you heedlessly**
> **Rend one another apart?**

And about the slaughter of animals for sacrifice he says: 'The father slaughters his own sons all the time praying, and is served with their flesh, the arrant fool! The son does the same slaying his father and the children their mother! The allusion is to the story of the House of Stireus as related in Greek mythology of which we have elsewhere said. Atreus killed his brother's two sons, and cutting up their limbs boiled and served their flesh to their father. The other ghastly killings were in revenge. Empedocles also believed that the soul acquires various bodies in transmigrating on death from one to another, putting on bodies off and one as one changing and old shirt with a new one. The souls are thus flung hither and thither, and he also includes himself in this tossing about, 'I too am one of these, a exile from God and a roamer'. He says:

The pangs of birth depict the cry of the soul in the newborn babe: 'I wept and wailed when I came to this unaccustomed place unfamiliar and comfortless [ἀσυνηθεα ξῶρον]'. As soon as the soul comes down to this world, the roofed-in cave, it encounters the evil demons of disaster:

..... that place bereft of joy
Where there is murder and rancour
Calamity, ills, putridity and floods
And darkness and a host of troubles ....
Mother Earth was there and the all-seeing Sun
Dissension and Harmony of Sober face
Fairness and Ugliness, Haste and Delay
Adorable Truth and dark-eyed Obscurity.

The soul encounters these pairs of opposites when it enters the babe's body. This is the consequence of furious Strife of which the outcome is bloodshed, and Empedocles bemoans it in his poem:

Alas O miserable mortals, unblest,
Such are the strifes and groans that have given you birth.

From this unhappiness only religion can relieve men. When Love triumphs it brings salvation. Then, he says:

The blood of bulls is not poured on altars;
And to destroy life to fill one's belly
Was considered the height of abomination ....
All creatures where tame and did not fear men,
Beasts and birds were well disposed to them
And the light of friendly fellowship shone.

In his poem *On Nature*, Empedocles bemoans the short-sightedness of men who reach a judgment during the brief period they come into the world:

> **They have hardly lived a few years here**
> **When Fate snatches them and they are gone like smoke;**
> **Believing only that which eachone has here experienced**
> **Yet firmly convinced they have known the whole!**
> **But not thus are things realized, heard or grasped by the mind.**

Empedocles discovered the Divine firstly in the imperishable in perishable existence, secondly in Love and Hate, the two forces governing physical life and which can only be grasped by the spiritual, and thirdly when goodness and perfection reach their zenith in the cosmic cycle. Empedocles' theology, therefore, is a synthesis of Xenophanes' monism and the polytheism of the Eleatics. He finds in his *Katharmoi* divinity in the human soul and they sway of Love and Strife is traced by him to the soul's existence.

Empedocles has been dubbed by modern critics as a charlatan and a medicine-man, indulging in boastful self-praise. But these critics have failed to see the earnestness of his belief, the consciousness of the Divine, the constant struggle between Love and Hate which is surely and decidedly life's stark reality, his condemnation of cruelty to creatures and the kinship of the soul in all beings. These derogatory remarks do him great injustice. His was a colourful and magnetic personality and in his view of the soul's divinity a precursor of Plato and Plotinus. He was not a conceited braggart as some critics view him to be. In his *Katharmoi* he was a poet and a musician of the kind of whom the poet Browning speaks:

> **Why rushed the discords in, but that harmony should be prized......**
> **Each sufferer says his say, his scheme of the weal and the woe:**
> **But God has a few of us whom he whispers in the ear;**
> **The rest may reason and welcome; 'tis we musicians know.[23]**

Anaxagoras

With Anaxagoras for the first time philosophy turned from the colonies and sought Athens as its centre. He was born at Clazomenae in Asia Minor. Either by being invited by Pericles or by his own preference he left his native place and settled at Athens where he was a member of an enlightened circle formed by Pericles, the renowned administrator who lived in the mid-fifth century B.C. After being closely associated with Pericles for thirty years, the opponents of the administrator prosecuted Anaxagoras, the reason being political, as he was close to him. He was charged with impiety, strangely enough, for saying that the sun was not a god but only a white-hot stone larger by a great deal than the Peloponnese! Thereafter he retired to Lampsacus where he founded a school of philosophy and soon after that he died.

His was a personality as striking and remarkable as that of Empedocles but in quite another manner. With not the slightest trace of vanity or self-esteem, he had no desire to be popular or influential, no intent to swagger or to claim to be a notch above the rest of mankind. The pursuit of knowledge absorbed him completely and it was truth that he sought, though in the end it eluded him. He was entirely indifferent to worldly possessions, personal gains or the things that ordinarily attracted people; things like wheat, power honour or fame. He neglected his property, allowed sheep to pasture on his farm and finally distributed all the possessed among his relations. He was the first of cosmopolitans and on being upbraided with not caring enough for his country and his fellow-citzens, is said to have retorted 'Hold your tongue for I care very much for my country', and he pointed to the sky above. Someone asked him why was life worth living and he answered 'So that we may contemplate on the world-order and the universe'. When he was exiled from Athens and some friends sympathized with him, he said that the distance of any place of the world from Hades was the same! His last wish as he lay dying was that the school children of Lampsacus, the city where he died, might have an annual holiday on his death anniversary!

Anaxagoras was interested in astronomy and medicine too, apart from philosophy, as for example meteors and other natural phenomena. In medicine he was a dietician and emphasized the need at proper nutrition to maintain the body with specific foods, though his medical theories are of little account in the light of modern medicine.

His theory of the elements is based on the concept of mixture in place of the older concept of becoming. For him there is no absolute coming-to-be or passing away of things, but only coming together and separation underlying natural changes. In the beginning all things were together, infinite in number and minute in size, and they were indistinguishable. Everything was held down by vapour and either for they are also infinite. They formed one compact mass. Then vapour and ether separated and this separating out originated the world.

Further Anaxagoras said that the food intake of the body contains all the germs of growth it needs. Thus hair, flesh, bones muscles, veins, sperm and so forth, must exist in latent form in the food we eat, for something can't come from nothing. But he was foxed when he came to consider the nature of the mind or spirit (*Nous*). If mind too was like the bones, flesh, hair etc., then why was it present in man as consciousness and not in other living creatures? It seemed that

Nous *could* not be accounted for by his aforesaid theory and that the limit of rationality had been reached. So he had to give an interpretation of mind which, even if he did not realize it, was distinctly metaphysical:

> 'Everything else is a share of everything. Mind, however, is infinite and self-ruling, and is mixed with nothing, but is alone, itself by itself. For if it was not by itself, but were mixed with something else, it would have a share in *all* things if it were mixed with *any*. For in every thing there is a portion of every thing, as I have said above; and if any other things were mixed with it, they would prevent it from controlling anything as it now does when it is alone by itself. For it is the thinnest of all things and the purest; and has every kind of knowledge about everything, and the utmost strength. And Mind controls all things that have soul both greater and smaller .... An many part so many things exist. But no thing is altogether separated off or distinguished from anything else except Mind. And all Mind is alike, both the greater and the smaller. But nothing else is like anything else; on the contrary each individual thing is and was most manifestly those things of which it contains the most'.[24]

Although Anaxagoras never refers to Mind as Divine as Anaximander did when he spoke of his *apeiron*, yet the term 'infinite', 'self-ruling', 'unmixed', and 'itself by itself' used for *Nous* clearly denote that the *Nous* or Mind is not conceived by him as an element or thing but as something beyond and of the nature of Divinity. *Nous* is that which understands every process of development of the past, the present and the future, including the revolutions of the meteorogical bodies, air ether etc., and it has preconceived and ordained every thing according to a definite plan (διεκόσμησε). Thus this *Nous* of Anaxagoras was nothing less than the controller of the Universe. It is the Divine in us which enables us to approach the Divine Mind and its scheme of the world-order. Plato is represented by Socrates as disappointed with Anaxagoras' concept, for though he introduced Mind in the beginning, he failed to make any further use of it to explain why things were just as they were. Indeed Anaxagoras' writings show that his concept of *Nous* was rather nebulous inasmuch as he veered between matter and the Divine in formulating it.

In his self-abnegation, his complete absence of self-pride, his scorn for riches and in his assiduous pursuit of knowledge and truth, Anaxagoras was a remarkable man. A Hindu saint and reformer, Swami Dayananda (b. 1824, d. 1883), had read some religious books which gave descriptions of anatomy and the nervous system. But with his passion for truth, he got hold of a corpse and cut it open with a knife. He found that the anatomy etc. of the dead man was quite different from the account of them in these religious books (*Siva-sandhya, Natha-pradipika, Yoga-bijak* and *Kesharani Sangit*). So he tore up the books and threw them in the river along with the dissected corpse. So was the case with Anaxagoras, an equally earnest seeker of truth. It is said a soothsayer when told that someone had presented Pericles a ram with only one head, interpreted this as meaning that Pericles would triumph over Thucydides, his political rival. The rationalist, Anaxagoras, could never give credence to this cock-and-bull story. He had the animal's skull dissected and showed that the single horn of the bull was due to an abnormality in its brain for it was smaller than the usual size, egg-shaped and connected with the root of the single born. Plutarch tells us that the gullible people, however, even while giving credit to Anaxagoras, reserved their admiration for the soothsayer when Thucydides was ostracized! Although his effort toward rationalization was praiseworthy. Anaxagoras could not keep to it, and ultimately had to turn to the metaphysical to explain the mystery of creation. he spoke of mind by applying to it the epithets *katharos* ('pure') and *leptos* ('thin', 'fine', 'small', i.e. finely ground or light material). The real reason why he had to abandon the rational for the metaphysical was that the solution of the reality of existence and creation did not lie in reason but in belief, for our senses can cognize the world of wakefulness, but beyond that the domain is that of faith. Anaxagoras was trying to squeeze in the mind (*Nous*) along with material things, forgetting that it is more linked with the soul than with the body, for as the soul is the controller of life, which ceases on its exit; the mind is the controller of the body while the body exists and all the body's functions are dependent on the brain, the mind's repository. Flesh, bones sinews and all that, remain and function where they are, but the mind can wander at will, as Arjuna, Lord Krishna's favourite warrior and disciple said: 'The mind, O Krishna, is restless, obstinate and stubborn. It seems as difficult to curb as the wind'.[25] It was long after that the Greek philosophers could turn to the non-material and the spiritual and realize the truth of what the Bard said:

> **'There are more things in heaven and earth, Horatio**
> **Than are dreamt of in your philosophy.'[26]**

The Cynics and Diogenes

Two of the schools of philosophy the Cynic and the Cyrenaic were inspired by the Socratic influence. The rise of the Mecedonian kings and the conquests of Alexander the Great put an end to the self-contained life of the Greek city-states. There was a transformation in Greek thought too. Compared to the systems evolved by the old philosophers the ones following were rather crude. The Hellenistic schools were of the Stoics and Epicureans. The founder of the Stoics was Zeno and they got their name from the painted Stoa or Colonnade at Athens. The derived a great deal of their attitude to life from the Cynics. The word 'cynic' in Greek means 'doggish' and the members of this schools were called in general *keyness* ('dogs'). The founder was Antisthenes who distinguished the one φύσει θεός from the many θεσει θεοί, among the latter gods about whom poets sang. Antisthenes lived about C. 440-370 B.C. The most famous disciple of Antisthenes was Diogenes of Sinope (c. 412.323 B.C.) who is said to have lived n one of the large earthenware jars which were used in ancient Greece for storing water, oil or grain, not in a tub as popular tradition has it. According to Seneca, however, it was a tub. Legend has it that Alexander the Great so admired him that he said 'If I was not Alexander I would wish to be Diogenes'. However, another version is that he offered to the philosopher whatever he desired and Diogenes told him, 'I wish you would move the other side for you are blocking my sun in which I am basking'. Butler mentions about Alexander and Diogenes:

> **The whole world was not half as wide**
> **To Alexader, when he cried**
> **Because he had but one to subdue**
> **As was a paltry tub to**
> **Diogenes.**[27]

Of Socrates we are told that he wore one garment only summer and winter, walked barefoot even in the snow and lived a simple life and that too supported by his friends, bearing cheerfully all hardships, having immense capacity for enduring them. The Cynics, at least in their living, went one better. The believed that people were unhappy because their wants outstripped their possessions. So the way to contentment was to get rid of want altogether and reduce living to the barest simplicity, the nearest approach to which was a dog's life. So the followers of Antisthenes wandered about like dogs. They had no house, slept in the porticoes of temples or in other public places, lived on scraps of leftovers which people threw away, and did not bother about decency when performing the natural functions. The Cyrenaics were seemingly just the opposite of the Cynics and declared that the single aim of life was pleasure. They could be likened to the Chāravāka hedonists of Indian philosophy. However, the aim of both the Cynics and Cyrenaics was the same, namely the pursuit of happiness. Only their means were different. Aristippus, the founder of the Cyrenaic school thought pleasure to be the means not renunciation. 'Enjoy in full' he said 'what you have without a care for the morrow'. Riches, splendid garments, sexual pleasures, delicious food-all such enjoyments, should not be spurned but enjoyed to the full, and if they are taken away there should be no regret, only a watch for such opportunities in the future. One should live for the present only and grab what Fortune offers, but not be enslaved by her, as the Bard of Avon says:

> **'There is a tide in the affairs of men,**
> **Which, taken at the flood, leads on to fortune,**
> **Omitted, all the voyage of their life**
> **Is bound in shallows and in miseries.**
> **On such a full sea are we now afloat,**
> **And we must take the current when it serves,**
> **Or lose our ventures'.**[28]

This doctrine was further developed by the Stoics and Epicureans. But before we go on to them, we proceed to briefly tell about the philosophy of Diogenes.

Diogenes lived for long in Athens. He made a study of nature, as Anaxogoras did, but he was also interested in the world and particularly in religious beliefs. If there were certain elements like air, water, fire and so forth they could not combine unless there was intrinsic similarity between them. Of these he chose air to be the most fundamental and basic for as breath it is that which sustains life. The soul inhabits the body only till breath lasts and the mind along with all mental powers associated with it depend on the breath. Air is thus the controller of all things, he said. It is really the power of God extending everywhere and in which every thing has a share. it has the capacity to know [νόησις]. He describes this primal thing as 'great, mighty, eternal, undying and of great knowledge'. In his treatise On Nature Diogenes mingled theology with anatomy, discussing the nature of the veins. His concept is the doctrine of *anima mundi* (that phenomena of animal life are produced by an immaterial soul). This animization has different stage occurring in a certain order. The Divine Mind has produced this order of itself. Matter and Mind are not opposed but united and Mind works from within outwards. Diogenes was the first to conceive a purposeful divine thought in nature, an idea contained in the theology of the Stoics later Socrates, who was dissatisfied with Anaxagoras' theory of the Mind, was more favourably inclined to Diogenes. He considered him to be the repository of a higher wisdom. Earlier thinkers had raised the controversy about the form [μορφή] of the Divine, insisting that its nature and form was like the expressed in folk-religion. Diogenes speaks, however, of the works (ἔπya) of the Divine. Socrates also says that it is difficult to determine the form of the gods but their works reveal their power. Th Divine can be known only indirectly for it is hid behind its works, just as the soul is not perceived but it is man's guide. Diogenes adds new dimensions to theology and his thought is remarkable in many ways. He spoke of the 'inner air' [ὁ ἐνγὸς αήπ] in man as distinct from the outer air. This inner air was that by which sense perception was possible and thus it was analogous to the soul. He called it 'a small part of God' [μικρὸν μόριον θεοû].

Democritus and Leucippus

We now come to the concept of atoms and motion. Although touching the fringe of philosophy and the concept of God and the soul-Democritus considers happiness or unhappiness of the soul to dwell 'not in flocks nor gold: the soul is the dwelling-place of the divine' - the Greek thinkers are yet not out of the mazes of materialism.

Leucippus was the founder of what is known as the atomistic school. This system was to later influence Epicurus in his ethical content and expounded by Lucretius in his renowned poem *Nature*, But in the atomic doctrine the disciple. Democritus became much better known than Leucippus, the guru. In fact some modern scholars even doubt the existence of Leucippus. But such cannot be the case for a fragment of his writing has come down to us in which he says 'Nothing takes place at random, (i.e., by chance, but reason and necessity are the causes of all happenings'. Surely it can't be said that he didn't at all exist, If a bit of his work, however fragmentary remains. It could be that he only initiated the theory of atoms and Democritus dealt with it exhaustively. Democritus' theory is remarkable as it was scientifically confirmed centuries later by modern experimentation. The Greeks at that distant time had no means of such testing and their genius lies lies in instinctively arriving at conclusion which were scientifically proved as late as A.D. 19th century! However it was only later they could move from the material to the spiritual, which was in a way surprising because the mystery of birth and death and that which causes them, namely that unseen, unknown entity, the soul, and the equally unseen power which keeps the entire universe in order, namely God; had been revolving in the minds of men ever since the beginning of civilization. Leucippus was a contemporary of Anaxagoras, Empedocles and Melissus. Democritus belonged to the period of the Sophists and Socrates and lived in Plato's time too. He was a northern Greek from Abera in Thrace, born about 460 B.C.

Parmenides had denied that there was anything called motion. What is fills all else. There is nothing besides it. So there cannot be an empty space or void anywhere. The atomists flatly denied this. They said there is being just as there is non-being. The absence of a body at one place is as much a fact as the presence of another body in another place. The only true realities were the elements which were tiny particles too small to be perceived by the senses of humans. These particles keep clashing as they have the capacity of motion and are separated from one another by emptiness. These atomoi (meaning 'that which can't be split', were the smallest particles of matter existing, solid, hard and indestructibe. Being different from one another in size and shape, relative positions and distances, they make the senses aware of the divergence in quality, texture, nature, feel and even taste of various things. In things that are hard the atoms are closely packed together in soft things wider apart. Sweet things are made up of smooth atoms, harsh or bitter ones by sharp-pointed ones causing an unpleasant pricking sensation in the tongue. Colurs are explained by the varying positions of atoms which reflect in different ways light which falls on them. Those atoms which are perfectly round and hence the greatest mobility, form the souls of animals and men. Hera a parallel may be drawn between Democritus' theory and that of the Vaisheshika of the Indian philosophy of Kanāda also dating back to several centuries before the Christian era, which postulates that atoms are the ultimate particles which cannot be further sub-divided. Ultimately all substances are made up of atoms - *tasya kāryyam lingam*.[29] However Kanāda does *not* include the soul as one to which his atomic theory applies. In this way all substances are considered in the light of materialism and all sensations are ultimately said to be the sense of touch. Even sight is explained this way. Object are said to be radiating from their surfaces fine films of atoms which convey their shapes to the eyes' sight. But in objects seen from a distance these films might become distorted, presenting a distorted image to sight. Since atoms were of various shapes including the hooked and branched ones and also infinite in number, moving in all directions they could collect together in masses. The atomists held that the world was formed in this manner.

Epicurus developed this thought two centuries later, but he said that due to gravity the atoms moved downwards, never in any other direction. But if this was so, how could their collision be possible? And if there was no collision how could the world of objects be formed? Epicurus sought to overcome this difficulty by asserting that gradually, due to some reason, the atoms falling downwards through space swerved a little this way or that, and so such collision was made possible. This, however, was a stretch of the imagination. Aristotle accused the atomists of 'lazily shelving' the question of how motion originated. They illustrated this point of movement, nevertheless by comparing it to motes seen in a sunbeam. Though these motes could not be atoms as they were visible while atoms were not, but it showed the way atoms also moved. Before we go on to the Sophists and Socrates, we will pause to consider the Hellenistic schools and their philosophy.

The Stoics

It has already been mentioned that the Stoics got their name from the painted Stoa or Colonnade at Athens and their founder was Zeno (C. 340-264 B.C.) whose teaching was developed by his successors at Athens - Cleanthes (C. 300 - 220 B.C.), a Greek inhabitant of Asia Minor, and Chryssippus (280 - 207 B.C.) a Cicilian Greek. The aim of the Stoics was to end the fear and misery oppressing men. Happiness they said, did not lie in external things because they were beyond one's control and if we were deprived of what we longed for the result would be restless anxiety, craving and frustration. So one must seek happiness within oneself. That way one became independent of chance and outward circumstances. All the happened to men was by the will of God (whom the Greeks personified as Zeus) clean thes expressed this thus:

> **O Zeus, O Destiny be my guide**
> **Whether willingly or with weak will,**
> **I will still follow without faltering**

One should joyfully yield to what comes about for God who controlled the universe was perfect Reason. However, strangely they believed that dog was a material substance! He was a kind of fiery gas, other or breath. But he had properties of a spirit too. The universe kept changing from one state to another. At times God, the Divine Fire existed alone. Then part of it condensed and became matter - air, water and earth and formed our world. But part of the Divine Fire enveloped the earth and directed the world's course. This Divine Fire was present as a particle in men and was their power of reason. After the ordained period of the world was completed it was burnt up by the Divine Fire. After an interval it was refashioned and ran its ordained course and was then again consumed by the Divine Fire. This process kept on being repeated for ever (c.f. the Hindu concept of *Pralaya*). The Stoics were thus religious but believed in paganism, even in the crude obscenities of the Greek mythology. Many persons professing to be Stoics were imposters, but some were its genuine and distinguished exponents like the emperor Marcus Aurelius and Epictetus an ex-slave.

The Stoics divided philosophy into three parts: logic (including theory and knowledge), physics (including theology and psychology), and ethics, Stoic logic, even though covering a large field, is dry and devoid of interest. As has be said before the Stoics were thoroughly materialistic. According to them only bodies had real existence. Thus God and the soul were also bodies. The channels of knowledge are the sense organs. The object seen makes an impression on the soul as a seal makes on wax. These comprehension, tested by reason, and found stable, constitute knowledge and such certain knowledge can only be obtained by the sage or wise man. Obviously the wisdom of the sages has nothing to do with spiritualism. At birth the soul is like a clean slate and gradually acquires worldliness. We have already mentioned the Stoic idea of the Divine Fire. The active principle of the Stoics was called by then Nature as well as God, and they joyfully resigned to Divine Providence. They accepted astrology and also the gods of mythology and believed in Fate, which they said, was the Divine will. As aforesaid, the Stoics believed that one had to live as fate willed whether he liked it or not. He was, they said, like a dog tied to a moving cart. The dog will either have to trot cheerfully along with the cart or be dragged along comfortably, but must go along with it in any case. The power of reasoning is given to man as a duty to be exercised by him. Reason is virtue the passions, emotions and desires are perverted or irrational reason. They are wrong concepts of what is good and bad for us.

The sage has no desire for external things riches. Heath or power. He is indifferent to family and friends. There is no one half-good or half-bad. There are only the sages and the vicious men. The stoics said 'A man can drown when he's in water a few inches above his head as completely as in the sea's depth'.

External circumstances are classed as 1. preferred, 2. deprecated and 3. completely indifferent. Their favourite doctrine was that when a man found desirable circumstances in life permanently less than the undesirable one it was no use keeping alive and he should commit suicide as a man leaving a room full of smoke or a child abandoning a game of which he was tired. They actually put this doctrine into practice. Their tendency to perform works they considered suitable or desirable led them to play a prominent role in Hellenistic and Roman politics.

The Epicureans and the Sceptics

Epicureans

Epicurus (c. 341-270 B.C.) founded his famous school 'Garden' about 307-6 B.C. at Athens. The Epicureans divided philosophy (as the Stoics did) into three divisions -canonic, physics (including psychology and theology), and ethics.

unlike the stoics who advocated cheerfulness and happiness by submission to God's will. Epicurus sought to banish fear by disapproving supernatural interference in the world and denying a future life. he was a thorough materialist and considered the body only as real, as the Stoics to held. He was for a life based on reason whose end is tranquillity which he called *ataraxia*. This means getting rid of fear-fear of the gods, of arbitrary divine intervention in the affairs of men, the fear of death and of afterlife if any with its possibility of punishments and sufferings.

In the canonic part of his philosophy he puts forwards four test of experience, namely feelings of pleasure and pain, sensation, concepts and intuitive apprehension. Sensation, he asserts strongly, is infallible. Error arises only when we start judging what our senses disclose to us. Like Democritus, Epicurus also took up the atomic theory, but with a slight difference. The smaller atoms, he said, were imperceptible, but the larger ones are visible. The fine an subtle ones penetrate through the pores and reach the mind which is itself material and consisting of very small round atoms. The atoms which thus penetrate produce mind-pictures and particularly the dream we see in sleep. Sometimes the images get mixed up with one another and result in all kinds of fantastic dreams and hallucinations. Thus all that is seen has only material existence.

The physics of Epicurus is a repetition of the atomic theory of Democritus, which has already been mentioned, except that he says the atoms swerve slightly and collide with one another, and these collisions give rise to the world and all that there is in it.

Epicurus says that the gods exist. A continuous stream of atoms ceaselessly flowing ensure their immortality. So even the gods' stay is just atoms! The gods do not interfere in the affairs of men (the Greek mythology shows them frequently so intervening). They live in perfect tranguillity, and represent the ideal life which human beings ought to imitate.

As regards ethics Epicurus said that pleasure and pain were the outcome of the good and the bad. Pleasure is not that kind which is momentary, but that which rids one absolutely of pain and brings complete peace. The worst pain is the fear of death and of what may come thereafter. As the Bard says:

> **Ay, but to die, and go we know not where ....**
> **The weariest and most loathèd worldly life**
> **That age, ache, penury, and imprisonment**
> **Can lay on nature, is a paradise**
> **To what we fear of death.**[30]

So too, fear of the gods is one of the greatest fears. Excessive desires to cause pain. Desires are of three kinds - natural and necessary; natural but not necessary; and neither necessary nor natural. We should confine ourselves to the first kind of desires. In this way the Epicureans were for reducing desires to the bare minimum. But they cannot be said to be inclined towards ascetism as some seem to suggest for ascetism implies the giving up of all desires, not merely reducing them. Friendship was considered to be of significance by Epicurus. The Epicureans wee quiet people who kept away secluded in their 'gardens', as they termed their small exclusive circles of philosoper-companions. They did not preach in the marketplace like the Cynics and the Stoics. But they showed not gratitude for their teachers from whom they had learnt much, and even treated them with contempt. They owe little to Aristotle or Plato. The Sceptics of which we go on to briefly relate, come really under the broad head of 'Sophists' of whom we will speak later on in detail, before moving on to Socrates. Plato and Aristotle and thereafter to the revival of Platonism, the Greek-Christian thinkers and Plotinus all of whom belong to the earlier Roman empire (1st Century B.C. and 1st - 2nd Centuries A.D.).

Sceptics

The extreme dogmatic attitude of the Stoics and Epicureans resulted in a sceptical reaction. The followers of Pyrrho of Elea was one branch of the sceptics. He had gone east and met some brahmin ascetics called gymnosophists by the Greeks. Pyrrho said that all things were unstable and could not be discerned. Nothing was really good or bad. Nothing existed nor did it not exist. Nothing definite should be thought of an no statement positive or negative made. Silence and suspension of judgement is the best and when this is attained tranquillity follows 'as the shadow follows the body.' The other sceptic school whose chief protagonist was Arcesilas, was mostly destructive criticism and made no useful contribution. The Sophists, whom we will next relate also partly expressed views similar to the sceptics. These were Gorgias and Protagoras. Gorgias deliberately parodied the usual little given by Greek philosophers to their works which was *On Nature or the Existent* by giving his as *On Nature or the Non-existent*. In this he endeavoured to prove three things: 1. That nothing exists, 2. That if anything did exist we could not know it, and 3. That if we could not know anything we couldn't tell it to anyone. Protagoras said that it was not possible to know whether the gods existed or did not exist, for there is no way in which one could have knowledge of this. The matter is obscure and presents many difficulties and besides human life is too short to sort out the problem. He said 'Man is the measure of all things, meaning thereby men may differ about what they think is the truth yet it is truth though the point of view about it varies. Truth is thus purely relative. But though no opinion is truer than another it may be better than another. If one wrongly believes a thing to be right he has the freedom to do so. But one's endeavour should be to convince him to change his view so that his wrong thinking may become right thinking. Thus the thinking of the wrong belief should be changed so that the person's point of view becomes better.

The Sophists

With the Sophists we reach the second half of the fifth century B.C. Socrates is at this time in his middle life. Plato's birth is near after (he was born in 427 B.C.). So long the Greek philosophers were mainly materialistic, though the concept of the Divine had occasionally appeared in their philosophies as the 'Boundless' in the Milesian philosopher Anaximander, the 'Being' of Heraclitus and 'Mind' of Anaxagoras. These are not viewed as the entity having all the perfections (ἀρεγαί) in other words God or the idea of the All (ὅλον, πᾶν) In our times the words 'sophist', 'sophistry' and 'sophistical' have acquired a derogatory sense meaning an intention to deceive or mislead. But the Sophists used the words in the sense of imparting education or what they thought to be that. This knowledge they sought to inculcate was merely efficiency in doing a task devolving on any person (Greek, arete). That was the meaning given to efficiency by Socrates and his applying it to everyone, whatever his task was, humble or exalted, irritated Greeks who opposed him, for to them menials like shoemakers, carpenters and so forth were not included in free citizens but slaves. We shall speak of this further about this, meanwhile relating the contest in which the ideas of the Sophists caught the Greek intelligentsia's attention and inclined them to this way of thinking.

From the year 431 B.C. Athens, which were one of the foremost centres of Greek culture, was drawn into war which led to its downfall thirty years later, and that along with the outbreak of a plague epidemic caused a great deal of devastation. it seemed their was nothing certain except uncertainty. Athens was no longer the state in which life proceeded at a leisurely pace. Human problems and matters relating to human life were becoming prominent. Athens was a small-sized democracy and its citizens and complete freedom in holding on to their view. Every citizen had the opportunity to play his part in politics which remained the foundation of Greek life from Solon to Pericles. At this turbulent and troubled age oratory, the main acquisition of politicians assumed importance, so greatly indeed, that like our modern Indian education today, it became a marketable commodity. Many aspiring politicians and advocates were readily willing to make their speeches and argument convincing by being tutored in effective language and pay a fee for such tuition. Protagoras of Abdera who visited Athens about 450 B.C. taught the art of rhetoric on payment of a fee. Prodicus of Ceos, Hippias of Elis, Corax in Sicily, Tisias and Gorgias educated would-be orators by such paid tuition. Isocrates was a pupil of Tisias. and Gorgias delivered speeches at Delphi and Olmpia which amazed and impressed his audience. He charged a hefty fee for giving lessons. Not only an artful style, and exactness of meaning of words used was in demand Prodicus taught the finer points of grammar, and protagoras the semantics of diction. Exact word usage was sought by those taught Prodicus, Antiphon and other fulfilled this need, for they were well up in both philosophy and rhetoric. Thus they became the endowers of wisdom as well as of oratory, and their specific kind of wisdom was rationalistic in method and agnostic in belief. These sort of educators became known as sophists. They found a ready market for their teaching in wartime Athens for the state provided no facilities for systematic education and all that children and youngmen learnt was by study in their homes. The younger generation readily turned to the Sophists, scorning the older one for its ignorance of rhetoric and the new wisdom the Sophiststaught. A new wave of learning swept through Greece in the arts, humanities and the sciences. But while benefitting this also led to the infiltration of strange and backward concepts. Thrasymachus, for example, said 'justice is the interest of the stronger', thus pushing back the history f mankind to thousands of years before civilization began, and the law of the jungle prevailed! Similarly, callicles declared that might was right, and Critas that religion was invented by a shrewd man in his own interest to foist religious beliefs on others! This was of course Sophism run wild. But it was not the real creed of Sophists in general.

There was a dissatisfaction felt about the traditional religion with the fantastic array of gods. The word 'sophistes' meant 'one who practiced wisdom ' and so did not originally have any bad sense. it was only the unpopularity of the fifth century B.C. Sophists which degraded it. Their teaching, indeed was practical. As we have said they emphasized being expert in doing what was one's job or profession. This they called *arte*. Unless one had first a clear idea of what he was out to do or make, it was pointless proceeding to make it. It was necessary firstly to visualize the thing and also the use to which it would be put such knowledge was individual. it could not be shared. Besides it was self-taught. No one could teach it to another. These were two points, which Socrates insisted on which, among others, incensed his opponents. His equating all classes, high and low in his concept of arte was, as we have said, another irritant. To illustrate the true sense of arte, the Sophist, Hippias, appeared at the Olympic games wearing nothing that he had not himself made even the ring on his finger! unfortunately most of the Sophists confined *arte* to what had practical use only, although many of the Sophists were men of great learning, and had as their friends people who were prominent in Greece, like Pericles and Thucydides. Such practical teaching the Sophists gave was to acquire power, wealth and renown and was not really spiritual even though Protagoras said 'man is the measure of all things' (as we have quoted in the section on the Sceptics). In a way the Sophistic attitude can be likened to the transformation currently taking place in Indian publishing. The old-fashioned books seeking to impart spiritualism have given place to practical ones on self-improvement aimed at efficiency in public speaking, ways of success in 'winning friends and influencing people', improving one's language, computers, business management and so forth. And just as our publishers are eager to give what the readers want so too the Sophists of Greece were fulfilling the needs of the people and the main incentive was money-gold omnipotent gold. But as we have some, like the indological and oriental publishing houses, who have undeterred sought to keep to the spiritual, so too the successors to the Sophists, Aristotle an Plato, refused to sacrifice spiritualism on the altars of utilitarianism and expediency. Aristotle said, 'Sophistry is the appearance of knowledge without the reality; and the Sophist is a man who makes money by the appearance of knowledge without the reality'.[31] The Sophists never bothered about the nature of truth or about the inculcation of character. All they aimed at was making money and the amount they could thus rake up depended on their popularity. Thus they were philosophers in name only and merely the products of their age. All human actions were to them based only on expediency. Right and wrong, wisdom, justice and goodness were not their guide and had no significance for them.

Socrates

Life and Death

At this time in the midst of this confused pragmatic and opportune thinking there came Socrates, son of Sophroniscus (470 - 399 B.C.). He loved wisdom passionately though he made no claim to it. He was a philosopher most unconventional in his thought. He had no school and he never taught for money as the Sophists did. He went about Athens moving among all kinds of men, high and low, questioning them. He left no writings but we know of his views through his disciples, chiefly the greatest of them, Plato, in most of whose dialogues Socrates is the main speaker, However, this being so, there will always remain a doubt about what he really said and what ideas Plato put in his mouth.

He was a singularly ugly man - thick-set, with full lips a broad flat nose and bulging eyes. He was indifferent to hardships, went barefoot on snow and practised such self-control as amazed the Greeks of his time, even though he could sit at a banquet with young men drinking with them nightlong. Wine seemed to have no effect on him. His needs were most probably provided for by his friends. His personal wants were few and the bare minimum, wearing only one garment both in winter and summer. He was very robust and had great powers of endurance. He was married but the ill temper of his wife Xanthippe spoilt his domestic life. May be the small means of subsistence was the reason for her surliness. It was possible he was taught music and gymnastic and was expected to take up his fathers profession of sculptor. But he believed he was divinely ordained for an education task and he earnestly set out to accomplish it. He frequented the busiest places - streets, markets and gymns - and talk to people of all shades of society - orators, statesman, artists, traders, commoners and men of wealth and position; and he held them spell bound by his words, like the Ancient Mariner the wedding-guest, as Plato records in his *Symposium* through Alcibiades whose words exemplify the magnetic personality of Socrates:

> 'When I listen to Socrates it is worse than being in a religious ecstasy: his discourse makes my heart beat wildly, and the tears stream from my eyes; and I often see others affected in the same way. Now when I listened to Pericles and other great orators, much as I admired them, I felt nothing like this; my soul was not stirred to its depths, nor was I tormented by the realization of my own degraded condition. But *he* has often made me feel like this, and has convinced me that life as I now am living is not worth it ..... and even now I am not quite sure that if I were to listen to him I

> could not resist him, but the same thing would happen to me again. For he compels me to confess that though I am very far from being what I ought to be, yet I go on neglecting myself, and giving my attention to Athenian politics. So against my will, I stop my ears and run away, as men try to escape from the Sirens, for fear that I may go on sitting here beside him till I grow old. He is the only man who has ever made me feel, what you might think it was impossible for me to feel, a sense of shame; no one else makes me feel like that. I know perfectly well that I can give no excuse for not following his advice; but when I leave his presence the desire for vulgar renown gets the better of me. That is why I run away and try to avoid him: and when I see him I feel ashamed because of the confession he has forced from me. Often I should be glad if he were no longer among the living; but on the other hand if he were to die, I am sure I should be still more distressed In short, I don't know what to make of him'.[32]

Such was Socrates, declared by the Delphic Oracle to be the wisest man in Greece. But he refused to be touched by pride when this was conveyed to him by an admirer. He said he did not himself know anything and he was wiser than others only in the sense that he was conscious of his own ignorance while others were not. This, in fact was the Socratic method, that by a serries of searching questions he convened the other person in the dialogue that while he thought he knew something in reality he did not. If one thought he already knew a thing there was no need for him to seek to know it. So ignorance precedes knowledge. True as this was, it did not appeal to the Athenians who resented that he went around convincing people of their ignorance. They thought him to be a super-sophist for the Sophists had also held that knowledge was impossible. In this the people of Athens were completely mistaken, for Socrates did not believe that knowledge was not possible. In fact he firmly and positively thought it was. The only thing he said was that the dark cobwebs of ignorance had first to be swept away from the mind before knowledge could be implanted in it. He was opposed to the sceptical view that 'and ideal of knowledge was not to be attained'.

Scorates was a great thinker with immense power of concentration. Once while serving in the Athenian army at Potidaea he stood without moving for a day and a night thinking out a problem oblivious of his surroundings and the needs of his body. He said and did what he thought right fearlessly and without any regard to its consequences. it was said that his conversation had the sting of the sting-ray (narke). People talked of ethical notions like justice, courage, temperance and so forth without knowing what these words really meant. Socrates' questions about them were searching, and he concluded that these persons had actually no clear notion of what such terms really meant Socrates was of the view that one ought to have a clearidea of the implication of words before using them. For instance one could not talk of acting wisely unless he knew what wisdom was. if men had differing concepts about what the same thing meant this would only result in confusion of thought both in the intellectual sense and the moral. He sought to express this b y his saying 'virtue is knowledge'. If one could see this truth they would instinctively choose the right his second famous observation was that no one did wrong willingly. Virtue in knowledge and vice is just due to ignorance.

Socrates had strong serenity which resulted from his devotion and confidence towards his friends. Though aware of the weaknesses and follies of men he never showed any contempt towards mankind. He was thoroughly human, had sympathy for all, was kind, patient and even had a sense of humour. He prized learning and was quick to find out who was sincere and eager to learn. he spoke of himself as a learner, even with all his knowledge and made no claim to be a teacher.

His devotion to truth was so sincere and passionate that he never paused in its pursuit. He went on and on in its quest. As in Plato's *Republic* Glucon is made to say in agreement with Socrates, 'Concerning philosophical natures we may surely agree to this, that they are lovers of whatever learning will reveal to them anything of that reality. Which always is, and is not driven too and fro by generation and decay ...... truthfulness; that is a determination never voluntarily to receive what is false, but to hate it and to love the truth....... And can you find any thing more akin to wisdom than truth?' 'Surely not'. 'Then is it possible that the same nature should be a lover of wisdom and a lover of falsehood?' 'Certainly not'. 'Then he that is a really a lover of learning must from his earliest year strive with all his heart after all truth?'[33] Socrates believed in knowledge and goodness and that these were attainable. And he never ceased in the pursuit of their attainment. One charge among others against Socrates which led to his being condemned to death was that did not recognize the gods recognized by the Athenians and introduced other strange gods. But this charge was absured for he did have piety-lots of it. Only his piety was not of the narrow kind which the Athenians wanted it to be. It lay in the God-ward direction of life and behaviour. He believed in the trust in and the presence of God; in the inner divine voice of conscience which stay one from doing what is wrong (what Indian philosophy terms the *antāhkarana*). He consistently believed in God's goddness and rejected everything in the traditional mythology which was inconsistent with it. He strongly believed in the immortality of the soul and that God's designs could never be against truth and goodness or to the detriment of mankind. In all this there was certainly no impiety at all. Athens and the AThenians never really understood the cosmopolitionism of Socrates. 'I am a citizen of the world.' he said 'not of Athens or of Greece' [Oὐk 'Αθηναῖos, oὐδ' "Ελληὰ kὸσμιos].[34] 'Impiety' was in fact the usual excuse for the Athenians to eliminate those who were either political misfits or nor-conformists in disregarding the plethora of the anthromorphic gods of Greek mythology. Anaxagoras was prosecuted for impiety because of his closeness to Pericles and he got more clemency than Socrates for he was only banished from Athens. The observation about Socrates put forth by a writer is amazing: 'Yet possibly the instinct of conservative Athens was right in regarding Socrates' influence as dangerous and subversive as far as the state religion was concerned. A sincere appeal to the spiritual basis of religion necessarily weakens the hold of anything gross or meaningless or merely conventional in established religious usages'.[35]

The acceptance of such a view would justify the fanaticism of Islamic jihad, the 'Sword of Mohomet' as Mill says 'Socrates was put to death, but the Socratic philosophy rose like the sun in heaven, and spread its illumination over the whole intellectual firmament. Christians were cast to the lions, but the Christian church grew up a stately and spreading tree, overtopping the older and less vigorous growths and stifling them by its shade. Our merely social intolerance kills no one, roots out no opinions, but induces men to disguise them, or to abstain from any active effort for their diffusion. With us, heretical opinion do not perceptibly gain, or even lose, ground in each decade or generation; the never blaze out far and wide, but continue to smoulder in narrow circles of thinking and studious persons among who they originate, without ever lighting up the general affairs of man kind with either a true or deceptive light'.[37]

Thus the senseless execution of Socrates was by no means 'right' as Margaret E.J. Taylor has it. It was not a matter of pride for Athens or Greece, it was their great shame, and a repudiation of the liberality in thought which was the special hallmark of the Greek psyche. And the more so for it was a brutal act against a gifted and courageous man who lived a life which was a beacon to other, and one entirely untouched by self-pride; of whom it was said: Eἰδέναι μέν μηδέν, πλήν αὐγὸ γοῦο, μηδέn εἰdέναι 'He knew nothing except this one thing, that he knew nothing'.[38]

When Athens needed him in her wars he fought in its battles. In peace he gave the highest gift he could give, the gift of wisdom, knowledge goodness and truth. He served God and persuaded others to do so. He upheld the laws of Athens. His ultimate obedience was doubtless to his inner soul and the voice of God which spoke in him when his intellect did not. But his obedience to God did not clash with his loyalty to Athens which he ever loved.

In 399 B.C. Socrates was prosecuted on a charge of impiety 'for not worshipping the gods whom the city worshipped, for in treducing religious innovations, and for corrupting the young men'. The prosecutor, Meletus, was supported by the moderate democrat, Anytus. We have already shown how unjustified the charge on religion was. As regards corrupting the young all that he urged was that young men should think for themselves even though such thinking may not be in consonance with that of the elders that could hardly be said to be 'corrupting the young men'. The punishment for this so-called 'impiety' was proposed to be death, by a majority of 60 votes in a court comprising about 500 jurors. According to Athenian custom it was open to him to suggest a lighter punishment, the judges being left to choose between the two. He suggested he should be given free meals for life in the Prytaneum. In any case he said he had no money to pay an adequate fine. When Plato and other friends of his earnestly instigated him to declare he would pay a fine which they would of on his behalf, he agree to it but added that he could give no guarantee that he would not educate and guide you men 'corrupt' them as his accusers termed it, for this was more important to him than life itself. That did. The judges condemned him to death and he was sent to prison to await the execution. His friends came to him there with a plan that would make his escape easy, for even many of those who disapproved of him would not wish him do die, rather leave Athens and live somewhere else. he replied that he had always had the advantage of the laws of Athens even as other citizens had, and now that those very laws decreed that he should die, it would be unjust and ungrateful for him to evade them. Socrates had never been frightened of death, for he viewed it much as Seneca did - *Interim poena est mori sed saepe donum* 'Death is a punishment sometimes, and yet often to die is gain',[39] and later Socrates' disciple Plato said 'I shall never act differently, even if I have to die for it many times'.[40] Socrates, not only felt that way but demonstrated it too, most vividly, had observed: 'To fear death, gentlemen, is nothing other than to think oneself wise when he is not; for it is to think one knows what one does not know. No man knows whether death may not even turnout to be the greatest of blessings for a human being; and yet people fear it, as if they knew for certain that it is the greatest of evil'.[41] To his friends he said,, 'Be of good hope in the face of death. Believe in this one truth for certain, that no evil can befall a good man either in life or in death, and that his fate is not a matter of in difference to the gods.'[42] And so he refused the cowardly alternative to escape from prison for he was the very embodiment of courage both in war and peace, life and death and told his well-wishers: 'And now the time has come when we must depart: I to my death, you to go on living. But which of us is going to the better fate is unknown to all except God'.[43] A month after being in prison, Contemptuous of the body's death and confident of the soul's survival, Socrates drank the cup of hemlock as the last rays of the sun lingered on Mount Hymettus. As a historian very rightly observes:

> 'As a citizen he obeyed the laws but not the dictates of those in power.... In equity Socrates was innocents. In attic law he was guilty of the charge preferred against him, and he refused stubbornly to accept the

mitigation of sentence which the law allowed to him. He died a martyr to his fath that the individual is to be guided by his own intellect in every field of human life. His martyrdom inspired the greatest philosophers of antiquity. In their eyes it discredited the restored democracy of Athens'.[44]

The execution of Socrates was doubtless and most atrocious crime of which the Athenians were guilty. There had also a political angle to it. The trial took place just after a group of nobles had seized power by violence. Though democracy was later re-established some young men who were associates of Socratcs considered him to be an opponent to them and wanted him out of the way. The motive behind his trial and conviction was thus mainly political. Religion was only a scapegoat. The act made Plato averse to democracy for he has seen it at Athens and he saw in its working all that he abhorrednoise, disorder, ignorance, shifting of stands a clear sign of insincerity and unreasoned decisions as the condemnation of Socrates. Most democracies in which the majority of people are corrupt, illiterate, unemployed and unscruplous seekers of wealth, like those of the developing an underdeveloped nations, of which unfortunately ours is one, are of the kind that would have incited Plato's disgust; as the poet says:

> **Ill fares the land, to hast'ning ills a prey,**
> **Where wealth accumulates, and men decay.**[45]

Teaching

We have commented on the Socratic method of teaching. He would, now and then, stop some well-dressed Athenian and ask him a simple questions or two. The hearer's first reaction would be 'who is this ill-clad uncouth man to question me?' and he would consider it beneath his dignity to be thus accosted. Soon others would crowd round for in Athens, as indeed in most of the other Greek city-states, men flocked to marketplaces, talking, discussing and exchanging views. However many would not walk away disdainfully but respond and when they did they realized this was no ordinary man for he caught them in the maze of their own making and showed the inconsistency of their answers. We have quoted from Plato's account in the Symposium about the magnetic effect Socrates had on the young and aristocratic military genius Alcibiades who said of him, 'His nature is so beautiful, golden, divine and wonderful within, that everything he commands surely ought to be obeyed even like the voice of a god.'

Socrates had studied the old philosophers but was disillusioned by their doctrines. They gave inconclusive and contradictory arguments and they hardly ever spoke about life and its significance. They speculated about nature and natural phenomena but about the inner self they said not a word. Socrates laid emphasis on the knowledge of this inner self, in other words the soul. He was the first man in Europe to have a clear idea about the soul. The soul was to Socrates a man's moral and intellectual personality and it was his bounden duty to make it as good as possible. When the soul knows goodness it acts rightly. Virue is nothing else but knowledge of the good. Right action results from right knowledge. All wickedness is due to ignorance, that is say absence of goodness and right knowledge. Lack of correct knowledge and of goodness made life lack direction. By knowledge Socrates did not mean abstract knowledge, but insight and realization, a turning of the soul's eye toward the vision of the good. All virtue is really one. A man is unaware of this universal virtue unless he knows it as a whole, unless he has a comprehensive and whole vision of human goodness which will guide him in every thing - give him courage when required by circumstances, self-restraint where there is temptation and respect for the rights of his neighbour. For example, as often happens in our country even today, one takes out a marriage procession with deafening loudspeakers blaring at the loudest pitch or some religious act or function with loudspeaker late through the night quite unmindful of the other people whose circumstances like illness, the desire to sleep etc., would necessitate peace. Such insensibility in human conduct would horrify Socrates. A man had to set himself right and turn his soul toward goodness by his own conviction and effort. It cannot be taught externally but only by persuasion as Socrates himself used to do by his discussions.

Although Socrates did not study nature it was not because of any disinclination to do so, but because firstly he was interested only in knowledge which had concern with human life and secondly because he considered that nature is beyond man's control It may be that afterwards man has been able to harness nature in many ways by scientific means, as for example flying in planes, sailing in ships, building dams and so forth. But just because a man is on a plane it doesn't man him any better just because of that. In fact because man's nature has in the sum total moved towards evil instead of goodness he keeps on devising more things for his own destruction than for peaceful progress. Socrates would say that such a destructive tendency in mankind is due to an unclear and confused idea of the truth of human conduct. If one values life and weighs it in the scales of goodness he could never do what is disastrous and evil, causing his rain. So wrongdoing is the consequence of false and confused teaching and wrong ideas of life and conduct either arising from one's own mind or instilled in it by others. He has in the latter case not exerted his own mind and has therefore not been able to combat such wrong thinking. The pursuit of right knowledge will invariably lead to goodness and truth.

Though it can't be said with certainty what Socrates believed about the destiny of the soul and a future life, one can be reasonably sure that he believed in the immortality of the soul. It may be mentioned that our knowledge about Socrates' teaching is mainly from the writings of Xenophon and more particularly of Plato in the latter's 'Apology', 'Crito' and 'Phaedo', for as has been said before, Socrates himself wrote nothing. but he spoke with an inner conviction which was intensely religious and that's why people listened to him as though mesmerized. He believed he had a mission assigned by God and he felt he had an inner divine voice which checked him doing wrong. What became know as the *daimon* or *daimonion* by the Greeks, an inner superhuman power.

Plato

In Diogenes Laertius Plato is quoted as saying Τέλος μέν (ἔλεγεν) εἶναι ρήν ἐξομοίωσιν γῷ θεῷ 'It is man's goal to grow into the likeness of God'. Plato was born in 427 B.C. and died at the age of 81 in 347-6 B.C. He was one of the greatest philosophers of Greece and a distinguished disciple of Socrates. Like Socrates he was an Athenian but unlike him he was highly connected, belonging to an aristocratic family of Athens. Some years after Socrates' death he founded a school of philosophical studies in the neighbour hood of Athens near a lovely grove dedicated to a mythical hero, Academus. Because of this the school was later known as a Academy (Akademeia), which went on for nearly nine centuries till it was abolished by the emperor Justian in A.D. 529. Plato was the first Greek philosopher whose works have come down to us in a more complete form that those of others. Yet he himself said in a letter that he never wrote a philosophical work. it could be, therefore, that his teaching was verbally given in the Academy to his disciples. In his Dialogues he never speaks of himself by name. We only find the expression the 'Athenian Stanger' in the laws. He often puts his words into the mouth of Socrates. Plato was critical of the world of change, its unrest and confusions. So he sought the stable in the midst of change, and this led him to a mystic craving to seek that was changeless and unchangeable. Socrates had taught that there was something like moral goodness and its knowledge would make men good. But he never defined what exactly this goodness was. Plato tried to define the nature of this goodness and the nature of the soul which when one knows, he can know what goodness is. In this way he combined the doctrine of Socrates with the Pythagorean teaching. This led to his doctrine of ideas or Forms.

The Theory of Ideas

Normally in English 'idea' is something that exists in the mind. But Plato thought of idea (*eidos*) as something having a real existent a part from the human mind. It was the ideal on which all ideas are based. As the poet says:

> **What was good, shall be good, with, for evil,**
> **So much good more;**
> **On the earth the broken arcs; in the heaven,**
> **a perfect round.**[46]

Facts as we know them existing in the world only partially embody things. But thought sees the reality beyond things. The realities of this world remind us of the spiritual. There is a *real* goodness to which all our imperfect notions of human goodness belong and the spirit of man can directly communicate with it. The spirit *knows* the ideas for it belongs to the unseen world of Forms. So all that exists, all that happens in the world here in only an imitation of that Reality which is not perceptible or fully expressible. So is the case with beauty, because the beauty which we see here suggest that of which it is a mere reflection and is linked with a 'divine discontent' for the soul then turns itself to the real beauty of which the worldly one is a mere shadow. Therefore says Plato (Λέγωγὰρ) Tảya θòν kaλòν εἶναι 'The good is the beautiful'.[47] Plato was a mystic, moralist, artist and mathematician, and various representatives of these might view him from their own respective points of view. The reality of all of these transcends them. For him the ideal world was the sole reality. The soul when embodied in the body, has to cope with the material world but is spiritual as well. The *Gita* does not see any contradiction in the material and the spiritual. Nor does Plato. Faith does not oppose reason. If supplements it.

The Idea of Good

All persons are in some way seeking the Good. Socrates considered Good to be related to life and conduct. Plato condered it to be the summum bonum of all existence. It is self-existent reality and calls for unquestioned faith in it. Good is the only reality and God made the world because he was good, for God can never depart from righteousness, and can be in no circumstances the cause of anything that is not good. As we have quoted him saying in the beginning, he holds that the aim of life is to be godlike. Men should imitate God and become like him as far as is possible for man to become. However, we can't conclude that he was conceiving a personal God. He has simply identifying God with the Supreme good. As the sum gives light whereby one can see, yet it maintains it own light undiminished, so too God gives knowledge and truth but transcends them. Man has an affinity with the divine. He cannot know the real nature of the Supreme Being but at times the consciousness of the Divine comes to him like a lightning flash and that is the closest one gets to God-vision. Manilius says in *Astronomicon* 'Exemplumque dei quisque est in imagine parva' - 'Every man is a copy of God in miniature', and Phocylides in *Sententiae* 'The Spirit is the image of God and his means of communication with men'.

The Relation Between God and the World

Euripides wrote in *Bellerophon* 'Ωs ἔμφνγos μέν πᾶσιν ἀνθρώποιs kákη' 'How evil is innate in all mankind!' This was the problem arising out of Plato's idea of Good in relation to God. If God can be the cause of Good only how is it that there exists evil in the world? Also if only Ideas and the Good have only true existence why are there the world and creation at all. it seems that we, who are ourselves part of existence cannot discern why this is so. We cannot go behind what appears. If we try to answer such riddles like this with the help of reason, we cannot, for reason has its limitations. For example the question, is there a God or not? Reason can prove there is God, and it can also prove there is no God. Akin is the question about how is there evil. Plato deals with the problem of evil by a myth or allegory in *Timaeus*. God has made the world because of his desire to make a universe of supreme excellence. He wanted it to be an image of himself. Plato speaks of God as the Divine Craftsman who fashioned the soul and the body of the material universe out of pre-existing material according to the patterns he contemplates in the world of Forms. He made a living creature in his likeness having both soul and body. He made time meant to be 'a moving image of eternity'. The sun, moon and planets were made by God to control and regulate time. These too have both body and soul and are 'created gods'. God entrusted the making of other beings to these gods so that he himself may be absolved of the evil in these beings. To these 'created gods' he gave a portion of the divine and immortal substance out of which he had fashioned their own souls. This did not have the purity of the pristine soul, but a lesser degree of it. These 'created gods' were told to add a mortal component to this purity and unite it with the body. The *Timaeusian* allegory thus brings out the point that the intention of God was to create the perfect in *so far as is possible*. The universe was made thus by reason combined with necessity. While reason works towards perfection, necessity keeps resisting this perfection, so creation is perfection in imperfection. Plato's concept of God being the Divine Craftman and yet is untained by the evil of creation finds a parallel in the *Gita*.[48] In the same way the English poet Tennyson says:

Out little systems have their day;
They have their day and cease to be:
They are but broken lights of thee
And thou, O Lord, art more than they.[49]

Evil is that which is not-God or non-good. The laws of Nature are the work of Mind or God. But once these laws are made divine reason does not interfere with them. Plato calls necessity the 'errant cause' and if man becomes a slave to necessity he may pick out the worse way which is not in conformity with God's scheme. God is unalloyed goodness, but if necessity turns a man towards evil, the responsibility is man's not God's, for neither God nor the 'created gods of Plato's myth, the *Timaeus*, are concerned with twarting necessity, as Simonides says: - 'Ανάγκῃ δ' οὐδὲ θεοὶ μάξονγαι – 'Even the gods war not with necessity.'[50]

God, Man and Soul

There goes on an incessant conflict between spirit and matter. The soul is essentially divine but in file it is embodied and so the body and soul act on each other, and thus till the soul is not disembodied, despite its eternal nature, it takes on the virtues or defects of the person whose soul it is. In fact, however, the human spirit is one with the divine. The true destiny of the spirit is to work in tandem with God, to seek goodness, beauty and truth. This, however is easier said than done. True life does not mean passive surrender to emotions. It means much effort, struggle, patience, courage, discipline and contemplation . It means the vision of the good, By means of education and replacement of the false view by the true, this kind of ideal life can be affianced by the few who care for it.

In his famous allegory of the Cave Plato states his views about the nature of education. He imagines there are a row of prisoners facing the wall bound from birth in such a way that they cannot move or turn round, all sitting in a cave. Shadows of people and objects fall on the wall, The prisoners they are real and so they have no thought beyond them. The task of education is to make the bonds of the prisoners loose so that they can turn round and see the real of which these are the shadows. Thus every soul that enters the body has seen and known the reality. It has forgotten it, and education is aimed to recapture this reality. How does the soul do this when it instruments are restricted to the senses? Plato's solution to it is his famous doctrine of Anamnesis or Recollection. This is that the soul has known the Forms in its divine existence before its incarnation in the body and is reminded' of them by their knowledge through the senses. We shall speak of Plato's concept of the soul later, we go on to speak about the type of education Plato had in mind for men to grasp reality.

According to him education is a long and continuous process lasting the entire life from birth to the end of life. His scheme recalls the Hindu idea of the stages of life (*āsharaṃas*). Plato's division is roughly early education, higher education, public service, finally quiet meditation and taking up educational and political work. In the *Republic* he graded the citizens into classes in accordance with their abilities, as rulers, warriors and workers. Here again we find similarity in the *Gita's* division by nature (*svabhāva*) and occupation (*kārya*). According to Plato's *Republic* the citizens would have not family life or private property. Children would be brought up by the state, learn music, literature, gymnastics. Then there would be two years' military training and thereafter, subject to fitness, higher education, only a few going on to the study of philosophy which includes contemplation. It is these who become rulers of the state, serving it as a duty (which the *Gita* terms as *kartavya*). It is because of this that Plato says in his *Republic* 'Unless political power and philosophy join hands, troubles with not end.' These philosopher rulers consider kingship as a burden they willingly shoulder, not as a temptation to be in power. Unfortunately our India politicians consider position and power merely as an allurement, so in Plato's view they are fortunate but not happy. Any education necessitates the cooperation of the person who seeks it. If those who do not have the idea of the Good are made rulers it will mean the rain of the state, for such persons who are keen to rule but unwilling to see the vision of the God and are uncooperative, are in truth uneducated, whatever degrees they may have obtained. That is why Plato insists that neither society not the state can be on the right lines until philosophers become kings or kings become philosophers. In such rulers there can be no self-seeking, no love for power or office, and therefore their rule cannot be oppressive or arbitrary. This of course implies that men and women who are entrusted with the work of government must have a spiritual bent of mind.

In the *Laws* Plato put forward a regime of education of a more detailed and practical kind. Children were to stay at home with their parents till they were six years in age. From age three they were to go a nursery school run by women teachers recruited from other states. After six boys and girls were to live in separate domitories and their education would be the same but approved by the ministry of education of the government. If a child misbehaved both the child and teacher concerned! were to get corporal punishment. Attendance in school was compulsory and comprised dancing, music, literature, wrestling, arithmetic, geometry and astronomy. Women magistrates were to oversee education in nursery schools and also act as marriage counsellors during the first ten years of married life. Men and women were provided public meals at state expense. both sexes were to participate in all activities, but maintain impeccable behaviour in all in which they took part including sexual relations. Religion and the training of the intellect were essential in Plato's system of education in the *Laws*. Plato's system might seem to us too rigid, illiberal and cut-and-dried, but it was aimed at drawing out the finest in men. It was also based on ethical principles and spiritualism. At the end of the *Laws* Plato said, 'No mortal man will ever turn out to be God's true devotee unless he is convinced that the soul is prior to all that exists and that it is immortal and superior to all that is material; and also perceives the Mind of the universe amid the constellations'. All education, particularly in the higher stages, should provide intellectual discipline and disinterested pursuit of truth. It should promote philosophic detachment, build character and inculcate discipline. Above all else it should lead to a vision of the Good which is also Beauty and Truth; as Keats the English poet wrote:

> **'Beauty is truth, truth beauty - that is all**
> **Ye know on earth, and all ye need to know.[51]**

And Plato observed that virtue is knowledge and the vivid realization of the good. Man should obey reason and control lust with the help of the nobler emotions. That's why he insists that one of the most important functions of education, particularly in the earlier stages, is the training of emotions and desires. The soul of man is his most important business. Plato does not believe in outward ascetism as practised by the Orphics and the eary Pythagoreans. He is for a Socratic indifference to bodily things. Here briefly we will speak about Platos's idea of the soul's divinity later it may be said that his idea of the soul does not appear to be borrowed from the Orphics, as a critic says: 'The Orphic soul-theory is a direct precursor of Plato's and Aristotle's view of the divine nature of soul or mind, though they have stripped away all the material features still clinging to this conception'.[52] Plato speaks generally of God not of the Greek gods of mythology. The origins of Orphism are obscure. The legend of *Bacchae* in Euripides is not truly Greek and in any case Orphism was a myth according to which the Titans ate up the limbs of the god Dionysus and were destroyed by the lighting of Zeus. From the ashes of the Titans mankind was believed to spring polluted by the act of the Titans but also containing a divine element arising from Dionysus. Hence arose the impure body of man containing the divine soul. The soul left the body on death and those who had lived impure lives got terrible punishment. But the Greeks did not believe the god created the universe. It was the other way about. The universe created the gods. Before there were gods, heaven and earth had been formed. They were the first parents. Dionysus had a dual aspect. he was a god of joy, the wine god and also heartless and savage. The allegory is from wine, a little of which can be pleasure-giving but excess causing violence and destruction. So how could Diony sus be associated with divinity as in the Orphic myth? Besides Plato had seen the unreasoned condemnation of Socrates for not believing in the gods of Athens, and he had a natural revulsion for such a whimsical and thoughtless act. He didn't therefore speak of the gods nor was his concept of the soul's divinity have any reaction to the fantastic Orphic myth. It was reason which guided him in the concept, not mythology. An it was logical, for surely when the human body remained with all its organs, the heart, brain and so forth, if something not of the world left it, why was there death? Plato's political teaching was simply an extension and elaboration of his moral. The philosopher was not to remain detached from the world but live a full life in the political community. He has a special responsibility for he alone knows the truth. He must take on himself the burden of ruling for the good of his fellows and the entire society.

There is a cycle is civilizations. When decadence Sets in thing go on getting worse and worse till the lowest depth is reached. Then the reverse process sets in and there is progress towards battlement. This leads to Plato's concept of stability. The smallest change may result in deterioration. So once a civilization has progressed it must be maintained at that level. All change should be firmly resisted. So particular was Plato about this that in his Laws he insists that even the pattern of children's toys must be kept unchanged from generation to generation!

The degeneration of the state takes the following course: from the rule of the philosopher kings to military aristocracy; thence to oligarchy or plutocracy; then through the revolt of the poor against the rich to democracy; and last of all to tyranny, the rule of one who has utterly abandoned himself to the foulest passions and unbridled lust for power. This tyranny is the exact opposite of the rule of philosopher kings.

There are two things worthy of note in the aforesaid views of Plato about civilizations and the state (he was speaking only about the small and compact Greek city-states). First, in rigidly combating change when 'stability' had been reached he was assuming that the state had reached the apogee of civilization when from that condition it could not be forecast that there would not be any better thereafter. Second, Significantly he puts democracy only above the final stage of degeneration. In other words military aristocracy, oligarchy, even anarchy were better than democracy. Many may not agree. But what is to be noticed is that those nations which extol democracy do not themselves - with very few exceptions - adopt it. Plato had seen the very arbitrary and disgusting trial and condemnation of Socrates by the members of Athenian democracy and Aristotle though then a youth (Socrates drank the cup of hemlock in 399 B.C. and Aristotle was born 384 B.C.), must have known of it. This was an act worse than the horrors of the guillotine in the French revolution. So perhaps both of these renowned philosophers. view of democracy was a truism. Plato wrote in the Republic, 'Οὐk ἐx ἆ λλης' πολιγείας γνραννις καθίσγαγαι ῆ ἐk δημοkραγίας' – Tyranny is the natural outcome of democracy.[53] And also that excess of liberty whether in states or individuals let to excess of slavery.[54]

Aristotle similarly observed 'H δημοkrapía ἡ γελενραία γυραννίs ἐσρίν' – Democracy is the acme of tyranny. Plato's insistence on the state control of education was motivated by the desire to make citizens good and useful to society. He was so particular about this that he said 'No man should bring children in the world unless he is prepared to ensure that he will see they are nurtured and educated to the very end'.[56] It is difficult to say whether societies influence the individuals or the individuals society. Perhaps it is the interaction of the one on the other. However nothing is achieved without character and character is moulded by the right type of education. That is why Plato put so much emphasis on it.

The Divinity of the Soul

Cicero says in *De Senectute*, 'The divine soul is drawn down form its lofty home, and, so to say, plunged into the earth, an abode which is by its nature the antithesis of divinity and eternity', and Ancharsis also speaks of the divine nature of the soul: 'ψνχῆs γὰρ ὄpγavov γὸ σῶ δ' ἡ ψυχή' The body is the implement of the soul, and the soul of God.[57] Both Pythagoras and Empedocles believed in the soul's divinity and immortality as well as in its transmigration into bodies, not necessarily human. Though Plato has the same view and also refers to previous thinkers like Heraclitus, Parmenides and Anaxagoras, it should not be supposed thereby that the lacked originality. That in fact showed his magnanimity, not his lack of originality. He acknowledged that each one of them was striving to reach the truth in his own way, but they saw only a particular aspect of it and philosophy necessitates comprehensiveness and completeness of vision. Heraclitus was right about the material world but materialism was not the whole reality. Parmenides thought unity and the real only as the corporeal and denied change altogether when change is also experienced as something real. Plato viewed the world and existence as a whole. There was good as well as evil, the material and also the spiritual, the beautiful as well as the non-beautiful, man's lower instincts and so too the higher. It was up to man himself to reject the own and turn his mind to the other - accept the good, the beautiful, the virtuous and the spiritual, and reject the evil, the unbeautiful, the vicious and the material. In such acceptance or rejection lay his victory or defeat. The struggle of life to achieve such an end was not in stages. The entire life was such a struggle, from birth to death, as a good builder starts with a strong foundation and then builds up and up on it turning nothingness into majestic splendor. And throughout this struggle towards the good there are two helpers - the mind and conscience. The mind could be likened to an unruly horse which can be made to go on the right path only when a tight rein is kept on it, and conscience to a signal on the railway track. The signalman gives the signal but thereafter it is for the driver to heed it and carry the train and its passengers safely to their destination or to disregard it and plunge them into destruction. But the mind as well as the conscience are very sensitive things. Therefore Plato devises stringent means to control them, education for the mind for the conscience hearkening to the voice of the soul. According to him the soul consists of three parts. The first is reason whose abode is in the head, in other words the mind. In the noble soul, this is the ruler and guide. Here the soul's eyes perceive the truth and direct the man on its path. Then there is the heart, the seat of the higher emotions like love, generosity, goodness, sympathy, gentleness and so forth. The third part, the 'savage hydra' whose abode is in the belly and the adjacent regions. Carnal lust and vicious prompting reside here. The spiritual in man is obedient to reason. The animal part in him is inclined to carnal and base lusts and craving and is overpowered by reason only after a firm and determined struggle.

Besides the control of reason another force which drives the knowing soul is the desire for good. The enlightened soul pursues this right upto the end. But when this desire turns into the baser or lower lusts it is destuctive. When it is for the higher and nobler ends it takes the philosopher to the 'great sea of beauty', the absolute and changeless beauty of the World of

Forms. Then it attains its true end. Plato says, 'Tὸ μέν γὰρ γἀληθέs δοξάζειν kaλὸν, γὸ δέ ψενδεσθαι aἰσχρὸν'. – To think truy is noble and to be deceived is base.[58]

Plato's doctrine of the soul is closely allied to that of Forms, Socrates had said it (soul) was the most important part of man Plato, completely reversing the previous Greek idea giving prominence to the body, said that the sail is far more real than the body. it was truly divine (θεῖον). He says God (θεόs) is a Soul, thus equating the two. The soul is divine in the Greek sense, and it is immortal in its own right, not the gift of any higher divinity. It is ever-existent, even before it inhabited any body. After it has attained final release from its chain of incarnations, it will contine to exist. It is a completely higher entity and has nothing in comon with the world of senses to which it descends. Any 'this-worldliness' or accommodation to existence on earth is for it a sin to be punished in the periods of its purification in the other worlds intervening between its successive incarnations. This doctrine of rewards and punishments, is greatly emphasized by Plato, particularly the punishment of these wicked. The soul's eternity was also later reflected in the poetry of Robert Browning, the English poets:

> **Fool! All that is, at all,**
> **Lasts ever, past recall;**
> **Earth changes, but thy soul and God stand sure:**
> **What entered into thee,**
> **That was is, and shall be:**
> **Time's wheel runs back or steps: Potter and clay endure.**[59]

As we have said, barring a couple of thinkers, in general the Greeks gave greater importance to the body than to the soul (psyche). The turnabout by Plato was therefore viewed by them as something incredulous. Ordinarily the Greeks believed that on death the soul, bereft of its home, become just a shadowy existence and got lost like an abandoned child, as Homer said 'like smoke' going up. Plato firmly believed that the body was like a prison or tomb for the soul which longed to be set free from it to fly back to the world of ideas. The body's death is not, therefore, evil. It means only another life. Philosophy is a kind of 'preparation for death' and aimed at making the soul stay for ever in the world of ideas, in other words be emancipated from repeated rebirths. As aforesaid, Plato's view of the soul's incarnations and its final release is a significant feature of his belief and so top his doctrine of reward and punishment in the hereafter. His views about the soul find place in the *Phaedo*, the *Meno* and in the myth of Er at the end of the *Republic*, where in the dialogue between Socrates and Glaucon, Plato says:

> 'But virtue has no master, and as a man honours or despises her, so will he have more of her or less. The responsibility is on him that chooseth. There is non on God!
>
> *Plato goes on to say that the prophet cast lots and each man took it up save Er. These men lived differt kinds of lives, some good others evil. And then he goes on to say:*
>
> 'There were lives of famous men also, (apart form tyrants as so forth) some famed for their comeliness and beauty, or for their strength and prowess, others for their lineage and the virtues of their ancestors; similarly there were the lives of unknown men; and also the lives of women. But there was no determination of soul, because of necessity the soul becomes different according as she chooses a different life. All other things were mixed with each other, and with wealth and poverty; some with disease and some with health, and there were also mean conditions of these things. An it is here, it seems, my dear Glaucon, that man's greatest danger lies; and for those reasons

> we must give all heed that each of us, putting aside all other learning, may search after and study this alone, if in any way he may be able to learn and discover who will give him capacity and knowledge to discern the good and evil in life, and always and everywhere to choose the better according to his ability ..... And so, Glucon, the tale was preserved and did not perish, and it will preserve us if we take heed to it and cross the river of Lethe [River in Hades producing forget fulness of the past] safely and keep our souls undefiled. But if you will listen to me, and believe that the soul is immortal and able to endure all evil and good, we shall always hold to the upper road, and in every way follow justice and wisdom. So we shall be friends to ourselves and to the gods, both while we remain here and when, like victorious athletes who go about adding to their prizes, we receive the rewards of our justice; and here, and in the journey of a thousand years, which I have described to you, we shall fare well.'[60]

We have mentioned that Plato firmly believed in the doctrine that the good persons will be rewarded and the wicked severely punished for their deeds in afterlife. This is also stated in Plato's *Republic* (Book X) where he again refers to the valiant warrior, Er, who after having been declared dead came back to life on the twelfth day. He told those round him that his soul went to a place with two openings, one leading up to heaven, the other downwards. The judges sat in the middle of the two openings. Socrates says:

> 'There ware many things, Glaucon, which would take long to relate. But this, he [Er.] said, was the sum of it. For all the unjust deeds that each man has ever done, and for all the men to whom he has done injustice, he pays penalty in due course, ten times for each (now this is once in every hundred years, for so long as the

> span of human life), in order that he may pay a tenfold ransom for his wrongdoing. If there by any who have caused the deaths of many men, either by betraying cities or armies, or by casting men into slavery, or taking part in any villainy, for all these crimes they suffer torments tenfold for each; and on the other hand, if they have done any deeds of kindness and have been just and holy, they get their reward on the same terms'.[61]

The Good and the Pleasant

Plato was strongly against the Sophists and countered them by his theory of Forms. Secondly he insisted on the health of the soul of which the main element was orderliness (*kosmos*) or orderly arrangement (*taxis*). In the early Greek city-states the citizens were law-abiding and disciplined. Socrates himself respected the laws of Athens and in proof thereof sacrificed his life for them. But later tyrants and bandits appeared. The men who were strong and powerful and they insisted that what they did was right and all they sought was pleasure, becoming the first hedonists of the transformed Greek city-states.

Socrates and thereafter Plato repudiated this doctrine holding that he who thinks only of the pleasant and discards the good causes great harm. But often what is good and true may be unpleasant particularly when it is aimed at correcting people. Socrates solves this difficulty by saying that the good must be what is beneficial. In this way even if something is done in self-interest, but also in so doing benefits others, it will still remain good. Good means good values-what is spiritual. And wisdom consists of the knowledge of good as distinguished from evil. When guided by wisdom all enterprises lead to happiness, when by folly they cause distress. The nous ('spirit' or 'mind') can discriminate what appears to be right on the surface and what is really, lastingly and in truth so. Justice is that when the spirit is in good order and when it is not that is injustice. The just results in inner harmony and so a proper response to the outer world. In any conflict between reason and desire, the spiritual part of human character (which the Greeks called *thymos*) awakens indignation when a wrong is done because man has *nous* (unlike beasts who haven't) which possesses the capacity to think and discriminate. When reason and desires are in conflict *thymos* sides with reason, and provides the incentive to the man to do what reason tells him is right. Physical desires of the body ought to be subordinated to the intellect. Plato's philosophy as contained in the *Symposium* and *Phaedrus* is not confined to the world only. As we have said, he believed in the soul's divinity and in the hereafter. Yet the contemplation of beauty devoid of all desires of the flesh, deathless and immortal, in which beauty becomes identical with truth, was his ideal, as we have quoted him as saying in *Lysis* 'The good is the beautiful'.

ARISTOTLE

The Universe and nature

A writer says 'To turn from Plato to Aristotle is like coming down from the mountain-tops to a well-fenced and carefully cultivated land of fields and gardens. Aristotle was never at home on the summits: he dwelt by preference in the plain'.[62] That is true; but only half-true. He began by criticizing Plato, whose pupil he was, and refuting most of what he said. He soon realized, however, that he ought to have remained on the mountain tops, for when he came down and took the path of reality he was lost in its labyrinth and found his way out only when he reverted to Plato's spiritualism and his concept of the soul and God. Mind is the beginning of knowledge he said, in *Analytica Posteriora* - Noûν ἀρξήν ἐπισγήμης and in *Ethica Eudemia* ended up by the belief - ''Ομοίως ἔξχι ψυξή πρὸς σῶμα kaì γεξνìγης πρὸς ὄρψανον kaì δεσπόγης πρòs δοûλον 'The relation of the soul to the body is similar to that of the workman to his too, and the master to his servant'.

Aristotle was born in 384 B.C. at Stagia in northern Greece. His father was a member of the medical guild of the Asclepiads and was the physician to philip II's father resident of Macedon. He joined Plato's Academy while he was yet a youth of seventeen and was in it till Plato's death, after which he left Athens and went to Assos, a city on the coast of Asia Minor opposite the island of Lesbos. He became a lecturer in a school there for three years. When he was forty years old he lived for two years at the island of Lesbos. From there he went to Pella in 342 B.C. where he became tutor to king Philip's son Alexander who was then a boy fifteen years old. After Philip's death and Alexander's accession in 336 B.C. and his conquests, he returned to Athens where he founded the Lyceum which was so named because of its nearness to the precincts of Apollo *Lyketos*. He started here the Peripatetic school which took its name from the *peripatos* or covered walk of the Lyceum. Here he also established a library, which according to strabo's account was the first in history. Apart from philosophy, the pursuit of science was particularly its objective.

Alexander was a born general and conqueror. Philip had humbled Athens but not fully subjugated it. Alexander continued to establish a huge empire defeating Darius, winning the Perians, over-running Babylon and even attempting unsuccessfully to wage war with the Indian emperor, Chandra Gupta Maurya, by whose forces he was defeated, thus disproving the appellation of 'World Hero' often applied to him. We are not concerned here with the historical part of Alexander's achievement, but with his sudden death due to fever in 323 B.C. the Athenian assembly proceeded to free the Greek city-states from a Macedonians. Aristotle, Alexander's tutor, and having a Macedonian connection, became a suspect, and the usual Greek device to get rid of unwanted people namely the charge of impiety, was sought to be levied against him. Aristotle had neither the courage to face death, nor the contempt for life which Socrates had, to whom in the words of Euripides would most aptly apply– 'Tís δ' οîδεν, εì ζ̂ν̂ν γοûθ' ο̋ κε̕κληγαι θανεîν, γò ζη̂ν δε̕ θνήσκειν ε̕σγὶ'

> **'Who knows that't is not life which we call death.**
> **And death our life on earth?'[63]**

So he went away to Chalkis in Euboea as before him Anaxagoras had gone to Lampsacus to escape the same charge of impiety, in order to 'prevent the Athenians as he said, 'from committing a second sin against philosophy'. He died in Chalk is only a year after at the comparatively early age of sixty-two in 322 B.C.

It has been said that Aristotle's strong point is 'robust common sense'. However philosophy can never be undiluted common sense for that is a pragmatic way of thinking and can be the quality of politicians, administrators and business executives. Philosophy in Greek meant a wise man or *sophoi* and from the fifth century B.C. onwards philosophy or *philosophos* meant speculation about the universe an about human good and evil. That in fact is the main reason why Aristotle began his thinking by rejecting Plato's theory about Forms being apart from what is material and the Soul bridging the material world and the world of forms. Aristotle sought reality in the world itself. He also criticized Plato's idea of the Good and had no belief that faith and intuition supported reason, or that there was any higher reality than what the material world represented. There was nothing beyond the things experienced, nothing divine or transcended. He never explained *why* the world order was as it is, but only dwelt on *how* it was. The world was constantly changing, yet there was something which did not change and this basic thing is the true subject of philosophy. Here we see how close he is coming to Plato. He says that there could not be anything self-moved. Yet he holds that it was God who caused the first moved to move. God was the unmoved Mover. He did not move the world by any act of his will. He would hardly care to take any notice of such a material thing as the world. It was the world which was drawn to him as 'a lover is drawn toward his beloved'. It is not God who loves the world. it is the world which loves God. Thus the materialist who began by denying anything beyond was material became the spiritualist making a sudden turnabout to mysticism! Plato had conceived the soul as divine an incarnating in various bodies till its final release from existence. Aristotle defined it as 'the first actuality of a natural body potentially having life; that is organic'. It is that which make a living body, a living body. In *De Anima* he says 'If the eye was an animal, its sight would be its soul'. Without life-giving form a body is mere dead matter. It is this form which makes it potentially actual and true. The form of a material body is immaterial. Aristotle makes a threefold classification of life-plants. animals and man. Plants have nourishment and growth. Animals have in addition sensation, desire and the capacity to move in order to satisfy that desire. Man has all these and in addition, reason. Body is matter and soul form. They are two aspects of one thing separable only in thought. There can be no life of the soul after death, except that of 'separable reason'. Having said this, apparently he discerned that it would not be a wholly satisfactory view of the soul. He must have realized what his guru had before him, that if the soul was lifeless what gave the body life while a man lived and why there was no life when the soul had left the body. So he put in, as a kind of corrective to his materialism, the idea of an intelligence separate from matter, imperishable and eternal and the human being could not go on if he parted with this active 'intelligence'. It will at once be seen that this is pure and simple quibbling with words, and Aristotle's 'active intelligence is only a sort of euphemism for the soul. No wonder then that he recognized this in his *Physica*-"Εσγι δέ ἡ ψνχή γοû χῶνγos aìgía και ἀρχή 'The soul is the cause and the beginning of the living body'.[64] Aristotle was doubtless a philosopher and one of Plato's most renowned pupils, but he was a little different inasmuch as he was tutor to the famed general and conqueror, Alexander the Great and although an Athenian, had a Macedonian connection too. His father was a physician, and Aristotle had a scientist's blood in his veins, his interest lying in biology, logic, epistemology, aesthetics, metaphysics and political philosophy also. So, much of his thought is based on the knowledge of these too.

In the *Organon* he divides sciences into three classes - theoretical, practical and productive according to their ends or ultimate purposes. These are knowledge of truth, the nature of a good human life and the making of useful or beautiful things. Logic is apart from these, but is a preparation for the study of all sciences. Its object is knowledge of rational thought which leads to truth . Its study is to know the meaning of words, the various realities to which they refer, and so arriving at the list of categories - substance quantity, quality, relation, place, date, position, state, action and passivity. Thereafter he goes on to analyze propositions, statements, sentences and syllogisms.

While Plato considered that knowledge cannot be got by the senses alone and that only thought could give one knowledge, Aristotle held that general causes and principles can be reached only through the act of perception. The steps to knowledge are thought then knowing and ultimately generalizing. For example a mango tree is just one such tree. But are many kinds of mango trees and they bear various types of mangoes. We cannot know about mango trees by just one such tree. We can know only by knowing all its kinds., Thus this universal knowledge of mango trees in general is the thru knowledge. In this way Aristotle substituted Universals for Plato's ideas. However when he followed his own argument to its logical conclusion he has to explain *how* did one arrive from the particular to the general. it would imply that what Aristotle called the 'universal' was always existing. Ultimately he had to conclude that the highest principle of reason was a matter of intuition.

Ever creature must have a parent. This thinking has a two fold application. The first is the act of begetting. That is to say a woman begets a child, a cow a calf and so forth and the specific form of each is according to that of the parent. Besides the form must have pre-existed in the parent; in the egg the chick in the seed the tree. The world is does not exist in time. Had it been so it would be hard to say what came first-the egg or the chicken, the plant or the seed and so forth. Aristotle says it (the egg, seed etc.,) has existed eternally and this existence as a whole is ensured in pure form or absolute perfection that is God. This knowledge which was spoken of in Europe by Aristotle was enunciated much earlier round about 8th century B.C. in the *Chāndogya Upanishad*, in the conversation of Shvetaketu and his father.[65]

Aristotle believed that form (unlike Plato's Idea) exists only *in* things, in other words in combination with matter. The form in the thing is its reality. The form *apart* from the thing is its universality. Form and matter go together and are inseparably connected. Making something implies giving form to matter. For example if a man wishes to make a painting he first conceives in his mind what he wants to put on the canvas. Then he puts the canvas on the easel and executes the painting in conformity with his conception. He gives the matter (canvas, paint and brush) form (the finished painting). Aristotle distinguishes between potentiality and actuality, the process of nature. When form finds expression in matter the mere possibility becomes a reality.

Then there is his theory of causes. These are enumerated as four. The first is formal cause, which is the thing, the character it possesses in common with others of its kind. The second is the efficient or motive cause. This is the form pre-existing as for example the chicken in the egg or the tree in the seed or the concept of a statue existing in the statue. The third is the end-product that which is made or achieved. Apart from these three there is the matter of which the three causes arise, i.e., the material cause, thus making the number of causes four.

This continuous process of the transformation of matter into form is Nature's life-process, which is beginningless and endless. When a living creature is perfected it starts movement in matter. This brings in other forms which are not yet in the stage of perfection. Aristotle takes this natural impulse towards perfection for granted without conceiving an ordering Mind to account for it. Thus his conception of the progress of the imperfect toward perfection does not rise to the intellectual level and remains unexplained. He is also very eager to espouse the cause of free will as against inevitable destiny.

A distinction is made by him between two stages of actuality : firstly when a thing has all powers but, like a man asleep, is not necessarily exercising them; secondly when not only are powers possessed, but fully exercised also, as a man awake and going about his work. The Unmoved Mover is of the second type and this eternal self-sufficient object is the Divine Mind having no knowledge outside itself. But because of his belief that the spheres of the universe were rotating in opposite directions, Aristotle had to postulate fifty-five Unmoved Movers instead of one.

Aristotle's view of the mechanism of perception was that it is a link between the object perceived and the particular sense that perceives it. When the eye sees white the whiteness of the object seen activates sight and singles out this whiteness. But between perception and knowing two stages intervene - the perception of the 'common sensibles', and the perception of the 'incidental sensibles'. The former is the perceiving of objects as having specific size, shape, number and whether they are in movement or at rest. The latter is comparing the object seen with the memory or resemblance of another, as distinguishing the whiteness of paper from the sattiness of salt or the perfume of a rose. Sense-perception activates the intellect and gives a mind-picture These mind-pictures or images are not thought but that which gives rise to thought through perception or memory, as Aristotle says in *Analytical Posteriora* (II., 19, 4.):

'Εκ μέν οῦν αἰσθήσεως γίνεγαι
μνήmh, ὥσπερ λέγομεν, ἐκ δέ
μνήμης πολλάκις γοῦ αὐοῦ γινομένης
ἐμπειρία'–'From perception therefore springs memory, as they say, and from memory often refreshed comes experience.

The mind becomes what it thinks. When one thinks of a thing the thought imprints itself on the mind. Single concepts can be linked to form a whole concept, e.g. 'the swift horse galloped away' is a combination of the thought of a 'horse', 'swiftness' and 'galloping'. Some power is required to make the thought existing in the mind actualize. This power is 'Separable Reason' which is changeless and eternal an can exist separate from the body. It is analogous to the 'First Mover' but not identified with God and it dons not exist when the body is no more.

A significant part of Aristotle's psychology is his idea 'pneuma' which is similar to ether. It is though 'pneuma' that sense perceptions reach the soul. It is present in the sense organs as well as in the channels and veins connecting them with the heart. Here again we find the frequent confusion in Aristotle's thinking between the heart and the soul. He introduces a new form of thought or mind which is prior to all thinking. This is divine and immortal. So he is back to the fundamental doctrine of Plato that in the soul of man there is something which can be explained only by supposing that it is divine and comes from God.

Ethics and Politics

Man, said Aristotle, is by nature a political animal - 'Ο ἄνθρωπος φύσει πολιγικὸν ζῷον ἐσγί'.[66] In his political views he remains confined to the Greek city-state, which is strange considering that he was in touch with the Macedonians, and Hermeias ruler of a small kingdom under the great king of Persia was his patrom. Nevertheless he was centred in Athens which was a kind of model Greek city-state. All the ills of the Greeks were therefore typified in him, the foremost being slavery. In the *laws* he said that in his ideal state he would like to have an adequate number of slaves. His political thought is narrow and entirely limited to the framework of the Greek city-states and therefore precludes him from taking a universal view of politics. The state's objective is the common endeavor of its citizens to work for the good of all. He allows private property but under social control, which again is a contradiction in terms, for if property is under state control how can it be termed as private? Citizenship, he said, was a full time job and confined to the leisured class, excluding labourers and artisans - another Greek characteristic which differentiated people as high and low (as downgrade as the Hindu institution of caste). He favoured a mixed democracy and oligarchy in which power is kept in the hands of the middle class, landowners and moderately well-to-do. Importance is given to education which produces men of good moral character. But in his *Politics* he does not give any information about higher education and so lacks the comprehensiveness of Plato's scheme. His emphasis is more on physical development and training aimed at character-building. Male chauvinism finds its best advocacy in Aristotle. Women, he considers as not being capable of the best life, and likens them to slaves and the lower orders. The only relieving feature in this dismal picture of Arostotle's state is his firm view that the aim of citizens of the state is the good, active and beautiful life not wealth, power, material gains or craving for territory and conquests. This noble thought is watered down, however, when he precludes women, slaves and the lower rung of society from sharing that kind of higher life, so that only the priviledged are entitled to it and as compared to others they are in a negligible minority. For the majority, work in such a state is pure drudgery.

Ethics

The politics of the city-state so greatly dominated Aristotle that ethics was relegated to a subordinate position. Bréhier remarks that it was the morality of a middle class lady in comfortable circumstances who is determined to make the best use of her social advantages'. He emphasizes character as preliminary to a study of ethics. Man's energy should be directed to find out that for which is suited and then to do it to the best of his ability. All men aim at wellbeing (*eudaemonia*) and the greatest wellbeing is the 'activity of the soul in accordance with reason'. Thus activity should be according to 'virtue', which in the Greek sense meant efficiency or expertness in a particular work According to his Nicomachean belief Aristotle's definition of virtue was 'a condition obtained by persistently doing good acts while discharging the bad ones; acts which have a balanced proportion of goodness; and which a man of good sense and judgement would approve'. In *Ethica Nicomachea* he puts it thus:

Τῆς γὰρεγησ μᾶλλον ρὸ εὖ
ποιεῖν ἤ γὸ εὖ πάσχειν, καὶ γὰ
καλὰ πράγγειν μᾶλλον ἤγὰ
αἰσχρὰ μὴπράγγειν – 'The province of virtue is rather well-doing than wellbeing, and the practice of good rather than

the avoidance of evil'.[67] It is our own power, Aristotle says to practise virtue and reject vice. Pleasure is not an evil. It is a necessary element in a man's activity. But it should not be directed to base ends. It should be allied to the higher activity, the highest being intellectual contemplation. He says, 'We must not, as people advise, think humanly, being human, nor as mortals, being mortals, but as far as possible we must put on the life of the Immortals, and do all we can to live according to the best in us'.

Virtue should guide one's entire life A little wealth, health, good birth, tidiness in personal appearance and a smooth family life are desirable. Aristotle, however, realizing that all of these could not be in one's control says that goodness 'shines through' misfortunes and the loss of any of these if such setbacks are endured with courage. As we have said, goodness is the cornerstone of Aristolean ethics. He says 'Ε̈ὐχεσθαι μένγὰ ἁπλῶs ὰyaθὰ και αύγοîs a γαθα εîναι'' - We should pray that the absolute good may be also our own good'.[68]

It has been said that every man is born either a Platonist or an Aristotelian. That is an exaggeration and maybe European thought is limited by such barriers, but it can't be said for the world's philosophy. Plato was far in advance of Aristotle. He was consistent in his philosophical views while Aristotle kept wavering between the spiritual and the material, desperately trying to stick on to the latter but in the final analysis going back to the spiritual.

In his views of the universe he held that the earth was fixed and unmoving at the centre while the stars and planets moved in perfect circles round it with uniform velocity. This was a retrograde view. Much is made of his biological knowledge, but most of it just 'words, words, words. For example:

'But of a truth every realm of nature is marvellous. It is told that when strangers, finding Heracleitus at the kitchen fire, hesitated to go in, he bade them enter since, he said, "gods were even in the kitchen'. So should we venture on the study of every kind of animal without distaste, for each and all will reveal something natural and beautiful. Absence of hazard and conduciveness of everything to an end are to be found in nature's works to the highest degree, and the resultant of her generations and combinations is a form of the beautiful.[69]

However his ideas about systematic embryological investigations of the developing chick, his observations about the habits of fishes, octopuses and squids, certain kind of dog-fish and of cat-fish, deserve praise, as of Plato's mathematical theory of the anaytical method. He considered mathematics allied to philosophy though with scant justification, and is said to have got inscribed over the entrance of his Academy 'Let none who has not learnt mathematics enter here'.

Aristotle also speaks about the bees, though taking the queen-bee to be the male of the species. He mentions the various varieties of honey, the way the bees built the honeycomb, the egg-laying, the provision of the larvae for food. The different kinds of flowers yielding their own varieties of honey and many facts about bee-keeping are mentioned by him. He speaks of various other insects like the house-fly, gnats, the transformation of the caterpillar into a butterfly, the silkworm and its cocoon.

In natural science and biology he was more a home than in his philosophy which can be only termed as mediocre. In that the genius was his renowned master, Plato.

The Philosophy of the Earlier Roman Empire-Revival of Platonism

In the first century B.C. and the first two centuries A.D.

there was a revival of Platonism. The Stoic doctrine became humanized and Platonism book much from it. Posidonius of Apamea emphaisized the world's organic unity a the universal sympathy which binds all things to man and acts as a bridge between animal life and the divine. Lucius Annaeus Seneca (C. 4B.C. - A.D. 65) was a renowned exponent of the Stoic philosophy besides being an essayist and dramatist. His passion was philosophy. His non-stoic doctrine on questions like firmness, providence, tranquillity of the mind and happiness in life were remarkable, as were his learned essays on Anger or Benefits and the Moral Epistles. In his Epistolae XXXV., 1 he says: 'Qui amicus est,amat non utique amicus est. Itaque amicitia semper prodest, amor etiam aliquando nocet' [He who is your friend loves you, but he who loves you is not always your friend. Thus friendship always benefits, but love sometimes injures]. Seneca's philosophy usually found expression in wise sayings and epigrams. In Phaedra, 615., he says, 'Curae leves loquuntur, ingentes stupent' [Small troubles voice themselves, great woes are struck domb], and is De Moribus, 74 'Magna res est vocis et silent tempora nosse' [It is a great thing to know the time for speech and the time for silence]. Also in his Epistolae, LXXIV., 20, he observes, 'Placeat homini quicquid deo placuit' [Whatever pleases God should be man's pleasure also]. Other philosophers with about the same angle as Seneca, were Musonius Rufus, Epictetus and Marcus Aurelius. The period now being considered was a sort of twilight zone in philosophy, in which some philosophers as those afresaid, expressed themselves in Latin, and others continued to do so in Greek. Epictetus (2nd century A.D.) used Greek and so did Marcus Aurelius Antonisus (121-18 A.D.). Epictetus observe about laugher, 'Τέλως μή πολὺς ἔσγω, μή ἐπὶ πολλοὶs, μηδέ ἀνειμένοs'. (*Enchiridion*, XXIII., 4) [Do not laugh much or often or unrestrainedly]. About self-control he says in *Stobaeus, Floriegium*, I., 50 "Κόλαζε γὰ πάθη, ἵναμή ὑπ' αύγῶν γιμωρῆ" [keep your passions in check lest they take vengence on you]. In *Enchiridion*, VIII he says 'Do not seek to bring things to pass in accordance with your wishes, but wish for them as they are, and you will find them'. In our times when with us the joint against brother, what Epictetus says in his *Enchiridion*, 43, assumes significance: 'If your brother wrongs you, remember not so much his wrongdoing, but more than ever that he is your brother'.

Marcus Aurelius was of the Stoic school of philosophy of which we have already spoken aforesaid. His real name was M. Annius Verus and he was a scion of a family claiming descent from Numa, second king of Rome. He was a warrior and fought valorously for the Roman empire and died while encamping in a battle. He wrote his Meditations amid the clangour of arms.

The Stoics owed much to Zeno and Chrysippus, so much so that it was said 'If Chrysippus wasn't there would be no Stoa (the Porch, from which the Stoics got their name)'. About philosophy Marcus Aurelius said 'Φιλοσοφια μόνα θέλει; ἅἡ φύσισ σον θέλει' [Philosophy only wills what your nature wills].[70] In *Quod sibi ipsi Scripsit* he also says 'We should so order every action, word and thought, as though we were already able to depart this life', and in the same tract, 'Nothing proceeds from nothingness and also nothing passes away into non-existence'. The world, he says is change and life an alternation - 'Ο κὸσμοσ, ἀλλοίωσις όΒίος ύπόληψις'. In *Quod sibi ibsi scripsit* IX., 42, he says 'Ο ἄνθρωπος εύερψεγικὸσπεφυκως' [Man is by nature disposed to do good]. Other observations of his are, 'If we would be secure, we must avoid being conspicuous', 'You are not far from forgetting all men, nor are you far from being forgotten by all'. Marcus' Meditations are remarkable in their wisdom, and the more so as they were written in the midst of the din of battles. On the evanescence of things he observes:

> 'Consider how quickly all things are' dissolved and resolved : the bodies and substances themselves, into

the matter and substance of the world: and their memories into the general age and time of the world. Consider the nature of all worldly sensible things; of those especially which either ensnare by pleasure, or for their irksomeness are dreadful, or for their outward lustre and show are in great esteem and request, how vile and contemptible, how base and corruptible, how destitute of all true life and being they are...

'The time of a man's life is a point; the substance of it ever flowing, the sense obscure; and the whole composition of the body tending to corruption. His soul is restless, fortune uncertain, and fame doubtful; to be in brief, as a stream so are all things belonging to the body; as a dream, or as a smoke, so are all that belong unto the soul. Our life is a warfare, and a mere pilgrimage. Fame after life is no better than oblivion. What is it then that will adhere and follow? Only one thing, philosophy. And philosophy both consist in this, for a man to preserve that spirit which is within him, from all manner of contumelies and injuries, and above all pains or pleasures; never do anything either rashly, or feignedly, or hypocritically: wholly to depend on himself, and his own proper actions: all things that happen unto him to embrace contentedly, as coming from Him from whom he himself also came; and above all things, with all meekness and a calm cheerfulness, to expect death as being nothing else but the resolution of those elements, of which every creature is composed. And if the elements themselves suffer nothing by this their perpetual conversion of one into another, that dissolution, and atteration, which is according to nature can be evil....

'The time therefore that any man both live, is but a little, and the place where he liveth is but a very little corner of the earth, and the greatest fame that can

> remain of a man after his death, even that is but little, and that too, such as shilst it is, is by the succession of silly mortal men preserved, who likewise shall shortly die, and even shiles they live know not what in very deed they themselves are: and much less can know one, who long before is dead and gone....
>
> 'As a part hitherto thou hast had a particular subsistence: and now shalt thou vanish away into the common substance of Him, who first begot thee...'[71]

Aristotle had said that philosophy was knowing things by their causes, but now it became a substitute for religion and the immoral conduct shown to have been assigned to the Greek gods and goddesses came in for criticism. Lucretius was of the view that bowing and prostrating before attars was not justified. Philosophy's domain was now to sharpen the conscience and propriety in human conduct. Marcus Aurlius said:

> 'As Surgeons keep their instruments handy so should one be ready to test the divine and human in everything, For both (the divine and human are allied and interact on each other'.

Seneca wavered between the concept of the Divinity as fate and as the internal power which makes man tread the righteous path. He conceived man as a brotherhood and deplored the institution of slavery. Why should we complain if the state is deprived of liberty, he said if we deny it to the individual? Epictetus, about whom too, we have mentioned, was a slave of Nero's Freedman Epaphroditus and while in his service heard the lectures of Musonius Rufus. He was freed from slavery and lived at Nicopolis in Epirus in his old age. His discourses given at that time show him to be pious and God-fearing, fully depending on the Almighty. Unlike Seneca he condemned suicide which was a common practice with the Romans, 'Wait for God, friends' he said. 'When he shall give the signal and release you from his serviced, then go to him;

but for the present endure to remain where he has put you. Wait then; do not depart without a reason'. Curiously Epictetus considered Diogenes and the Cynics to be the ideal model for living, but his discourses depict his earnest faith in God:

> 'We should sing God's praises always while engaged in our tasks. He is great. It is he who has given us hands to work organs to breathe and digest our food. What other should one do but to sing hymns to him? Having been born as a human rational being my duty is to praise God and I will ever do so. I call on you, friend to do likewise'. However a certain hardness was part of Stoicism also. Seneca says 'Only weak eyes shed tears on knowing of the misfortunes of others', and Epictetus says 'When you console those bereaved 'you may sigh, but take care that the sigh does not come from the heart'!

The main groups of Platonists at this time were three. The first was represented by Atticus. They were much influenced by Stoicism and were against Aristotle's teachings. The second were represented by Alibinus and facourable to Aristotle's views on logic and metaphysics and hostile to the Stoics, though also to some extent not uninfluenced by them. In the third group were those who went back to Pythagoreanisim. The main characteristics of revived Platonism were:

1. It was primarily theological and was for a life that stressed religion and the knowledge of the divine and of that which 'has the greatest possible likeness to god'.

2. It postulated a hierarchy at the head of which was an exalted God who was Supreme Mind which combined Aristotle's Unmoved Mover with Plato's Form of the Good. After him come the intermediary beings - the Second Mind, the lesser gods, the stars, the *daemones* - ruling and ordering,

and some of them inhabiting the visible universe which itself is animated by a World-Soul.

3. Though some of the Platonists believed that the universe was formed at a definite moment in time, others believed in the world being eternal. It was the latter view that prevailed.

4. It was an Evil Soul that was the cause of evil. This soul was immanent in matter and so the whole material universe was under its domination. Thus materialism was the cause of all evil.

5. These middle Platonists were far removed from mysticism. Man was so greatly distanced from the Supreme Mind that any degree of contemplation on his part could not reveal it to him. Therefore such meditation on it was purposeless.

6. The main contribution of these Platonists was in theology. They tried to harmonize the ideas of Plato and Aristotle in regard to the universe and divine things.

Greek-Christian Thought-Philo and St Justin

The Greek view of virtue was very different from that of the Christian. The doctrine of the soul's immortality was Greek not Jewish. Nevertheless the concept of a sacred rite or sacrament by which the soul was purged of sin belongs to the Orphic tradition as also the ideas of hell, heaven and purgatory. But despite the claims of certain Christians about this superficial similarity, there was a vast gulf between the two. Christianity owes much more to the Greeks than the Greeks to Christians. Dean Inge traces back to Plato 'the religion and the political philosophy of the Christian church and the Christian type of mysticism'. Modern Christianity was greatly alien to the Greek view. The Greeks were neither bound to a church nor to any scripture. Ecstasy and enthusiasm as in the Dionysus cult or in the Bacchae are connected with Hellenism. But the higher religious consciousness of the

Greeks was compounded of metaphysics, ethics and the emotion of piety. The idea of a number of churches was quite foreign to the Greeks. In the ancient city-states of Greece the church and state were one. Anyone considered guilty of impiety would be punished not by the priesthood or the church but by the authorities of the city as Soctrates was in Athens. A church was unknown to the Greeks but a state religion was familiar to Greek theology was reality reached by human reason alone. According to Christian theology divine truth was beyond the reach of human intelligence and it was disclosed only by God's help in the form of grace and revelation.

The philosophers who reinterpreted Greek ideas in the Christian manner were firstly Philo and secondly the Apologists - Fronto, Celsus, Porphyry, Julian, Tertullian, Minicius, Felix Aristrides and St Justin. Of these St Justin was the most prominent.

Philo

Philo believed in the Jewish doctrine of God, the ruler and creator of the universe. God, as conceived by him acts through various intermediary powers called 'Logos' which he identified with Plato's world of Forms. Other doctrines of his are, 1. 'Pneuma' by which God breathes into man part of his divine substance which becomes God's image in man, and 2. Mystic union whereby the human spirit or intelligence may even in this life obtain mystical union or direct vision of God.

The Apologists

St Justin believed that only divine grace can bring on in immediate contact with God. With him we are nearer to the Christians than to the Greeks, despite his professed affinity to Plato and the Platonists and the Stoics. His view was that God plants the seeds of Goodness in the minds of good men. This he calls the 'seminal - Logos', using the Stoic term but in a different sense. And then he goes on to claim an exclusive privilege for Christians in a very unGreek manner, saying that the Christians put non-Christians into the shade as they have not merely the seeds of truth but the Logos Himself and hence Christian Revelation transcends the teachings of the philosophers. He also expressed his belief, though nebulously in the doctrine of the Christian Trinity of the Father, Son an the Holy Ghost.

Following the Apologists there came the School of Alexandria who preached Christianity. Pantaenus, Clement and Origen belonged to this School.

Plotinus

We have already briefly mentioned the views of Plotinus in the introduction to this book as contained in his *Enneads* where he speaks of the World Soul, the Divine Mind and finally the ecstatic union of the Soul with the One. The revival of Platonism reached its zenith in the philosophy of Plotinus in the third century A.D. Nothing is reliably known about his race or parentage for a Pophyry says about him 'he was like a man ashamed of being in the body and would never speak of such things' In his *Enneads* (*De Providentia*) he says Πâσα δέζωήένέρψεια, καὶ ἡ φαυλή 'All life, even in its lowest form, is energy'. Matter, according to him remains unchanged by the forms imposed upon it. It is a formless darkness and the very principle of negation. The universe is a noble work of the higher. Soul ordered and ruled by it and held together by Nature in a organic unity or order. It is only the beautiful soul which can perceive beauty, as he says in *Enneades*:

Οὐγὰρ ἂν πώπογε είδεν ὀφθαλμὸs
ἥλιον ἥλιον ἡλιοειδήγεγενημένοs,
οὐδέ γὸ καλὸ ἄν ἴδοι ψυχήμή
καλή γενομένη.

'The eye which is not of the nature of the sun has never seen the sun, nor can the soul which is not itself beautiful perceive beauty'.

Plotinus is the most difficult of Greek philosophers and is said to have had a genuine mystical experience. Commentators and critics have interpreted his thought in various ways.

1. According to some he was an extreme pantheist, opposed to rationality, for whom the end of spiritual life was a denial of all reality. The self he held dissolved into a formless nothingness.

2. Others think he was a Christian or Sufi mystic and conceived God as unified with love and with the transcendental Good.

3. Yet others see in his philosophy a kinship with Hindu thought - the realization of man's pre-existing identity of the soul with the Cosmic Absoule, much as Plato thought, and Cicero said in *De Senectute*:

'The divine soul is drawn down from its lofty home, and so to say, plunged into the earth, and abode which is of the nature of the antithesis of divinity and eternity'.[72]

The religion and philosophy of Plotinus are one. At the topmost is the transcendent First Principle, the One and the Good. It is beyond mind and being, language or thought unknowable and indescribable. It is the Unity-Absolute and beyond non-duality. It is pure will and It loves Itself and is the cause of Itself. The knower and know and their duality are not in it.

He speaks of the 'higher' and the 'lower'. The higher produces the lower. Contemplation is the primary activity and where contemplation stops production too stops. That which is produced is lower than the producer and the producer is not diminished by giving forth the product. It remains unchanged. It is as the fire generating heat, the flower yielding perfume or the sun its light. The lower proceeds to the higher in stages. At first it is not fully realized. But when it returns in this half-realized state to the higher it is perfected and fully formed before returning to the lower and this is through contemplation, thus:

The soul is the between the higher spiritual world and the materials world. There is the Higher Soul (the World Soul) and the Lower Soul (Nature). Mind is the source of the Soul's reality - the good, intelligent and beautiful. The Soul is higher when its activity is contemplation and then it is attuned to the Divine Mind. In its lower capacity it is concerned with the material universe. The Soul, says Plotinus, contains the body not the body the Soul.

The spiritual state of the Soul depends on its attitude. If it is directed to the body and entangled in the needs of the body, it becomes isolated from the whole and when continually entrapped in bodily needs it finally sinks into brutishness. The mere fact of being embodied is not of consequence but its fall come when it identifies itself with the body and surrenders to it. The Soul thus ennobles or demeans itself according to its own attitude. It can pass from the narrowness of earthly life to the universality of the transcendental and then even beyond to take its rightful place in the world of the Divine Mind, and from there even higher, though in rare cases, to ecstatic union with the divine. The Katha Upanishad and the Gita have also the same idea.

Prayer, says Plotinus, is 'the setting in motion through the universal sympathy of a celestial force proceeding from a star-god, by means of incantation or magical ritual.

Evil and suffering are inevitable inliving. The individual who suffers has no right to complain for suffering is a natural consequence of human life and indeed of all life. The wise man is beyond suffering not because his body is invulnerable to it but because of his detachment. His most significant self abides above in the spiritual world and away from the turmoil of bodily life. For the ordinary man who is not a philosopher and cannot thus rise to the higher world, Plotinus has little hope. Those weak and vile suffer for their own fault. They get what they deserve, and cannot expect those good or the gods to aid them.

Embodiment itself is a regrettable necessity, and one gets and existence lower than human because of his own sins. Then the soul is cast into lower wombs. Lord as Lord Krishna says in the *Gita* (16:19) Plotinus's whole moral teaching is directed to soul-purfication. Though the soul must abide for its appointed time in a body it should remain detached as though out of the body. It is his most important teaching that we can and should live almost wholly in the higher realms of spiritual and intellectual life while still living in the world.

Summing Up

Marcus Aurelius says (*quod sibi ipsi scripsit*) Φιλοσοφία μόνα θέλει, ἅ ἡ φύσις σον θέλει. 'Philosophy only wills what thy nature wills', and Socrates as in Plato's Theatetus XI, 'Wonder is what a philosopher feels and so philosophy begins in wonder'. The Greeks considered that philosophy was the search for truth and knowledge about the nature of the universe and of man. It started with the lonians round about 600 B.C. and three persons all from Miletus, the richest and most powerful of the lonian cities, namely Thales, Anaximander and Anaximenes, were the first philosophers. But because their interest was mainly in astronomy, geography and land-survey, they spoke more about the world's origin than about life and the soul. Thales called this first reality 'moisture', Aniximander called it Apeiron', i.e., the unbounded or indefinite. Anaximenes called it vapour. The world came out of these substances by separation and recombination of different forms of opposites, and this was governed by a law or rhythm of balance called *Dike* (Justice).

Thus philosophy was still in its rudiments and never yet came near its real inquiry which, as will Durant says is to inquire into what is beyond science - 'problems such as good and evil beauty and ugliness, order and freedom, life and death' and one might add, the nature of the soul.

In 546 the Persian invasion saw the decline of lonia and ended in the destruction of Miletus in 494 B.C. The centre of intellectual life moved to South Italy and Sicily. Here Pythagoras founded the Pythagorean Brotherhood at Croton (South Italy). The ascetism and other worldliness of their beliefs were far removed from the normal Greek beliefs and religions practices. It was based on Orphism and the Orphic cult whose founder was the mythical singer Orpheus. The world was believed to emanate from a kind of World-egg. Man was a blend of the earthly and eivine. The immortal soul imprisoned in the body has to go round its chain of reincarnations in various bodies unless released by following the Orphic life. For the Pythagoreans the next world was more real and important than this one It was a place of bliss for those blessed and of torment for those not blessed. That which makes the soul divine is the intellect, the power to know eternal unchanging truth. With the Pythagoreans philosophy took a great step forward, inasmuch as it first though of life and soul, the One and the many, which is the true realm of philosophy. In Stobaeus, *Florilegium* (1., 23) Pythagoras wrote, Πέπεισο μήεὶναι σὸν κγῆμα, ὅπερ μὴ ἐνγὸs διανοίαs ἔχειs 'Be sure that nothing is yours save what you posses intellectually'.

The 5th century B.C. begins with Heraclitus and Parmendes. There is a coming down from the study of the Soul and the universe again becomes the object of thought. Reason replaces faith and belief. The thinking, which with Pythagoras had assumed an un-Greek colour, becomes Greek again. But while it gains in insularism inasmuch as it is back home, it loses in universality, for as Cicero

Says in *De Officious* (II., 2, 5):

'Philosophy, if you ask the meaning of the word, is nothing else but the love of wisdom'.

Heraclitus believed in an ever changing world much like Buddha. There is perpetual change anc conflict. Yet he conceded that there is order in the world. He called this 'Logos' and it held the opposites together. It was, he said, the 'Ever-Living Fire' or 'the thunderbolt that steers all things. Heraclitus, in this way contradicts his own doctrine of change. But having postulated change he had to explain why despite this change there is yet what is changeless. He says there is no eternal rest yet admits a harmony of conflict and contrast, 'a counter-pulling harmony like that of a bow or a lyre'.

Parmenides' thought is entirely different. There is no Absolute non-existence. That which is *is* and it cannot be said not to be. His primal One is changeless, immovable, continuous, homogeneous and indivisible. He calls his one 'divine' but does not attach any religious significance to it. Thinking is identical with being says - Tò yàp aúγò νοιεῖν ἐσγί γε καὶ εἶναι.

The two greatest post-Parmenidean thinkers (Pluralists) were Empedocles of Agrigentum and Anaxagoras of Clazomanae and besides them a group of younger Pythagoreans who considered all reality as ultimately being made up of indivisible mathematical units. Empedocles is the first great philosopher after Pythagoras. He considered fire, earth air and water, the standard four elements of later Greek philosophy, to be the four roots of elementary bodies (the Hindus had in addition the firmament or ether, *gagan*). There are two moving causes, the principle of unification (Aphrodite or Love) and the principle of division (Ares or Strife). The cosmic cycle moves with these two alternating, sometimes Love predominating, sometimes Strife. The universe exists when the two are balance, i.e,. when there is neither complete separation nor complete fusion of the four basic elements.

With this cosmology Empedocles combined the Pythagorean doctrine of the soul's divinity, its reincarnation and its final return to the company of the gods. Empedocles's greatness lies in speaking of the soul, for philosophy consists in conceiving the unknown; the known need no knowledge or reflection, it being in the domain of the senses being clear as the day's light and night's darkness. To know is to cognize what is beyond the five senses and that which is got only by meditation, as Virgil says in *Aneid* (VI., 124).

Know first, the heaven, the earth, the main,
The moon's pale orb, the starry train,
Are nourished by a soul,
A bright intelligence, whose flame
Glows in each member of the frame
And stirs the mighty whole.[73]

Anaxagoras, the central figure in the intellectual life of the Athens of Pericles's times comes back to the theological indifference of the Milesians. His moving cause was '*Nous*' (Mind). This was formed of the finest and subtlest matter. The parts are always like the whole and so there is 'a proportion of everything in everything'. He said Noûv ἀρχὴνκινησέως. 'Mind is the beginning of motion'. To begin with the elements were in chaos. Intelligence started a 'vortex' leading to separation and resulting in the universe we know. Heat, cold, light and so forth are experienced by the presence in us of their opposites.

The Atomists, represented by Democritus (about 460 B.C.) got over Parmenides's difficulties by just ignoring them. All bodies, they said, are simply atoms which cannot be further divided and which are spontaneously in perpetual motion. The souls of human beings and all else, even the gods, are just atoms in movement. This crude materialism could only give a very distorted and base sense of reality.

After the Atomists came the Sophists. This was a period of great material prosperity in Greece, but also one of disintegration. The age of Sophocles and Euripedes when everything - the world, heaven and earth - was considered to be full of evil and not worthy of trust. It was the time of tyrannical rule and of cynical nihilism as that of Critias. But in this age of mental bankrutcy came Socrates why bravely faced life and died a noble death a marty to Athens' cruel injustice. He said he was wiser than all as the Delphi orache declared, only because he 'at least knew that he knew nothing'. He was the first man in Europe to have a clear idea about the soul. Virtue he said was knowledge of the good. Right action follows right knowledge. All vice is due to ignorance. Knowledge implies turning 'the eye of the soul to a direct and compelling vision of the good'. As Plato said in *Sophist* (XXXIX) - Tà yàρ γῆν πρὸs γῶν πολλῶν ψνχῆs ὄμμαγα καργερεῖν πρὸs γὸ θεῖον ἀφορῶνγα ἀδύναγα. 'The eyes of the soul 'The eyes of the soul of the multitude are unable to endure the vision of the divine'. The health and the goodness of the soul is attained when it really knows goodness a by knowing it acts rightly. And how does one act rightly? By overcoming evil tendencies and knowing what really is salutary, what valueless. For example he says Tòν φθόνον (εἶπεν) ἕλκοs εἶναι ρῆs ψυχῆs - 'Envy is an ulcer of the soul'. He cared nothing for riches and as we have said, wore only one garment be it summer or winter and had few needs, those too provided by his friends. Those who had the fewest needs, he said, were nearest to the gods - Ελαχίσγων δεόμενοs, ἕγγισρα εἶναι θεῶν. Although he refused to bypass the Athenian law, preferring death to such a course, he said (Plutarch, de Exilio, V.) (600 F) 'I am a citizen, not of Athens or of Greece, but of the world. And sure enough his condemnation to death was a disgrace to both Athens and Greece a sad commentory on both. As Ralph Waldo Emerson says in *Self-Reliance* 'Pythagoras was misunderstood, and Socrates... and every pure and wise spirit that ever took flesh. To be great is to be misunderstood'. By his life and his death, he demonstrated the truth of what he said. He belonged to the world of great men. He did not favour indoctrination. Everyone had to discover right and truth and goodness on his own. He taught by the persuasive method as his discourses disclose. One must have a comprehensive vision of virtue and goodness. A man does not really know unless he knows virtue as a whole. By his entire thinking one can positively conclude that he believed in the soul's immortality. If this was not so he would not have said just before his death that he was confident the gods would be his friends in the next existence and that in the other world he would be able to converse with the great men of the past as he had conversed with his contemporaties.

Plato immortalized Plato in his Dialogues. He believed unshakably in the soul's divinity and its reincarnation and also in the doctrine of reward and punishment for one's deeds. His theories of 'Forms' or 'Ideas' and of Amnesis or Recollection were unique. In *Meno*, XV, he says: Οὺμανθάνομεν, ἀλλὰ ἡν kaλοῦμεν μάθησιν ἀνάμνησίs ἐσγιν - 'We do not learn, and what we call learning is only a process of recollecion'. The care of the soul is of fundamental importance. The Divine Craftsman makes all things good. Evil and imperfection are due to the lower element in the soul.

Proper and systematic education was emphasized both by Plato and his pupil Aristotle. Aristotle criticized Plato's theory of Ideas. He sought reality in the world not in spiritualism as Plato did and he established his Peripatetic school in place of Plato's 'Academy'. Aristotle gave prominence to the perception of the senses. The world, he said, was reality and the search of truth is confined to the world, not as Plato said to spiritualism. But ultimately he found such a stand untenable and had to revert to Plato's spiritualism and admit that the highest principle of reason was intuition. He kept coming back to Plato's doctrine of Ideas which he set out to reject initially. He also came back to the idea of God. The world could not go on by itself. It needed some external force or power God thus becomes a necessity. Aristotle tried to avoid God's relation to the world by holding that while God was necessary to the world, the world was not necessary to God. It was mere quibbling with words, a vain attempt to get out of the maze into which he had got himself. It could not hold water and his thought cultivated in the existence of a God who is entirely external to the world!

After Aristotle came the two great schools of Hellenistic philosophy, the Stoics and Epicureans. Allied was Diogenes and the Cynics. The Stoics were Zeno (the founder), Cleantes, Chrysippus and others. They seemed to believe more in thought than in speech, unlike the Sophists. Zeno said in *Diogenes Laertius* 'We have two ears and only one mouth so that we may hear more and speak less', and Chrysippus in Stobaeus Florilegium : Τήνδιάνοιαν εἶναι λόγου πηγήν εφη - 'Thought is the fountain of speech'. Stoic philosophy was undiluted materialism. Their active principle was Nature as well as God. The Divine Fire permeates all, proding 'tension'. The world is created, destroyed and recreated in cycles. The Stoics believed in Fate which is the Divine Will. No one can avoid what is destined. So the best thing is joyful acceptance. The word is divided into sages and vicious men, everyone being the one or the other. There is no halfway house between the two. External circumstances were preferred, deprecated or calling for complete indifference. Life and death were in the last category and some Stoics took that view and being fed up with living committed suicide. They were just the opposite of the Platonists.

Epicurus believed that sensation was infallible. There was nothing spiritual in his philosophy. Everything consists of atoms. Tranquillity is freedom from pain, trouble and fear, particularly the fear of death, and possible punishment in afterlife. The Epicureans believed in pleasure, but not that which is momentary.

The sceptical reaction which followed in the wake of the Epicureans produced pyrrho, Arcesilas, and the Sophists who taught those eager to learn, not so much for knowledge's sake as for teaching oratory and turning out would-be political aspirants. There was very little philosophy if one understands it as the pursuit of the knowledge of the soul and spiritualism. Pyrrho said in Diogenes Laertius, Oî νεγαι ρὰ πράγμαγα, μή γοιαû γα εἶναι γ ῇ φύσει, ἀλλὰ μόνον φαίνεσθαι. 'Things are not in nature, but only seem to be, as they appear to the senses'.

In the first century B.C. and the first two centuries A.D. there was a revival of Platonism. Posidonius, Seneca, Rufus and Marcus Aurelius belong to this period. This was followed by the Greek-Christian thinkers, with whom Greek ideas were reinterpreted in the Christian manner. Philo and the Apologists (Celsus, Tertulian and others, particularly St Jusin) were among these. Greek thought was completely changed by them, and traces of the doctrine of the Father, Son and the Holy Ghost, the Christian Trinity, appeared. The Christian Revelation transcended the teaching of the Philosophical schools. After the Apologists the Alexandrian School Continued to widen the limit of Christian thought. This School is represented by Pantaenus, Clement and Origen.

The highest water-mark in the revival of Platonism was reached with the philosophy of Plotinus and the predominace of the soul was re-established. Spiritualism as exemplified by Plato's doctrine was restored.

The Greek city-states and their civilization depicted the triumph of the spirit of reasoning for the first time in Europe.

Europe, not the world as some historians seem to think. H.A.L. Fisher rightly says:

> 'It has been said that almost all that lives and moves in the world outside the blind forces of nature is Greek in origin. The statement is clearly an exaggeration, for it takes no account of the intellectual and emotional forces which have gone into the making of Indian, Chinese and Japanese civilization; but if we interpret the word "world" as meaning Europe and the sum of European influence in other continents, then the proposition is substantially true. The origins of European civilization are in fact to be found in ancient Greece, in the work of the Greek thinkers and artists who discovered Man and first interpreted the riddles and displayed the beauties of nature'.[74]

This is true of Greek philosophy also. But when the writer goes on to say 'the conception of the soul as the spiritual substance of human personality was a *Greek discovery*', one can concede this only if we add 'in Europe' to this statement. The soul's divinity was known to the Aryans of India much before the Greek civilization. So was the case with wealth. The Greeks seemed to have wavered in their concept of it. Diogenes (in *Erasmus, Chiliades Adagiorum* "*Amor*") speaks about 'Golden fetters' - Χρυσὶ πεδαι, and Naumachius (*Nuptialia Monita*)

Gold is but dust, and silver like the stones That, worthless, lie upon the pebby beach.[75]

However it is apparent that what the Greek philosophy conveyed was not always practised by them for as said before Solon who introduced many salutary reform in the interest of the Athenlans 'was mocked for not exploiting his position and securing wealth for himself'.[76] Solon said in his Fragment:

Χρήμαγα δ' ἱμέρω με̋ν ἔ̋χειν, ἀδικως δέ πεπâσθαι ούκ ἐθελω πάνγως.

I nowise covet'

And so too Menander says in Monosticha: Οὐδεὶς ἐπλούγησεν γαχὺ δίκαιος ὤν - 'No man of honour ever grew wealthy quickly'. On the other hand in Aristophanes (Plutus, 144. - (Chremylus) we find:

> **'If there is anything**
> **Illustrious, graceful or fair in man**
> **It is because of wealth**
> **For all that is, is subservient to it'.**

Thus the Greek attitude to wealth was uncertain and contradictory. And this disaccord is evident in the attitudes of their philosophers too. The Cynics, like Diognes, Antisthenes etc. lived on scraps and preached the abandonment of all luxuries as not obtaining them was the cause of unhappiness. The Cyrenaic school whose founder was Aristippus of Cyrene said on the contrary that the acquisition of pleasure was man's only objective. In reality the Greek philosophers veered between materialism and spiritualism and so did the Greek civilization which wavered between democracy and tyranny. Slavery was not particularly confined to Greece. It seemed to have been prevalent in most civilizations both of the East as well as of the Wast. But what was peculiar to Greece was the very large number of them. In *Politica* (VIII, 9) Aristotle surprising says: Οὐ γὰρ δεῖ οἴεσθαι δουλείαν εἶναι γὸ ζῆν προς γήν πολιγείαν, ἀλλὰ σωγηρίαν - 'A life lived for the state must not be considered slavery but a safeguard'. The only real philosophers from the spiritual angle in Greek could be considered to Socrates Plato, Plotinus, Pythagoras, Diogenes and to a certain extent, Empedocles and Xenophanes. Philosophy's true nature is the knowledge of the soul and its source, God, as A.M.S. Boethius says:

Grant, Father, that our minds. Thy august seat may scan,
Grant us the sight of true good's source, and grant us light
That we may fix on Thee our mind's unblinded eye.
Disperse the clouds of earthly matter's cloying weight;
Shine out in all Thy glory; for thou art rest and peace
To those who worship Thee; to see Thee is our end,
Who art our source and maker, lord and path and goal.[77]

REFERENCES

1. EURIPIDES. *Phrixus, Fragment* II.
2. *ishāa vāsyam idam sarvam yat kiṁ cha jagatyām jagat Ishāvāsyopanishad* 1..
3. Aristotle. *Physics* iii. 4, 203b6 (Anaximander). Quoted Werner Jaeger. *The Theology of the Early Greek Philsophers*. Oxford, 1947, p., 25.
4. K.C. Guthire. *The Greek Philosophers From Thales to Aristotle*. London: Methuen & Co. Ltd., 1950 p., 28.
5. Simplīcius. *Physics* 24, 13 f. (Anaximander A9). Quoted, Werner Jaeger. *The Theology of the Early Greek Philosophers*. Oxford, 1947, p., 34
6. William Wordsworth. *Ode. Intimations of Immortality*.
7. William Shakespeare. *King Henry VIII*, iii. 1.3.
8. W.K.C. Guthries. *The Greek Philosophers* etc. London: Methuen, 1950, p. 35.
9. Margaret E.J. Taylon. *Greek Philosophy*. Oxford, 1924, p., 20.
10. *Bhagavadgita* 2 : 22.
11. Werner Jaeger. *The Theology of the Early Greek Philosophers*. Oxford. 1947 Tran.; from the German by E.S. Robinson, p., 147, op. cit.

12. William Shakespeare. *Merchant of Venice*. Act V Scene 1.
13. London : Oxford University Press, 1924, p., 22.
14. See W.G. Orr. *A Sixteenth Century Mystic*. London & Redhill: Lutterworth Press.
15. Werner Jaeger. *The Theology of the Early Greek Philosopher*. Oxford, 1947. Trans; Edward S. Robinson, p., 112, op. cit.
16. Aeschelus *Proem*. 447. Quoted Werner Jaeger. The *Theology of the Early Greek Philosophers*. Oxford, 1947, p., 97.
17. ibid Werner Jaeger. p., 99, op.cit. [Slightly amended].
18. Margaret E.J. Taylor. *Greek Philosophy*. London : Oxford University Press, 1924, pp., 34-35.
19. Eduard Zeller. *Philosophe der Griechen*, i, p., 1001.
20. Hermann Diels. *U*ber die Gedichte des Empedokles*, 1898, pp., 396 ff. and Jean Bidez. *La biographie d' Empedocle*. Ghent, 1894.
21. Ettore Bignone. *Empedocle*. Turin. Chapter 1. 'Considerazioni generali'.
22. Both 'Love' and 'Hate' figure in Hesiod's *Theogony* (224-6).
23. Robert Browning. *Abt Vogler*.
24. W. Jaeger. *The Theology of the Early Greek Philosophers*. Trans.; E.S. Robinson. London : Oxford University Press, 1947. op. cit. (Anaxagoras).
25. *Bhagavadgita*. 6 : 34.
26. William Shakespeare. *Hamlet*. Act 1, scene S.
27. *Hudibras*. I. iii
28. William Shakespeare. *Julius Caesar*. Act 4, scene
29. Vaisheshika Chapter 8, Book 4 *Sutras* (aphorisms) 2 and 5.
30. William Shakespeare. *Measure for Measure*. Act 3, scene 1.
31. *Greek Philosophy, an Introduction*. Margaret E.J. Taylor. London : Oxford University Press, 1924, p., 58-op.cit.
32. Margaret E.J. Taylor. *Greek Philsophy*. London : Oxford University Press, 1924, p., 65, op. cit.
33. The *Republic. Plato*. Trans.; A.D. Lindsay. Heron Books. J.M. Dent & Sons Ltd pp., 176-77.

34. *Plutarch, de Exilio*, v, (600, F.).
35. Margaret E.J. Taylor. *Greek Philosophy*. Oxford, 1924, p., 68.
36. Francis Bacon. *On the Unity of Religion*. Oxford University Press. London.
37. John Stuart Mill. *On Liberty*. London : John W. Parker and Son, West Strand. M DGCC LIX, pp., 65-66.
38. SOCRATES. (*Diogenes Laertius*, II., 5, 16.)
39. SENECA. *Hercules Oetaeus*, 933. - (*Deianira*).
40. PLATO. *Apology*.
41. SOCRATES. Trans.; katheleen Freeman. Fighting Words. Beacon Press, 1952.
42. Ibid.
43. Ibid.
44. N.G.L. Hammond. *A History of Greece* to 322 B.C. Oxford University Press, 1967, p., 449.
45. Oliver Goldsmith. *The Deserted Village*. I. i 1.40-41.
46. Robert Browning. *Abt Vogler*, IX.
47. Plato *Lysis*, XIII (*Stephens*, p., 216 D.) - (*Socrates*).
48. *Bhagavadgita*. 9 : 4-5.
49. Alfred, Lord Tennyson. *In Memoriam*.
50. MONIDES OF CEOS (Stobaeus, Eclogues, Eclogues, I, 4,2,C).
51. John Keats. *Ode on a Grecian Urn*. Poems of John Keats. Thomas Nelson & Sons Ltd. p., 273.
52. Werner Jaeger. *The Theology of the Early Greek Philosophers*. Oxford Trans.; Edward S. Robinson, 1947, p., 87.
53. PLATO. *Republic*, VIII., 15. (*Stephens*, p., 564, A.) - (*Socrates*).
54. PLATO *Republic*. VIII.,.15. (*Stephens*, p., 564, A.) - (*Glauco*).
55. ARISTOTLE. *Ethica Magna*., I., 4, 3.
56. PLATO. *Crito*, V. *Stephens*, p., 45.D. - (*Crito*).

57. ANACHARSIS. (*Plutarch, Septem Sapientum Symposium*, XXI).

58. PLATO. *Theaetetus*, XXXIV. (*Stephens*, p., 194, C.) - (*Socrates*). Trans.; Jowett.

59. Robert Browning *Rabi Ben Ezra*.

60. Plato. *The Republic*. Trans.; and Ed., A.D. Lindsay. London: J.M. Dent & Sons Ltd. Heron Books, pp., 322-325.

61. ibid. pp., 318-319.

62. Margaret E.J. Taylor. *Greek Philosophy. An Introduction*. London : Oxford University Press, 1924, p., III.

63. Euripides. *Phrixus, Fragment* 11.

64. ARISTOTLE. *Physica*, II., 4.

65. *Chāndogya Upanishad*, chapter 6.

66. ARISTOTLE. *Politica*, I., 2.

67. ARISTOTLE. *Ethica Nicomachea*, V., 1, 7.

68. ARISTOTLE. *Ethica Nicomachea*, V., 1, 9.

69. *Universal History of the World*. Ed., J.A. Hammerton.

70. *Quod Sibi ibsi scripsit*, V., 9.

71. *The Meditations of Marcus Aurelius*. Trans.; Meric Casaubon. London: J.M. Dent & Sons Ltd. 1906, pp., 14, 17, 24 and 31.

72. Est enim animus coelestis ex altissimo domicilio depressus, et quasi demersus in terram, locum divinae nature aeternitatique contrarium. CICERO. *De Senectute*, XXI., 77.

73. Virgil. *Aneid*, VI., 724. Trans., Conington.

74. Rt. Hon. H.A.L. Fisher. *What the Modern World Owes to Greece. Universal History of the World*. Ed. J.A. Hammerton. London : The Educational Book Co. Ltd. CLIO, vol., 3. p., 1555.

75. *Diogenes. Erasmus, Chiliades Adagiorum* '*Amor*'.

76. N.G.L. Hammond. *A History of Greece*. Oxford University Press, 1967. p., 164.

77. Boethius, A.M.S. *The Consolation of Philosophy*. Trans.; W.E. Watts, England: Pengim Books, 1969, pp., 97-98.

